CAMBRIDGE SURVEYS OF ECONOMIC LITERATURE

PUBLIC CHOICE

CAMBRIDGE SURVEYS OF ECONOMIC LITERATURE

The literature of economics is expanding rapidly and many subjects have
changed out of recognition within the space of a few years. Perceiving the
state of knowledge in fast-developing subjects is difficult for students and
time-consuming for professional economists. This series of books is
intended to help with this problem. Each book will be quite brief, giving
a clear structure to and balanced overview of the topic and written at a
level intelligible to the senior undergraduate. They will therefore be
useful for teaching, but will also provide a mature yet compact
presentation of the subject for the economist wishing to update his
knowledge outside his own specialism.

First books in the series
E. Roy Weintraub: Microfoundations: The compatibility of
microeconomics and macroeconomics
Dennis C. Mueller: Public Choice

Public choice

DENNIS C. MUELLER

Professor of Economics, University of Maryland

CAMBRIDGE UNIVERSITY PRESS

CAMBRIDGE

LONDON   NEW YORK   NEW ROCHELLE

MELBOURNE   SYDNEY

Published by the Press Syndicate of the University of Cambridge
The Pitt Building, Trumpington Street, Cambridge CB2 1RP
32 East 57th Street, New York, NY 10022, USA
296 Beaconsfield Parade, Middle Park, Melbourne 3206, Australia

First published 1979
Reprinted 1980, 1981, 1982

Printed in the United States of America
Text set in Great Britain at The Pitman Press, Bath; printed and
bound by Vail-Ballou Press Inc., Binghamton, New York

Library of Congress Cataloguing in Publication Data

Mueller, Dennis C.

Public choice.

(Cambridge surveys of economic literature)
Bibliography: p.
Includes index.
1. Elections. 2. Democracy. 3. Social choice. 4. Welfare economics. I. Title.
JF1001.M78   324'.2   78–11197
ISBN 0 521 22550 7 hard covers
ISBN 0 521 29548 3 paperback

To my parents, Catherine and Anthony

CONTENTS

FOREWORD

This book is an extension of a survey article that appeared in the June, 1976, issue of the *Journal of Economic Literature*. All of the topics covered in that article are covered here, but in greater length. The amount of new material varies considerably, however, from topic to topic. Some are treated in almost the same way, others expanded and rewritten so as to be hardly recognizable as outgrowths of the earlier work.

One of the reasons for undertaking this work was to be able to address issues that were neglected or inadequately treated in the earlier survey. In addition to expanded material, there are several topics covered here that were not dealt with at all in the earlier survey, e.g. the new voting methods described in Chapter 4, and the supply side of the public weal discussed in Chapter 8. Articles have been appearing at an especially rapid rate in these areas, and their treatment here will probably still seem too brief, especially after the passage of a couple of years.

The book follows fairly closely the outline of the article. Some material has been shifted around, however. The normative discussion of majority rule has been placed in Part II where the rest of the normative work is discussed. The empirical work is discussed along with the theoretical hypotheses it tests rather than receiving separate treatment. In general, however, if one has read the article one should find the basic format of the book familiar.

The reader should keep in mind that, although longer and more comprehensive, the book is still, as the article was, a survey of the literature. I have attempted to present the major ideas reviewed here in such a way so that the reader would not have to consult the original texts to understand what was said. But the book should not be regarded as a substitute for the works reviewed. Instead, it is intended to give the reader enough of an understanding for what has been said on each subject to allow him to pursue those topics he finds most interesting in greater depth. And, if the book has succeeded it will whet the reader's appetite sufficiently to induce him to follow up some of this literature.

For the reader who is familiar with the literature surveyed here, it is hoped that the book may offer a useful perspective from which to view this literature, and may bring to the reader's attention some ideas or works with which he was unfamiliar. No claim is made to have covered all of the relevant literature, however. And that which is covered must inevitably exhibit certain selection biases reflecting the author's 'view of the world'. The latter is very much the view of the economist, albeit one with a marked intellectual debt to Wicksell.

For pedagogic purposes, I have tried to avoid direct statements of who said what. Often very important ideas are introduced with only a bracketed or footnote reference to the originator of an idea. Although this makes it difficult to evaluate the relative importance of some contributions, I think it makes it easier to understand what these contributions were. I have tried to make clear what the seminal contributions to the literature were, and the relative importance of the others should not necessarily be inferred from the mode of reference. The reader is again urged to consult the original texts and make his own evaluations of their merits.

I started writing the survey article in Ithaca in 1974, completed it in Berlin in 1975, started the book in Berlin in 1977, completing it in Washington, D.C. in 1978. During this period, I have been blessed with several good and tolerant secretaries, including in particular, Judith Murphy, Cheryl Wallace, and Elinor Waters. The bulk of the typing on the book was done by Helen Seifert of the International Institute of Management. My hearty and sincere thanks go to her for her cooperation, effort and skill. She has certainly lightened the burden of putting this manuscript together considerably.

I wish also to thank the International Institute of Management and the Science Center Berlin for supporting an important fraction of my work on this book. My contract with the Institute was to work in the industrial. organization area, and I am extremely grateful to the Institute and, in particular, Walter Goldberg, its co-Director, for allowing me to divert some of my energy to this project.

Several scholars in the Public Choice field were kind enough to provide comments on either the article or book manuscripts. Bruno Frey, Robert Goodin, Charles Plott, Steven Slutsky, Robert Tollison, Henry Tulkens, and Gordon Tullock all helped to improve the manuscript in various places. Peter Bernholz and Alan Peacock conscientiously read the entire book and made detailed suggestions for improvement. To these gentlemen I am extremely grateful. Given the nature of the work they are responsible for some of the ideas contained in the following pages. But, I know they do not all accept my interpretation of their work and other aspects of the literature, and the reader is advised of this possible discrepancy.

Finally, I would like to thank James Buchanan, who has read and commented on this work at several stages of its evolution. I owe him an unmeasurable debt of gratitute for the time and effort he has put into improving this book. Whatever level of success it achieves will be that much higher for his effort.

Berlin, July, 1978

1

Introduction

Public choice can be defined as the economic study of nonmarket decisionmaking, or simply the application of economics to political science. The subject matter of public choice is the same as that of political science: the theory of the state, voting rules, voter behavior, party politics, the bureaucracy, and so on. The methodology of public choice is that of economics, however. The basic behavioral postulate of public choice, as for economics, is that man is an egoistic, rational, utility maximizer.[1] This places public choice within the stream of political philosophy extending at

[1] For detailed justification of this postulate in the study of voting see Downs [1957, pp. 3–20]; Buchanan and Tullock [1962, pp. 17–39]; Riker and Ordeshook [1973, pp. 8–37]. J. A. Schumpeter's early use of the postulate also should be mentioned [1950]. One of the curiosities of the public choice literature is the slight *direct* influence Schumpeter's work appears to have had. Downs claims that 'Schumpeter's profound analysis of democracy forms the inspiration and foundation for our whole thesis' [1957, p. 27, n. 11], but cites only one page of the book (twice), and this in support of the economic man assumption. Most other work in the field makes no reference to Schumpeter at all.

Gordon Tullock has made, in correspondence, the following observation on Schumpeter's influence on his work: 'In my case, he undeniably had immense impact on me, although it was rather delayed. Further, although I read the book originally in 1942, I didn't reexamine it when I wrote The Politics of Bureaucracy [1965]. In a sense, it gave me a general idea of the type of thing that we could expect in government, but there weren't any detailed things that could be specifically cited.' I suspect that Schumpeter's work has had a similar impact on others working in the public choice field.

least from Thomas Hobbes and Benedict Spinoza, and within political science from James Madison and Alexis de Tocqueville. Although there is much that is useful and important in these earlier contributions, and much that anticipates later developments, no effort is made here to relate this earlier work to the modern public choice literature, for it is separated from the modern literature by a second, salient characteristic. The modern public choice literature employs the analytic tools of economics. To try to review the older literature, using the analytic tools of its descendants, would take us too far afield.[2]

Public choice's development as a separate field has been largely within the last three decades, and in response to issues and needs arising elsewhere in economics. Starting with A. Bergson's 1938 article, and spurred by K. J. Arrow's 1951 book [rev. ed. 1963] a large literature has grown exploring the properties of social welfare or social choice functions.[3] It focuses on the problems of aggregating individual preferences to *maximize* a social welfare function, or to satisfy some set of normative criteria, i.e. on the problem of which social state *ought* to be chosen, given the preferences of the individual voters. This research on optimal methods of aggregation has naturally spurred interest in the properties of *actual* procedures for aggregating preferences via voting rules, i.e. on the question of which outcome will be chosen for a given set of preferences under different voting rules. The problem of finding a social choice function satisfying certain normative criteria turns out to be quite analogous to establishing an equilibrium under different voting rules. Thus, both K. J. Arrow's study [1963] of social welfare functions and D. Black's seminal work on committee voting procedures build on the works of J. C. de Borda [1781], M. de Condorcet [1785], and C. L. Dodgson (Lewis Carroll) [1876]. We discuss the most directly

---

[2] See, however, Black [1958, pp. 156–213]; Buchanan and Tullock [1962, pp. 307–22]; Haefele [1971]; Ostrom [1971].
[3] For surveys, see Sen [1970a, 1977a, b]; Fishburn [1973a]; Plott [1976]; Kelly [1978].

relevant parts of the social welfare function literature as part of normative public choice in Part II.

The second development in economics fostering interest in public choice has been the work on market failures, again stemming from papers appearing in the 1940s and 1950s. This work centers on establishing conditions for efficient allocation in the presence of public goods, externalities and economies of scale, and leads directly to the study of nonmarket procedures for revealing individual preferences in these situations. The public choice approach to nonmarket decisionmaking has been (1) to make the same behavioral assumptions as general economics (rational, utilitarian man), (2) often to depict the preference revelation process as analogous to the market (voters engage in exchange, via voting individuals reveal their demand schedules, citizens exit and enter clubs), and (3) to ask the same questions as traditional price theory. (Do equilibria exist? Are they stable? Pareto efficient? How are they obtained? How are the economic functions of society performed?) This part of the literature resembles positive economics so closely that it is referred to here as positive public choice, although parts of it have normative implications. Positive public choice is reviewed in Part I.

Public choice and public expenditure theory share an ancestry in the work of the 'Continental' writers on public finance.[4] Of particular importance here are the papers by E. Lindahl [1919] and K. Wicksell [1896]. Lindahl's paper has had the greater influence on public goods theory; Wicksell's on public choice and public finance. Wicksell's view of government as a *quid pro quo* process of exchange among citizens underlies James M. Buchanan and Gordon Tullock's *Calculus of Consent* [1962], and much of the positive public choice literature. Richard A. Musgrave's [1959] influential separation of government activity into allocation and redistribution decisions is directly traceable to Wicksell. In Part III, we argue that this Wicksellian distinction constitutes the

---

[4] See papers compiled by Musgrave and Peacock [1958].

natural conceptual boundary between positive and normative public choice.[5]

Not surprisingly, given this background, many contributors to public choice have worked in or started from public finance. Despite this overlap, the amount of work on the interface between public choice and public finance remains small,[6] and little is said about it in this survey.

It is perhaps worth pointing out several other topics that might be considered part of the public choice area, but are neglected in this study. None of the rapidly emerging literature on law and economics, or property rights is addressed here. Nor do we have much to say about the literature on bureaucracy, except as it is related to the supply of government outputs (see Chapter 8). Our reason for omitting these topics is simply that bounds of time and space require drawing lines about what is defined as public choice. For the same reason, we shall not consider critiques of the literature from both the 'new left' and the 'new right'.[7] Our focus is on the main stream of the literature, that has used and paralleled developments in neoclassical economics.

Within the discipline of economics the methodological ground rules for developing and testing theories have become fairly well established and accepted. Man is a rational animal who maximizes (or perhaps satisfizes) an objective function. This objective function is defined over a few well-defined variables. The interaction of individuals can be characterized by certain fairly simple, analytical models, like those used in noncooperative games. And so on. These are all assumptions which are defended as coming

---

[5] This division of the literature also corresponds to a difference in views of the state as either an 'organic' entity, or a union of individuals engaged in *quid pro quo* exchange. The distinction was clearly drawn and the subsequent development of the literature anticipated in 1949 by J. M. Buchanan in an article that builds on Wicksell. See, also Buchanan [1975*b*, n. 10].

[6] Exceptions are J. M. Buchanan's book [1967] and Greene [1970]; Klevorick and Kramer [1973]. The general topic is reviewed and Wicksell's influence emphasized by J. M. Buchanan [1975*b*].

[7] For a discussion of the views of the 'new left', and a forthright presentation of the libertarian position see Rowley and Peacock [1975].

sufficiently close to reality to facilitate the explanation and prediction of certain kinds of *economic* behavior. In public choice, these assumptions are used to help explain and predict political behavior. Not surprisingly the recent efforts to explain and predict political behavior with highly simplified and abstract models have been challenged by some of those traditionally charged with that task.[8] The political scientist's view of man the voter or politician is, in general, quite different from that assumed in the public choice models. The environment in which these characters interact is usually assumed to possess an institutional richness far beyond that implicit in these abstract models. To many political scientists the public choice models seem but a naive caricature of political behavior.

The public choice theorist's answer to these criticisms is the same as the answer economists have given to the same criticisms as they have been raised against their 'naive' models of economic behavior down through the years. The use of the simplified models of political behavior is justified so long as they outperform the competitors in explaining political behavior. At this point, the degree to which economic models of democracy offer superior explanatory power is still in doubt [Toye, 1976]. Much effort has been devoted recently to testing various aspects of the public choice model of democracy, however, and an appraisal of its relative merits should soon be possible. We shall review some of the empirical results that have been obtained to date as we proceed through the various theoretical models.

On one empirical question, there can be no doubt. The level of government activity in the United States has grown large and continues to increase. Table 1.1 presents some representative figures on government expenditures between 1902 and 1970. These figures vividly indicate the growth in both absolute and relative importance of the government. They also indicate that this growth has taken place at both the federal and local levels. Table

[8] See, e.g., Macpherson [1961]; Stokes [1963]; Barry [1965, 1970]; Toye [1976].

Table 1.1. *Federal, state and local expenditures in constant dollars (1929) 1902–70*

	Billions of spending			Percentage of GNP		
	Total	Federal	Non-federal	Total	Federal	Non-federal
1902	3.2	1.1	2.1	6.8	2.4	4.4
1913	5.0	1.5	3.5	8.0	2.4	5.6
1922	9.5	3.7	5.7	12.6	5.1	7.5
1932	15.4	5.5	10.8	21.3	7.3	14.0
1940	25.0	11.8	13.2	20.3	10.0	10.3
1950	46.5	28.7	17.9	24.7	15.7	9.0
1960	79.9	48.9	30.6	30.1	19.4	10.7
1970	135.5	79.8	56.7	34.1	21.3	12.8

Source: Borcherding [1977b, p. 26, Table 7].

1.2 goes on to illustrate that no single type of government expenditure can be singled out as the *main* cause of this expansion. Although national security expenditures and transfer payments have grown faster than the other categories, all have increased relative to GNP.[9]

We shall discuss in passing some of the hypotheses of public choice that may be relevant in explaining this growth of government. In general, however, it has not been a major objective of this literature to explain the size of government, and it will not be of ours. Given the size of government, it is useful to understand how it operates, and to evaluate its normative properties, and these are our main objectives.

We shall proceed as follows: we first discuss the reasons why collective decisions are necessary (Chapter 2). We then proceed to

---

[9] For further discussion of the relative importance of the various types of government expenditures in explaining the growth in total expenditures, and an attempt to relate these to some of the hypotheses about government size, see Borcherding [1977b].

Table 1.2. Government spending as a per cent of total public spending and GNP 1902–70 (as a per cent of GNP in parentheses)

	Social welfare[1]	Government housekeeping	Transfers excluding interest	Interest	National security	Total
1902	40.9 (2.8)	36.3 (2.5)	4.5 (0.3)	4.5 (0.3)	13.6 (1.0)	100 (6.8)
1913	40.2 (3.3)	40.2 (3.3)	6.1 (0.5)	6.1 (0.5)	9.1 (0.8)	100 (8.0)
1922	41.2 (5.2)	28.2 (3.5)	7.1 (0.9)	15.6 (1.9)	9.4 (1.2)	100 (12.8)
1932	46.5 (9.8)	27.3 (5.8)	9.1 (1.9)	10.1 (2.1)	6.1 (1.3)	100 (21.2)
1940	47.5 (9.6)	26.0 (5.2)	5.9 (1.1)	12.8 (2.6)	12.8 (2.6)	100 (21.0)
1950	33.0 (8.2)	15.8 (3.9)	18.3 (4.5)	7.0 (1.7)	26.2 (6.5)	100 (24.8)
1960	30.2 (9.1)	14.4 (4.3)	17.4 (5.2)	6.2 (1.8)	30.8 (9.3)	100 (30.0)
1970	34.7 (11.8)	17.4 (5.9)	18.0 (6.1)	5.6 (1.9)	25.5 (8.6)	100 (33.8)

Source: Borcherding [1977b, p. 29, Table 12].
[1] 'Activities in this category are education, highways, welfare, hospitals and health care, local sanitation, parks and recreation, natural resources, housing and community development' [Borcherding, 1977b, p. 30]. These items are listed as 'big debate' items by Borcherding following the original classification of government expenditures along this line by Stubblebine [1963].

discuss the properties of the various voting procedures that have been used or proposed (Chapters 3–7). In Chapter 8 we take up some recently developed models of the government bureaucracy. Part II reviews the normative theories of the state, and of collective choice processes that have been developed. The positive and normative approaches are compared in Chapter 14.

PART I

Positive public choice

2

The reasons for collective choice

Probably the most important accomplishment of economics is the demonstration that individuals with purely selfish motives can mutually benefit from exchange. If A raises cattle and B corn, both may improve their welfare by exchanging cattle for corn. With the help of the price system, the process can be extended to accommodate a wide variety of goods and services.

Although often depicted as the perfect example of the beneficial outcome of purely private, individualistic activity in the absence of government, the invisible hand theorem presumes a system of collective choice comparable in sophistication and complexity to the market system it governs. For the choices facing A and B are not merely to trade or not, as implicitly suggested. A can choose to steal B's corn, rather than give up his cattle for it; B may do likewise. Unlike trading, which is a positive sum game benefiting both participants in an exchange, stealing is at best a zero sum game. What A gains, B loses. If stealing, and guarding against it, detract from A and B's ability to produce corn and cattle, it becomes a negative sum game. While with trading each seeks to improve his position and both end up better off, with stealing the selfish pursuits of each leave them both worse off.

The example can be illustrated with strategy Matrix 2.1. Square 1 gives the allocations when A and B trade and refrain from stealing, square 3 when they steal and trade. Both are better off

Matrix 2.1

B\A	Does not steal	Steals
Does not steal	1 A (10-cattle, 9-corn) B (8-cattle, 6-corn)	4 A (6-cattle, 5-corn) B (10-cattle, 9-corn)
Steals	2 A (10-cattle, 10-corn) B (5-cattle, 3-corn)	3 A (7-cattle, 5-corn) B (7-cattle, 5-corn)

when they both refrain from stealing, but each is still better off if he alone steals (cells 2 and 4). In an anarchic environment both may be induced to adopt the dominant stealing strategy with the outcome cell 3. The distribution of cattle and corn in cell 3 represents a 'natural distribution' of goods (so named by Winston Bush [1972]), the distribution which would emerge in an Hobbesian state of nature.

From this 'natural' state, both individuals become better off by tacitly or formally agreeing not to steal, provided that the enforcement of such an agreement costs less than they jointly gain from it. The movement from cell 3 to cell 1 is a Pareto optimal move that lifts the individuals out of a Hobbesian state of nature [Bush, 1972; Bush and Mayer, 1974; Buchanan, 1975a]. An agreement to make such a move is a form of 'constitutional contract' establishing the property rights and behavioral constraints of each individual. The existence of these rights is undoubtedly a necessary precondition for the creation of the 'postconstitutional contracts', which make up a system of voluntary exchange [Buchanan, 1975a]. Problems of collective choice arise with the departure from Hobbesian anarchy, and are coterminous with the existence of recognizable groups and communities.

A system of property rights and procedures to enforce them are a Samuelsonian public good in 'that each individual's consumption leads to no subtraction from any other individual's consumption of that good' [Samuelson, 1954].[1] Nearly all public goods, whose provision requires an expenditure of resources, time, or moral restraint, can be depicted with a strategy box analogous to Matrix 2.1.[2] National defense is the collective provision of protection against external threats; laws and their enforcement against internal threats; fire departments against fires. Replace stealing with paying for an army, or a police force, or a fire department, and the same strategy choices emerge. Each individual is better off if all contribute to the provision of the public good than if all do not, and each is still better off if only he does not pay for the good.

A pure public good is characterized by indivisibilities in production or jointness of supply, and the impossibility or inefficiency of excluding others from its consumption, once it has been supplied to some members of the community [Musgrave, 1959, pp. 9–12, 86; Head, 1962]. The joint supply characteristic creates the potential gain from a cooperative move from cell 3 to 1. Given jointness of supply, a cooperative consumption decision is necessary to provide the good efficiently. If it took twice as much resources to protect A and B from one another as it does to protect only one of them, collective action would be unnecessary in the absence of nonexclusion. Each could choose independently whether or not to provide his own protection. Failure of the exclusion principle to apply provides an incentive for noncooperative, individualistic behavior, a gain from moving from cell 1 to either cell 2 or 4. The impossibility of exclusion thus raises the likelihood that purely voluntary schemes for providing a public good break down.

One can envisage goods characterized by jointness of supply in which no exclusion problem arises. These are goods in which the participation of *all* members of the community is necessary to

---

[1] The extent to which individuals can be excluded from the benefits of a public good varies. One man's house cannot be defended from foreign invasion without defending another, but a house may be allowed to burn down without endangering another. Gordon Tullock has suggested that voluntary payment schemes for excludable public goods could introduce cases resembling the latter [1971c].

[2] See Runciman and Sen [1965]; Hardin [1971]; Riker and Ordeshook [1973, pp. 296–300]; Taylor [1976, pp. 14–27].

secure *any* benefits. The crew of a sail boat, a two-man bobsled, are examples. With such goods, cells 2, 4, and 3 collapse into one, and cooperative behavior is voluntarily forthcoming. Such cases undoubtedly make up a small portion of the set of all public goods, however, and almost always involve very small groups of individuals and constrained technological conditions. The more typical case is likely to be one in which at least one member of the community can benefit from noncooperation, if all others continue to cooperate. Thus, together, the properties of public goods provide the *raison d'être* for collective choice. Jointness of supply is the carrot, making cooperative-collective decisions beneficial to all, absence of the exclusion principle the apple tempting individuals into independent noncooperative behavior.

Matrix 2.1 depicts the familiar and extensively analyzed prisoners' dilemma. Despite the obvious superiority of the cooperative non-stealing outcome to the joint stealing outcome, the dominance of the stealing strategies ensures that the non-stealing strategies do not constitute an equilibrium pair, at least for a single play of the game. The cooperative solution may emerge, however, as the outcome of a 'supergame' of prisoners' dilemma games repeated over and over by the same players.[3] The cooperative solution can arise, even in the absence of direct communication between the players, if each player chooses a supergame strategy that effectively links his choice of the cooperative strategy in a single game to the other player's choice of this strategy. One such supergame strategy is for a player to play the same strategy in the present game as the other player(s) played in the previous game. If both (all) players adopt this strategy, *and* all begin by playing the cooperative strategy, the cooperative outcome will emerge in every play of the game. An alternative strategy, which achieves the same outcome, is for each player to play the cooperative strategy

---

[3] The best, short introduction to the prisoner's dilemma game is probably R. Duncan Luce and Howard Raiffa [1957, pp. 94–113]. Anatol Rapoport and Albert Chammah have a book on the subject [1965]. Michael Taylor presents in a collective choice context an exhaustive discussion of the possibilities of the cooperative solution emerging as an equilibrium in a prisoners' dilemma supergame [1976, pp. 28–97].

so long as the other player(s) does, and then to *punish* the other player(s) for defecting by playing the noncooperative strategy for a series of plays following any defection before returning to the cooperative strategy. Again, if all players begin by playing cooperatively, this outcome continues throughout the game [Taylor, 1976, pp. 28–68]. In both of these cooperative strategy, equilibrium solutions to the prisoners' dilemma supergame, the equilibrium comes about through the *punishment* (or threat thereof) of the noncooperative behavior of any player, in this case by noncooperation of the other player(s). This idea that non-cooperative (antisocial, immoral) behavior must be punished to bring about conformity with group mores is to be found in most, if not all, moral philosophies, and forms a direct linkage between this large literature and the modern theory.[4]

The appearance of cooperative solutions in prisoners' dilemma games has been found in experimental studies to depend on the number of players, number of plays of the game, size of gain from adopting the cooperative strategy relative to both the loss from the noncooperative outcome, and to the gain from successful playing of the noncooperative strategy [Siegel and Fouraker, 1960; Sherman, 1971]. The latter two need no elaboration. The first two factors combine to determine the predictability of the other player(s)' response. When the number of other players is small, it is obviously easier to learn their behavior and predict whether they will respond to cooperative strategy choices in a like manner. It is also easier to detect noncooperative behavior and, if this is possible, single it out for punishment, thereby further encouraging the cooperative strategies. When numbers are large, it is easy for one or a few players to adopt the noncooperative strategy, and either not be detected, since the impact on the rest is small, or not be punished, since they cannot be discovered or it is too costly to the cooperating players to punish them. Thus, voluntary com-

---

[4] For classical discussions of moral behavior and punishment, which are most modern and in line with the prisoners' dilemma discussion, see Thomas Hobbes, *Leviathan* [1651, chs. 14, 15, 17, 18]; David Hume [1751, pp. 120–7].

pliance with behavioral sanctions, or provision of public goods is more likely in small communities than large [Coase, 1960; Buchanan, 1965*b*]. Reliance on voluntary compliance in large communities or groups leads to free riding and the under or nonprovision of the public good [Olson, 1965].

In game experiments, cooperative solutions are reached only after a series of plays of the game (typically 6–8), and continue until shortly before the preannounced end. In the absence of direct communication and agreement, time is needed to learn the other player(s)' behavior. Generalizing from these findings, one can expect the voluntary provision of public goods and cooperative behavioral constraints to be greater in small, stable communities of homogeneous behavior patterns.

In the large, mobile, heterogeneous community a formal statement of what behavior is mutually beneficial (e.g. how much each must contribute for a public good) may be needed, for individuals even to know what behavior is consistent with the public interest. Given the incentives to free ride, compliance may require the implementation of individualized rewards or sanctions. Mancur Olson found that individual participation in large, voluntary organizations like labor unions, professional lobbies, and other special interest groups was dependent not on the collective benefits these organizations provided to all of their members, but on the individualized incentives to members they provided in the form of selective benefits for participation and attendance, or penalties in the form of dues, fines, and other individualized sanctions [1965, pp. 50–1, 132–67].

Thus, democracy, formal voting procedures for making and enforcing collective choices, is an institution that is needed by communities of only a certain size and impersonality. The family makes an array of collective decisions, without ever voting; a tribe perhaps only occasionally. A metropolis or nation state may have to make a great number of decisions by collective choice processes, although many of them may not correspond to what we have here defined as a democratic process.[5] Similarly, small, stable com-

---

[5] It must also be kept in mind that democracy is but one, *potential* means

munities may be able to elicit voluntary compliance with group mores and contributions for the provision of local public goods by the use of informal communication channels and peer group pressure. Larger, more impersonal communities must typically establish formal penalties against asocial behavior, like stealing, levy taxes to provide for public goods, and employ a police force to ensure compliance.

The size of the community, its reliance on formal sanctions and police enforcement, and the breakdown of the prisoners' dilemma may all be dynamically related. Detection of violators of the prisoners' dilemma takes time. An increase in the number of violations can be expected to lead to a further increase in violations but only with a time lag. If, because of an increase in community size, or for some other reason, the frequency of violations were to increase, the frequency of violations in later periods could be expected to increase even further, and with these the need for and reliance on police enforcement of the laws. James Buchanan has described such a process as the erosion of a community's legal (i.e. rule abiding) capital.[6] Michael Taylor has presented a similar scenario [1976, pp. 132–40]. Taylor relates the breakdown of the cooperative solution to the prisoners' dilemma not to the community's size, however, but to the level of government intervention itself.[7] Intervention of the state in the provision of a community want or in the enforcement of social mores, psychologically 'frees' an individual from responsibility for providing for community wants and of preserving its mores. State intervention leads to increased asocial behavior requiring more state intervention, and so on. The theories of Buchanan and

---

for providing public goods. Autocracies and oligarchies also provide public goods to 'their' communities. This survey has little to say about them, except to the extent oligarchs resolve their differences by voting.

[6] [1975a, pp. 123–29]. See, also, Buchanan [1965b].

[7] Indeed, at several points he seems on the verge of arguing that the likelihood of a cooperative outcome to the game is not dependent on the size of the community [1976, pp. 23–5, 27 n. 16, 61, 92]. But eventually he does concede its dependence on size [p. 92], and his discussion of anarchy is clearly couched in terms of the small, stable community [ch. 7].

Taylor might constitute one explanation for the rising government expenditures that have occurred in this century. Their theories would link these expenditures directly to the increasing mobility and urbanization that has occurred during the century, and the consequent increases in government intervention this has caused.

The scenarios by Buchanan and Taylor of the unraveling of the social fabric mirror to a remarkable degree the description by John Rawls [1971, pp. 496–504] of the evolution of a just society, in which the moral (just, cooperative) behavior of one individual leads to increasingly moral behavior by others, reinforcing the cooperative behavior of the first and encouraging still more. The dynamic process in these scenarios is the same, only the direction of change is reversed.

The game theoretic underpinning of the public choice process, as represented by the prisoners' dilemma game, and the different possibilities for arriving at the cooperative solution to this game have important implications for the selection of a set of democratic rules by a community, as will become apparent as we examine the properties of these rules under the positive theory of public choice. Some of the normative issues raised in this chapter are returned to in Part II.

3

Public choice in a direct democracy

This and the next two chapters explore the properties of various voting rules. These rules can be thought of as governing the polity itself, as when decisions are made in a town meeting or by referendum, or an assembly or committee of representatives of the citizenry. Following Duncan Black [1958] we shall often refer to 'committee decisions' as being the outcomes of the voting process. It should be kept in mind, however, that the word 'committee' is employed in this wider sense, and can imply a committee of the entire polity voting as in a referendum. When a committee of representatives is implied, the results can be strictly related only to the preferences of the representatives themselves. The relationship between citizen and representative preferences is taken up later.

A. The unanimity rule

Since all can benefit from the provision of a public good, the obvious voting rule for providing it would seem to be unanimous consent. Knut Wicksell was the first to link the potential for all to benefit from collective action to the unanimity rule [1896]. The unanimity rule coupled with the proposal that each public good be financed by a separate tax constituted Wicksell's 'new principle' of taxation. To see how the procedure might work, consider a world with two persons and one public good. Each person has a given initial income, Y_A and Y_B, and a utility function defined over the public and private goods, $U_A(X_A, G)$ and $U_B(X_B, G)$, where X is the private good, and G the public good. The public good is to be financed by a tax of t on individual A, and $(1 - t)$ on individual B. Given these taxes and a given quantity of public good, we can solve for the amount of the private good each individual can buy, given his budget constraint

$$X_A = Y_A - tG$$
$$X_B = Y_B - (1 - t)G$$
(3.1)

From (3.1) we can substitute into each individual's utility function and obtain utility functions for A and B defined over G and t

$$U_A = U_A(Y_A - tG, G)$$
$$U_B = U_B(Y_B - (1 - t)G, G)$$
(3.2)

Figure 3.1 depicts this mapping of A and B's indifference curves from the private–public good space into public good–tax space [Johansen, 1963]. Embedded in each point on an indifference curve is a quantity of private goods implied by the individual's budget constraint as given in the equation system (3.1). A_1 and B_1 are A and B's utilities in the absence of any public good. Lower curves for A (higher for B) represent higher utilities. If A_1 and B_1 intersect, a set of tangency points, CC', exists which is a contract curve mapping the Pareto possibility frontier (bounded by the zero public good level utilities implied by the initial endowments) into the public-good tax-share space.

To see that each point on CC' is a Pareto efficient allocation, take the total differentials of each individual's utility function with respect to t and G, holding the initial incomes (Y_A, Y_B) constant

$$\Delta U_A = \frac{\partial U_A}{\partial X}(-t)dG + \frac{\partial U_A}{\partial G}dG + \frac{\partial U_A}{\partial X}(-G)dt$$
$$\Delta U_B = \frac{\partial U_B}{\partial X}(-1+t)dG + \frac{\partial U_B}{\partial G}dG + \frac{\partial U_B}{\partial X}(G)dt$$
(3.3)

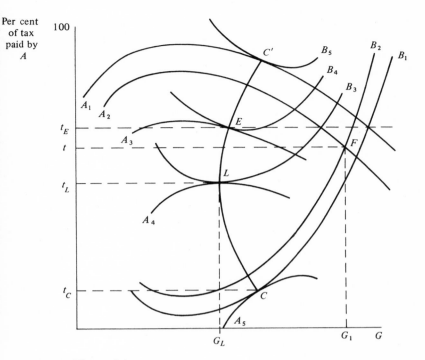

Figure 3.1

Setting the total change in utility for each individual equal to zero, we can solve for the slope of each individual's indifference curve

$$\left(\frac{\mathrm{d}t}{\mathrm{d}G}\right)^A = \frac{\partial U_A/\partial G - t\partial U_A/\partial X}{G(\partial U_A/\partial X)} \tag{3.4}$$

$$\left(\frac{\mathrm{d}t}{\mathrm{d}G}\right)^B = -\frac{\partial U_B/\partial G - (1-t)\,(\partial U_B/\partial X)}{G(\partial U_B/\partial X)}$$

Equating the slopes of the two indifference curves, we obtain the Samuelsonian condition for Pareto efficiency [1954]

$$\frac{\partial U_A/\partial G}{\partial U_A/\partial X} + \frac{\partial U_B/\partial G}{\partial U_B/\partial X} = 1 \tag{3.5}$$

Now consider the following public choice process. An impartial observer proposes both a pair of tax shares, t and $(1-t)$, and a quantity of the public good, G_1. If the combination falls within the eye formed by A_1 and B_1, both individuals prefer this proposal to no public good at all. Both will vote for it, if they vote sincerely. F now becomes the *status quo* decision and new tax share-quantity pairs are proposed.[1] When a combination falling within the eye formed by A_2 and B_2 is hit upon, it is unanimously preferred to F. It now becomes the *status quo* and the process is continued until a point on CC', like E, is obtained. Once this occurs, no new proposal will be unanimously preferred, i.e. can make both individuals better off, and the social choice has been, unanimously, made.

Note that for the tax shares inherent in the allocation E, each individual's optimal quantity of public good differs from the quantity of the public good selected. A prefers less of the public good, B prefers more. Given the tax shares t_E and $(1 - t_E)$, therefore, each is being 'coerced' into consuming a quantity of the public good that differs from his most preferred quantity [Breton, 1974, pp. 56–66]. This form of 'coercion' can be avoided under a slightly different variant of the voting procedure [Escarraz, 1967; Slutsky, 1977c]. Suppose, for an initially chosen set of tax shares t and $(1 - t)$, voters must compare all pairs of public good quantities, and a given quantity is chosen only if it is unanimously preferred to all others. This will occur only if the two individuals' indifference curves are tangent to the tax line from t at the same point. If no such quantity of public good is found for this initially chosen t, a new t is chosen, and the process repeated. This continues until a t is found at which all individuals vote for the same quantity of public good against all others. In Figure 3.1, this occurs at L for tax shares t_L and $(1 - t_L)$. L is the Lindahl equilibrium.

The outcomes of the two voting procedures just described (E

---

[1] Of course, the rule for selecting a new tax share or a new public good–tax share combination in the procedure described above must be carefully specified to insure convergence to the Pareto frontier. For specifics on the characteristics of these rules, the reader is referred to the literature on Walrasian-type processes for revealing preferences on public goods as reviewed in Tulkens [1978].

and L) differ in several respects.[2] At L the marginal rate of substitution of public for private goods for each individual is equal to his tax price

$$\frac{\partial U_A / \partial G}{\partial U_A / \partial X} = t \qquad\qquad \frac{\partial U_A / \partial G}{\partial U_B / \partial X} = (1-t) \qquad\qquad (3.6)$$

L is an equilibrium then, in that *all* individuals prefer this quantity of public good to any other, *given each individual's assigned tax price*. E (or any other point reached via the first procedure) is an equilibrium in that at least one individual, and perhaps only one, is worse off by a movement in any direction from this point. Thus, L is preserved as the collective decision through the unanimous *agreement* of all committee members on the quantity of public good to be consumed, *at the given tax prices*; E is preserved via the *veto* power of each individual under the unanimity rule. How compelling these differences are depends upon the merits of constraining one's search for the optimum public good quantity to a given set of tax shares (search along a given horizontal line in Figure 3.1). The distribution of utilities at L arrived at under the second process depends only on the initial endowments and individual preferences, and has the (possible) advantage of being independent of the sequence of tax shares proposed, assuming L is unique. The outcome under the first procedure is dependent on the initial endowments, individual utility functions, *and* the specific set and sequence of proposed tax–public good combinations. While this 'path dependence' of the first procedure might be thought undesirable, it has the (possible) advantage of leaving the entire contract curve, CC' open to selection. As demonstrated above, all points along CC' are Pareto efficient, and thus are incapable of comparison without additional criteria. It should be noted in this regard that if a point on CC', say E, could be selected as most preferred under some set of normative criteria, it could always be reached via the second voting procedure by first redistributing the initial endowments in such a way that L was obtained at the utility levels implied by E [McGuire and Aaron,

---

[2] For a detailed discussion of these differences, see Slutsky [1977c].

1969]. The informational requirements for such a task are obviously no mean thing, however.

We have sketched here only two possible *voting* procedures for reaching the Pareto frontier. Several papers have described Walrasian tâtonnement procedures for reaching the Pareto frontier when public goods are present.[3] These procedures all have in common the existence of a 'central planner' or 'auctioneer' who gathers information of a certain type from the citizen-voter, processes the information by a given rule, and then passes a message back to the voters to begin a new round of voting. These procedures can be broadly grouped into those in which the planner calls out tax-prices (the ts in the above example), and the citizens respond with quantity information, the process originally described by Erik Lindahl [1919] (see also Malinvaud [1970–71, sec. 5]); and those in which the planner–auctioneer calls out quantities of public goods and the citizens respond with price (marginal rate of substitution) information, as in Malinvaud [1970–71, secs. 3 and 4], and Drèze and de la Vallée Poussin [1971]. A crucial part of all of these procedures is the computational rule used to aggregate the messages provided by voters, and generate a new set of signals from the planner–auctioneer. It is this rule that determines if, and when, and where on the Pareto-frontier the process leads. Although there are obviously distributional implications to these rules, they are in general not designed to achieve any specific normative goal. The central planner–auctioneer's single end is to achieve a Pareto-efficient allocation of resources. These procedures are all subject to the same important distinction as to whether they allow the entire Pareto-frontier to be reached, or always lead to an outcome with a given set of conditions, like the Lindahl equilibrium. As such, they also share the other general properties of the unanimity rule.

The unanimity rule is the *only* voting rule certain to lead to Pareto-preferred public good quantities and tax shares, a feature

---

[3] For an excellent and thorough review of this literature, see again Henry Tulkens [1978], and of the public good literature more generally Milleron [1972].

which led Wicksell [1896] and later Buchanan and Tullock [1962] to endorse it. Two main criticisms have been made against it. First a groping search for a point on the contract curve might take considerable time, particularly in a large community of heterogeneous tastes [Black, 1958, pp. 146–7; Buchanan and Tullock, 1962, ch. 6]. The loss in time by members of the community in discovering a set of Pareto optimal tax shares might outweigh the gains to those who are saved from paying a tax share exceeding their benefits from the public good. An individual, who was uncertain over whether he would be so 'exploited' under a less than unanimity rule, might easily prefer such a rule rather than spend the time required to attain full unanimity. The second objection against a unanimity rule is that it encourages strategic behaviour.[4] If A knows the maximum share of taxes B will assume rather than go without the public good, A can force B to point C on the contract curve, by voting against all tax shares greater than t_C. All gains from providing the public good then accrue to A. If B behaves the same, the final outcome is dependent on the bargaining strengths of the two individuals. The same is true of the other equilibria along the contract curve.[5] Bargaining can further delay the attainment of the agreement as each player has to 'test' the other's willingness to make concessions.

The 'bargaining problem' under the unanimity rule is the mirror image of the 'incentive problem' in the voluntary provision of a public good. The latter is a direct consequence of the joint supply–nonexclusion properties of a public good. Given these properties, each individual has an incentive to understate his preferences and free-ride, since the quantity of public good provided is largely independent of his single message. The literature on voluntary preference revelation procedures has by and large side-stepped this problem by assuming honest preference revelation in spite of the incentives to be dishonest. The strongest result to justify this assumption has been that sincere message

---

[4] See Black [1958, p. 147]; Buchanan and Tullock [1962, ch. 8]; Barry [1965, pp. 242–50]; Samuelson [1969].

[5] See Musgrave [1959, pp. 78–80].

transmittals is a minimax strategy, i.e. sincere revelation of preferences maximizes the minimum payoff an individual can obtain [Drèze and de la Vallée Poussin, 1971]. But a higher payoff might be obtained through a misrepresentation of preferences, and some individuals can be expected to pursue this more daring option. If to remove this incentive one compels all citizens to vote in favor of a public good quantity–tax share proposal before it is provided, the free-rider problem does disappear. Each individual's vote is now essential to the public good's provision. This reversal in the individual's position in the collective decision alters his strategic options. Where an individual might gamble under a voluntary-revelation scheme on the rest of the group providing an acceptable quantity of the public good without his contributing, under the unanimity rule he might gamble on the group's reducing the size of his contribution rather than risk his continual blocking of the collective outcome. Although the strategy options differ, both solutions to the public good problem are vulnerable to strategic behavior.

Even if strategic behavior did not indefinitely delay the achievement of a unanimous collective decision, one might object to the unanimity rule on the grounds that the outcome obtained depends on the bargaining abilities and risk preferences of the individuals [Barry, 1965, p. 249; Samuelson, 1969]. Such a criticism implicitly contains the *normative* judgement that the proper distribution of the gains from cooperation *should not* be distributed according to the willingness to bear risks. One can easily counter that they *should*. An individual who votes *against* a given tax share, to secure a lower one, risks, under a unanimity rule, not having the good provided at all, or if so in a less than optimum quantity. Voting in this manner, expresses a low preference for the public good, in much the same way as voting against the tax share, because it is 'truly' greater than the expected benefits, does. Someone not willing to vote strategically might be said to value the public good higher, and therefore perhaps ought to be charged a higher price for it.

We are clearly in the realm of normative economics here, as we

were in comparing points E and L above, and need criteria as to
how the gains from cooperation *ought* to be shared.[6] Indeed, in a
full evaluation of the unanimity rule its normative properties must
be considered. Wicksell's advocacy of the unanimity rule was
based on its normative properties. The unanimity rule would
protect individuals from being coerced by other members of the
community he argued. Wicksell used 'coerced' not in the sense
employed by Breton of an individual's having a different evaluation of the public good *at the margin* than his tax price, but in the
sense of an individual being coerced through a collective decision
to pay more for a public good than its benefits to him are *in toto*.
This argument for the unanimity rule stems directly from Wicksell's view of the collective choice process as one of mutually
beneficial voluntary exchange among individuals, as is Buchanan
and Tullock's [1962] (see also Buchanan [1975*b*]). This emphasis
on the 'voluntary exchange' nature of collective choice underlies
the classic essays by both Wicksell and Lindahl and forms an
intellectual bond between them leading in Wicksell's case to the
unanimity principle, in Lindahl's to a set of tax prices equal to each
individual's marginal evaluation of the public good.[7] It also
explains the reference to 'just' taxation in the titles of each of their
essays. We shall return to these issues when we take up the
normative theories of collective choice in Part II.

---

[6] At least two normative proposals for sharing these gains are dependent
on the bargaining or risk preferences of the individuals [Nash, 1950;
Braithwaite, 1955].

[7] The seminal discussions of the 'voluntary exchange' approaches of
Lindahl and Wicksell are by Richard Musgrave [1939] and James
Buchanan [1949]. See also Head [1964].

The relationship between Wicksell's voting theory, and the Lindahl
equilibrium is taken up by Donald Escarraz, who first described a way in
which the Lindahl equilibrium could be reached under a unanimity
voting rule [1967]. Escarraz argues that the unanimity rule was a
necessary assumption underlying Lindahl's belief that the equilibrium
would be reached, and might have been implied in Lindahl's concept of
an 'even distribution of political power'. Under this interpretation
Lindahl's even distribution of political power, Wicksell's freedom from
coercion, the unanimity rule, and a set of tax prices equal to the marginal
rates of utility for the public good all become nicely integrated.

B. **The optimal majority**

When a less than unanimous majority is sufficient to pass an issue, the possibility exists of some individuals being made worse off via the committee's decision; Wicksell's coercion of the minority can take place. If the issue is of the public good–prisoners' dilemma variety, and there exist reformulations of the issue which could secure unanimous approval, the use of a less than unanimity rule can be said to impose a cost on those made worse off by the issue's passage, a cost that could be avoided through the expenditure of the additional time and effort required to redefine the issue so that its passage benefits all. This cost is the difference in utility levels actually secured, and those that would have been secured under a full unanimity rule. Buchanan and Tullock were the first to discuss these costs, and refer to them as the 'external costs' of the decision rule [1962, pp. 63–91] (see also Breton [1974, pp. 145–48]).

Were there no costs associated with the unanimity rule itself, it would obviously be the optimal rule, since it minimizes these external decision costs. But, the time required to define an issue in such a way as to benefit all may be considerable. In addition to attempting to find a formulation of the proposal benefiting all, time may be required to explain the nature of the benefits of the proposal to some citizens unfamiliar with its merits. On top of these costs must be added the time lost through the strategic maneuvering, which might take place as individuals jockey for more favorable positions along the contract curve as described above.

Most observers, including those most favorably disposed toward the unanimity rule like Wicksell and Buchanan and Tullock, have considered these latter costs sufficiently large to warrant abandoning this rule. If all need not agree to a committee decision, what percentage should agree? The above considerations suggest a tradeoff between the external costs of having an issue pass against which the individual is opposed, and the costs of time lost through decisionmaking. At the one pole stands unanimity, under which any individual can block any agreement until he has one with

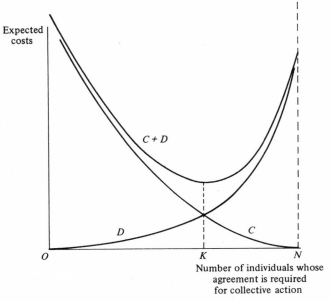

Figure 3.2

which he is satisfied, or which he feels is the best he can obtain. The external decision costs under this rule are zero, but the decision time costs may be infinite. At the other extreme, each individual decides the issue alone. No delays may occur, as with a pure private good decision, but the external costs of allowing each individual to decide unilaterally for the community are again potentially infinitely large.

These various possibilities are depicted in Figure 3.2, which is taken from Buchanan and Tullock [1962, pp. 63–91]. The costs of a particular collective decision are presented along the vertical axis, the number of people 0 up to N, the committee size, required to pass the issue along the horizontal axis. Curve C is the external cost function representing the expected loss of utility from the victory of a decision to which an individual is opposed under the committee decision rule. Curve D depicts the decision-time costs of achieving the required majority to pass the issue as a function of the size of the required majority. The optimal majority is the percentage of the committee at which these two sets of costs are together minimized. This occurs at K, where the vertical addition of the two curves reaches a minimum. The optimal majority to pass the issue, given these cost curves, is K/N. At this percentage, the expected gain in utility from redefining a bill to gain one more supporter just equals the expected loss in time from doing so.

Since these costs are likely to differ from issue to issue, one does not expect one voting rule to be optimal for all issues. The external costs will vary depending upon both the nature of the issues to be decided, and the characteristics of the community deciding them. *Ceteris paribus*, when opinions differ widely, or information is scarce, large amounts of time may be required to reach consensus, and if the likely costs to opposing citizens are not too high relatively small percentages of the community might be required to make a decision. The extreme example here is, again, the pure private good. In contrast, issues for which large losses can occur are likely to require higher majorities (e.g. Bill of rights type issues). The larger the community, the more individuals there are likely to be with similar tastes, and thus, the easier it is likely to be to achieve a consensus among a given *absolute* number of individuals. Thus, an increase in N should shift the curve D rightward and downward. But, the fall in costs of achieving a consensus among a given number is unlikely to be fully proportional to the rise in community size. Thus, for issues of a similar type, the optimal *percentage* of the community required to pass an issue K/N, is likely to be lower the larger the size of the community [Buchanan and Tullock, 1962, pp. 111–16].

Individuals whose tastes differ widely from most others in the community can be expected to favor more inclusive majority rules. Individuals with high opportunity costs of time should favor less inclusive majority rules. Buchanan and Tullock assume that the choice of the optimal majority for each category of issues is made in a constitutional setting in which each individual is uncertain over his future position, tastes, etc. Each views the problem in the same way, therefore, and a unanimous agreement as to which less than unanimity rule to use for which set of issues is achieved. When such a consensus does not exist, the knotty question must be faced of what majority should be required to decide the issue of what majorities are required on all other issues. Having now faced this question, we shall move on.

C. Majority rule

The method of majority rule requires that at least the first whole integer above $N/2$ support an issue before it can become the committee decision. Nothing we have said so far can indicate why $K/N = N/2$ should be the optimal majority for the bulk of a committee's decisions; and yet it is. As Buchanan and Tullock note, for any one rule, such as the majority rule, to be the optimal majority for a wide class of decisions there must exist some sort of a kink in one of the cost functions at the point $N/2$, causing the two curves to intersect in a substantial proportion of the cases at this point [1962, p. 81].

A possible explanation for a kink in the decisionmaking cost curve, D, at $N/2$ can be obtained by considering further the internal dynamics of the committee decision process. When less than half of a committee's membership is sufficient to pass an issue, the possibility exists for both the issue A and the issue's converse ($\sim A$) to pass. Thus, a proposal to increase school expenditures by 10 % might first achieve a winning majority (of say 40 %) and a counter proposal to cut expenditures by 5 % also receive a winning majority. The committee could, when less than half of the voters suffice to carry an issue, become deadlocked in an endless series of offsetting proposals absorbing the time and patience of its members. The method of simple majority rule has the smallest possible required majority to pass an issue, which avoids the possibility of self-contradictory issues simultaneously passing [Reimer, 1951]. It thus could be heavily favored as *the* committee decision rule by a committee whose members placed a relatively high value on the opportunity costs of decisionmaking time.

Most of the recent, and most persuasive arguments in favor of

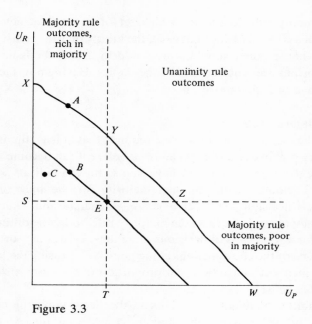

Figure 3.3

majority rule have not focused on its advantages in saving decision costs, however, but on its normative properties. Thus, a full treatment of the properties of majority rule, as with the unanimity rule, requires discussion of both its normative and positive properties. This is true, in the case of majority rule, because any issue which passes with a less than unanimous consent must almost inevitably leave some individuals worse off. Thus, a redistribution is effectively involved from those who are worse off through the issue's passage to those who are better off.[8] Any evaluation of these gains and losses, in defense of the less than unanimity rule, must depend on normative criteria. To see this point more clearly, consider Figure 3.3. On the vertical and horizontal axes are depicted the ordinal utilities of two groups of voters, the rich and the poor. All of the members of both groups are assumed to have

---

[8] For a discussion of the alternative argument, that significant redistribution is unlikely under the unanimity rule see George von Furstenberg and Dennis Mueller [1971], and Martin Faber [1973].

identical preference functions. In the absence of the provision of any public good, representative individuals from each group experience utility levels represented by S and T. The point of initial endowment on the Pareto possibility frontier with only private good production is E. The provision of the public good can by assumption improve the utilities of both individuals. Its provision thus expands the Pareto possibility frontier out to the curve $XYZW$. The segment YZ corresponds to the contract curve in Figure 3.1, CC'. Under the unanimity rule both groups of individuals must be better off under the provision of the public good for them to vote for it. So the outcome under the unanimity rule must be a quantity of public good and tax share combination leaving both groups somewhere in the YZ segment along the Pareto possibility frontier.

But there is no reason to expect the outcome to fall in this range under majority rule. A coalition of the committee's members can benefit by redefining the issue to increase their benefits at the expense of the noncoalition members, say by shifting the tax shares to favor the coalition members. If the rich were in the majority they could be expected to couple the public good proposal with a sufficiently regressive tax package so that the outcome wound up in the XY segment. If the poor were in the majority, the taxes would be sufficiently progressive to produce an outcome in ZW. Given the opportunity to redefine the issue proposed through the alteration of either the quantity of the public good provided, the tax shares, or both, one can expect with certainty that the outcome of the collective choice process *will* fall outside of the Pareto preferred segment YZ [Davis, 1970]. As long as the issue could be continually redefined in such a way that a majority still benefited, it would pass, and a stable majority coalition could, in principle, push a minority back as far along the Pareto possibility frontier as their consciences or the constitution allowed.

The process of transforming a proposal unanimously supported into one supported by only a simple majority resembles that described by William Riker in which 'grand' coalitions are transformed into minimum winning coalitions [1962]. In developing his theory of coalitions Riker makes two key assumptions: that decisions are made by majority rule, and that politics is a zero-sum game. He assumes that the allocational efficiency decisions (quantities of public goods) are all optimally resolved as a matter of course, and that the political process is left with the distributional issue of choosing from among the Pareto-efficient set (pp. 58–61). Thus, Riker takes the extreme position that politics involves *only* redistribution questions, and is a pure zero-sum game (pp. 29–31). Given that the game is to take from the losers, the winners can obviously be better off by increasing the size of the losing side, as long as it remains the losing side. Under majority rule this implies that the losing coalition be increased until it is almost as large as the winning coalition, until the proposal passes by a 'bare' majority. In Riker's description, the committee is made up of several factions or parties of different sizes, rather than two 'natural' coalitions are depicted above, and the process of forming a minimum winning coalition consists of adding and deleting parties or factions until two 'grand' coalitions of almost equal size are formed. In regular committee voting, the process would consist of adding and deleting riders to each proposal, increasing the number of losers and increasing the benefits to the remaining winners.

Several writers have described ways in which majority rule can lead to redistribution other than via the obvious route of direct cash transfers. The pioneering effort in this area was by Gordon Tullock [1959]. Tullock described a community of 100 farmers in which access to the main highway is via small trunk roads, each of which serves only 4 or 5 farmers. The issue comes up as to whether the entire community of 100 should finance the repair of all of the trunk roads out of a tax on the entire community. Obviously one can envisage a level of repairs and set of taxes on the individual farmers under which such a proposal would be unanimously adopted. But, under majority rule it is to the greater advantage of some to propose that only one half of the roads are repaired out of a tax falling on the entire population. Thus, one can envisage a coalition of 51 of the farmers forming and proposing that only the roads serving them are repaired out of the community's general tax revenue (there are other possible outcomes which Tullock discusses, and we take up below). Such a proposal would pass under majority rule, and obviously involves a redistribution from the 49 farmers who pay taxes and receive no road repairs to the 51 farmers whose taxes cover only slightly more than one half of the cost of the road repairs.

In the Tullock example redistribution to the 51 farmers in the majority coalition takes place through the inclusion in the larger community of 100's budget a good that is of benefit to only a subset of the community. Each access road benefits only 4 or 5 farmers and is a public good with respect to only these farmers. The optimal sized jurisdiction for deciding each of these 'local' public goods would seem to be the 4 or 5 farmers on each access road. The inclusion of private goods in the public budget as a means of bringing about redistribution was first discussed by James Buchanan [1970], and has been analyzed by several other writers. Building on Buchanan's paper Robert Spann has demonstrated that the collective provision of a private good financed via a set of Lindahl tax prices leads to a redistribution from the rich to the poor [Spann, 1974]. To see this, consider Figure 3.4. Let D_P be the demand schedule for the poor, D_R for the rich. Let X be a pure private good with price = marginal social cost = P_X. If the good is supplied to the market privately, the poor purchase X_P at price P_X, the rich purchase X_R. Assume next that the good is collectively purchased and supplied to the community in equal quantities per person, as if it were a public good. The optimal quantity of X is then given by the intersection of the community demand schedule, obtained by vertically summing the individual demand schedules. (We ignore here income effect considerations. The argument is not substantively affected by this omission.) The supply schedule under collective provision is obtained by multiplying the good's market price by the number of members of the community. If we assume for simplicity an equal number of rich and poor, the community will purchase X_C units of the good for each individual.

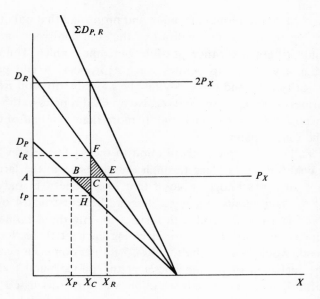

Figure 3.4

At this quantity, a poor individual places a marginal evaluation on the good of X_CH, and his Lindahl tax is t_P. A member of the rich group pays t_R. The poor receive an effective subsidy of $ACHt_P$, the difference between the price they pay for the good and its social cost multiplied by the quantity they consume. But their consumer surplus gain from the collective provision of the private good is only $ABHt_P$. Thus, there is a deadweight loss of BCH through the collective provision of X. In addition to the direct transfer of income from R to P (t_RFCA) via the subsidization of P's purchase of X, R is worse off by being forced to consume a less than optimal amount of X. R loses the consumer surplus triangle FCE [Buchanan, 1970, 1971; Spann, 1974].

This loss in efficiency comes about through the constraint placed on each individual's behavior, when all are forced to consume the same quantity of the private good. Given the costs of producing the private good all could be made better off by being allowed to maximize their individual utilities at the set of market prices for this and the other goods. The additional constraint that all consume the same quantity lowers the set of utilities possibly attainable. But, the poor are better off receiving the redistribution in this form than not at all, and if it is not feasible for them to obtain direct cash subsidies via lump-sum transfers, and it is possible to obtain them through the collectivization of private good supply, then the latter is worth pursuing.

The above illustration does not imply that redistribution will inevitably be from the rich to the poor,[9] or that it will take place at a set of Lindahl prices. It does help to emphasize, however, that the Pareto efficiency properties of the Lindahl prices are contingent on the constraint that all consume an equal quantity of the good being a natural (physical) constraint, and not one artificially imposed as in the collective provision of an essentially private good (see here again Buchanan [1960, 1971]; Spann [1974]).

Yoram Barzel [1973] individually and with Robert Deacon [1975] has taken up the specific case of education as a private good purchased and supplied as a public good, and has illustrated both the allocational inefficiencies and redistributive properties of this activity. Education is an example of a good which can involve redistribution from the bottom to the top (or middle) of the distribution. And redistribution may occur on the basis of criteria other than income (e.g. occupation, sex, race, geographic location, recreational preferences, political affiliation). What is required for redistribution to take place under majority rule is that the members of the winning coalition be clearly identifiable, so that the winning proposal can discriminate in their favor, either on the basis of the distribution of the benefits it provides (e.g. Tullock's unequal distribution of roads at equal taxes), or the taxes it charges (e.g. Buchanan and Spann's equal quantities of private good X at unequal taxes).

Regardless of what form it takes, and regardless of whether political choice under majority rule is a pure zero-sum game as Riker assumes, or involves allocational efficiency changes *plus*

---

[9] Davis argues that redistribution is generally toward the poor [1970]. We take up an alternative argument below.

redistribution, the fact remains that the redistributional characteristics of any proposal will figure in its passage, and that majority
rule creates the incentive to form coalitions and redefine issues to
achieve these redistributional gains. Indeed, from the mere knowledge that an issue passed with some individuals in favor and
others opposed, one cannot discern whether it really was a public
good shifting the Pareto possibility frontier out to $XYZW$ in Figure
3.3 coupled to a tax unfavorable to the poor, say, resulting in an
outcome at A; a pure redistribution along the private-good
Pareto-efficiency frontier resulting in B; or an inefficient redistribution from the poor to the rich via the collective provision of a
private good resulting in say C. All one can say with much
confidence is that the rich appear to believe they will be better off,
and the poor that they will be worse off from the proposal's
passage, i.e. that the move is into the region $SEYX$.

The redistributive properties of majority rule raise additional
ambiguities to which we now turn.

D. Cycling

Consider a three-man committee that must decide how to
divide a gift of \$100 among them using majority rule. This is a pure
distributional issue, a simple zero-sum game. Suppose that V_2 and
V_3 first vote to divide the \$100 between themselves, 60/40. V_1 now
has much to gain from forming a winning coalition. He might
propose to V_3 that they split the \$100, 50/50. This is more
attractive to V_3 and we can expect this coalition to form. But now
V_2 has much to gain from trying to form a winning coalition. He
might now offer V_1 a 55/45 split forming a new coalition, and so
on. When the issues proposed involve redistributions of income
and wealth, members of a losing coalition always have large
incentives to attempt to become members of the winning coalition,
even at the cost of a less than equal share.

The outcome of a fifty–fifty split of the hundred dollars among a
pair of voters is a von Neumann–Morgenstern solution to this
particular game [Luce and Raiffa, 1957, pp. 199–209]. There are
three such solutions to this game, however, and there is no way to

predict which of these three, if any, would occur. Thus, the potential for cycles, when issues involve redistribution seems quite large. It is always possible to redefine an issue so as to benefit one or more members and harm some others. New winning coalitions containing some members of the previously losing coalition, and excluding members of the previously winning coalition are always feasible. But, as we have seen from the discussion of majority rule above, when issues can be amended in the committee, any pure allocative efficiency decision can be converted into a combination of a redistribution and an allocative efficiency change via amendment. It would seem then, that when committees are free to amend the issues proposed, cycles must be an ever-present danger.

The possibility that majority rule can lead to cycles across issues was recognized almost two hundred years ago by the Marquis de Condorcet [1785]. C. L. Dodgson [1876] analyzed the problem anew one hundred years later, and it has been a major focus of the modern public choice literature beginning with Duncan Black [1948*b*] and Kenneth Arrow [1951, rev. ed. 1963].[10] Consider the following three voters with preferences over three issues as in Table 3.1 (> implies preferred). X can defeat Y, Y can defeat Z, and Z can defeat X. Pairwise voting can lead to an endless cycle. The majority rule can select no winner nonarbitrarily.[11]

If we define Z as a payoff to voters V_2 and V_3 of 60/40, Y as the payoff (50, 0, 50), and X as (55, 45, 0) the ordinal rankings of issues in Figure 3.5 corresponds to the above zero-sum pure distribution game. But it is also possible to get orderings as in Table 3.1 and Figure 3.5 for issues involving allocational efficiency. If X, Y, and Z are sequentially higher expenditures on a public good, then Voters 1 and 3's preferences can be said to be single-peaked in the public good-utility space (see Figure 3.5). Voter 2's preferences are double-peaked, however, and herein is the cause of the cycle. Change 2's preferences so that they are single-peaked, and the cycle disappears.

---

[10] For a discussion of these and other early contributions see Black [1958] and William Riker [1961].

[11] See A. K. Sen's discussion [1970*a*, pp. 68–77].

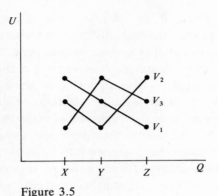

Figure 3.5

Table 3.1

Voters	Issues			
	X	Y	Z	X
1		>	>	<
2		>	<	>
3		<	>	>
Community		>	>	>

One of the early important theorems in public choice was D. Black's proof that majority rule produces an equilibrium outcome when voter preferences are single-peaked [1948*a*].[12] If voters' preferences can be depicted along a single dimension, as with an expenditure issue, this equilibrium lies at the peak-preference for the median voter. Figure 3.6 depicts the single-peaked preferences for 5 voters. Voters 3, 4, and 5 favor *m* over any proposal to supply less. Voters 3, 2, and 1 favor it over proposals to supply more. The preference of the median voter decides.

[12] G. H. Kramer has offered a rigorous proof [1972]. Kramer and A. K. Klevorick have established a similar result for local optima [1974], and A. Kats and S. Nitzan have shown that a local is likely to be a global equilibrium under fairly mild conditions [1976].

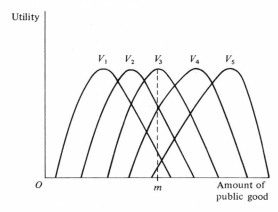

Figure 3.6

Single-peakedness is a form of homogeneity property of a preference ordering [Riker, 1961, p. 908]. People who have single-peaked preferences on an issue *agree* that the issue is one for which there is an optimum amount of the public good, and that the further one is away from the optimum, the worse off one is. If quantities of defense expenditures were measured along the horizontal axis, then a preference ordering as in Figure 3.6 would obviously imply that Voter 1 is somewhat of a dove, and Voter 5 a hawk, but a consensus of values would still exist with respect to the way in which the quantities of defense expenditures were ordered. The Black and Kramer theorems state that a consensus of this type (on a single dimensional issue) is sufficient to insure the existence of a majority rule equilibrium. During the Vietnam War, it was often said that some people favored *either* an immediate pullout or a massive expansion of effort to achieve total victory. Preferences of this type resemble Voter 2's preferences in Figure 3.5. It is preference orderings such as these that can lead to cycles. Note that the problem here may not be a lack of consensus on the way of viewing a single dimension of an issue, but on the dimensionality of the issue itself. The Vietnam War, for example, raised issues regarding both the United States' military posture abroad and humanitarian concern for the death and destruction it wrought.

One might have favored high expenditures to achieve the first, and a complete pullout to stop the second. These considerations raise, in turn, the question of the extent to which any issue can be viewed in a single dimension.

If all issues were unidimensional, multi-peaked preferences of the type depicted in Figure 3.5 might be sufficiently unlikely so that cycling would not be much of a problem. In a multi-dimensional world, however, preferences as in Table 3.1 seem quite plausible. Issues *X*, *Y*, and *Z* might, for example, be votes on whether to use a piece of land for a swimming pool, tennis courts, or a baseball diamond. Each voter could have single-peaked preferences on the amount to be spent on each activity, and a cycle still appear over the issue of the land's use. The introduction of distributional considerations into a set of issues can also, as already illustrated, produce cycles.

A great deal of effort has been devoted to defining conditions under which majority rule does yield an equilibrium. Returning to Figure 3.6, we can see, somewhat trivially, that *m* emerges as an equilibrium, because the other voters are evenly 'paired off' against one another regarding any move from *m*. This condition has been generalized by C. R. Plott [1967], who proved that a majority rule equilibrium exists, if it is a maximum for one (and only one) individual, and the remaining even number of individuals can be divided into pairs whose interests are diametrically opposed, i.e. any time a proposal is altered so as to benefit a given individual *A*, a given individual *B* must be made worse off. This condition is obviously too restrictive to offer much hope for insuring the existence of a majority rule equilibrium.[13] In addition, it is extremely vulnerable to strategizing, since any single voter can upset the equilibrium by slightly misrepresenting his preferences so that they no longer mirror his paired voter.

A second stream of literature has attempted to establish equilibrium conditions by placing restrictions on the preferences of the

[13] Although when buttressed by additional assumptions it may become more plausible. See Tullock [1967]; Arrow [1969]; Simpson [1969]. R. Saposnik's [1975] theorem is of the same genre.

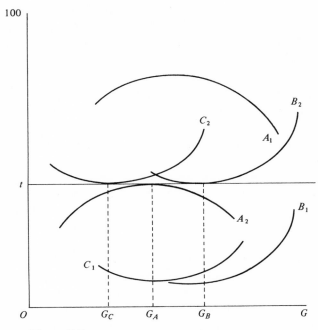

Figure 3.7

individual's voting as the single-peakedness condition does.[14] Not all of this literature is particularly relevant to public choice, since the conditions proposed often do not lend themselves to straight-forward interpretations, as single-peakedness does, nor is it clear that they can be plausibly assumed to exist in reality.[15] One of the most relevant attempts in the context of public choice to employ the single-peakedness condition to obtain a majority rule equilibrium has been presented by Steven Slutsky [1977*b*] (see also Bernholz [1974*b*]). Slutsky has proven that a majority rule equilibrium can exist, if voters are forced to choose from points along certain vectors in the public good–policy space. We shall

[14] For the most general statement of single-peakedness type conditions see A. K. Sen [1966]. See also, Sen and Pattanaik [1969] and Slutsky [1977*a*].
[15] This literature is surveyed in Inada [1969]; Sen [1970*a*]; Plott [1971]; Taylor [1971].

illustrate the point with a highly simplified example. Figure 3.7 represents the indifference curves of three individuals mapped into public good–tax shares space from private good–public good space as was done in deriving Figure 3.1. A's taxes are higher as one moves upward, B's and C's taxes are higher downward (assume B and C each pay one-half of $(100 - t)$. Instead of employing one of the voting procedures applied above with the unanimity rule, let the tax shares for A, B, and C be pre-assigned at the levels implied by t, and let the voters choose the quantity of public good via majority rule. A_2 is the highest utility level A can reach, B_2 and C_2 are the highest levels B and C can reach. The utility functions of the individuals are single-peaked in the one dimension in which they are free to choose (the quantity of the public good). G_A, the quantity of the good favored by median voter A, is the majority rule equilibrium. Note that there is no reason to expect that this equilibrium will be on the Pareto possibility frontier as was the equilibrium reached under the unanimity rule. Slutsky has proven that with more individuals and more policy dimensions, the same results can be obtained: a majority rule equilibrium exists, but it is non-Pareto efficient [1977*b*]. Slutsky's results illustrate the important distinction between the existence of an equilibrium under majority rule voting, and the normative properties of such an equilibrium. Under the constraints imposed in Slutsky's procedure, an equilibrium exists, but is non-Pareto efficient. Thus, it might be inferior to a non-constrained majority rule outcome, in which the outcome was chosen randomly but perhaps fairly, from a set of issues on the Pareto frontier over which there existed a cycle. This point is further strengthened when one considers the importance of the agenda setting step in Slutsky's procedure. Obviously the welfare effects of the procedure depend heavily on the initial choice of tax rate t. If B and C can control this step of the procedure and establish a high enough tax on A, the non-Pareto efficiency of the outcome will be of second interest to them. The role of the agenda step of the voting procedure has also been emphasized recently by Richard McKelvey [1976], and Michael Levine and Charles Plott [1977]. McKelvey shows that when conditions of diametric opposition as in Plott's theorem do not exist, 'it is *possible* for majority rule to wander anywhere in the space of alternatives. The *likelihood* of this occurring probably is strongly dependent on the nature of the institutional mechanisms which generate the agenda ' (italics in original [1976, p. 480]). Thus, if one voter can control the agenda at each step of voting 'he can construct an agenda which will arrive at any point in space, in particular at his ideal point' (p. 481). As a final observation on the normative properties of a majority rule equilibrium, note that a *sufficient* condition for there to be a majority rule equilibrium is for there to be $(N/2 + 1)$ voters with identical preferences [Buchanan, 1954; Kramer, 1973]. While the existence of such a natural coalition insures a stable outcome, the danger of such a majority coalition 'tyrannizing' over the minority of noncoalition members is likely to be great. This threat of a tyrannous majority has been a spectre haunting arguments for majority rule as long as these arguments have been made.

That irreconcilable conflict over tax shares and other direct redistribution measures can lead to cycles is perhaps not surprising. The reader may still feel, however, that between the Scylla of cycles, and the Charybdis of tyrannous majorities and manipulated agendas, there must still be types of issues which can be reasonably dealt with under majority rule. Unfortunately, this is not so. This can be seen most clearly in the recent attempt by Gerald Kramer [1973] to generalize the single-peakedness condition for majority rule equilibrium to more than one dimension. Kramer's theorem is of particular interest because, unlike much of the rest of the literature, which deals with preference orderings, Kramer postulates quasi-concave, differentiable utility functions as postulated in much of the economics' literature.

To see the significance of Kramer's theorem, consider Figure 3.8, adapted from Kramer [1973]. G and S are two public goods that can be provided in combinations of quantities as given along or within the production possibility frontier PP'. Let Y be the *status quo* point and W, X, and Z be three Pareto efficient alternatives to Y. Let U_1, U_1', U_2, and U_2' be indifference curves

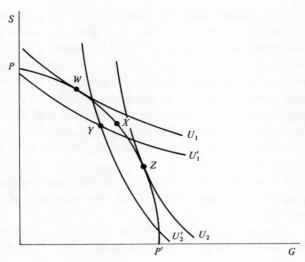

Figure 3.8

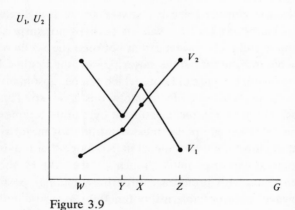

Figure 3.9

defined over G and S for two voters. The orderings of the four alternatives for the two voters in the dimensions of G are depicted in Figure 3.9. Voter 1's preferences are double peaked, and the stage is set for a cycle. When voters' preferences differ, any move to the Pareto possibility frontier can be a source of conflict, and the start of the cycle. 'The only obvious condition on individual preferences which will insure single-peakedness in two or more dimensions [and thus a majority rule equilibrium] is the condition of complete unanimity of individual preference orderings' [1973, p. 295].

And so we return to a unanimity condition. Recalling that what we seek at this stage of the discussion is a voting rule to reveal individual preferences on public goods, the options would appear to be as follows. A unanimity rule might be selected requiring a perhaps infinite number of redefinitions of the issue until one which benefited all citizens was reached. While each redefinition might, in turn, be defeated until a point on the Pareto possibility frontier had been reached, once attained no other proposal could command a unanimous vote against it, and the process would come to a halt. The number of times an issue must be redefined before a passing majority is reached can be reduced by reducing the size of the majority required to pass an issue. While this 'speeds up' the process of obtaining the *first* passing majority, it slows down, perhaps indefinitely, the process of reaching the *last* passing majority, i.e. the one which beats all others. For under a less than unanimity rule, some voters are made worse off. This is equivalent to a redistribution from the opponents of a measure to its proponents. As with any redistribution measure, it is generally possible to redefine an issue transferring the benefits among a few individuals and obtain a new winning coalition. The Plott 'perfect balance' condition insures an equilibrium under majority rule by imposing a form of severe symmetry assumption on the distribution of preferences which insures that any redefinition of an issue always involves symmetric and offsetting redistributions of the benefits leaving the winning coalition intact. Slutsky's constrained voting procedure reduces the effective decision at each stage to one of choosing along a single dimension, thereby achieving the kind of balance required by Plott's theorem. The Kramer 'identical utility functions' condition removes all conflict, and thereby eliminates all questions of redistribution.

The redistributive characteristics of less than unanimity rules explain the similarities between the proofs and conditions establishing a social welfare function and majority rule equilibrium (or the impossibilities thereof). Both flounder on their inability to choose among Pareto preferred points, i.e. to handle the question of redistribution (see A. K. Sen [1970*a*, chs. 5, 5*]). We shall return to these issues again when we take up the normative properties of the various voting rules in Part II.

Out of the frustration of seeking formal proofs for the existence of majority rule equilibria a large number of studies have explored, using simulation techniques, the probabilities that cycles would occur in practice. Their findings are dependent on the assumptions made about the likelihood of various preference orderings occurring. We are, to some extent, already prepared for these results. Cycles occur because of a conflict of interest over redistribution-type issues. When the conflict is not such as to yield Plott's 'perfect balance' of opposing interests the probability of a cycle occurring is very high, and approaches 1 as the number of alternatives increases.[16] We have also noted, that a cycle cannot occur if a majority of voters have identical preferences. Thus, we might expect that as various homogeneity assumptions are made about voter preferences, the probability of a cycle occurring decreases. And this is so. Niemi [1969] and Tullock and Campbell [1970] have found the probability of a cycle declines as the number of single-peaked preferences increases. Williamson and Sargent [1967], and Gehrlein and Fishburn [1976] have found the probability of cycles declines with the proportion of the population having the same preferences, and similarly Kuga and Nagatani [1974] find that it increases with the number of pairs of voters whose interests are in conflict. While these results are comforting, it is not clear how comforting they are. To the extent that the collective choice process involves only movements from off the contract curve to points on it, i.e. the kinds of decisions the unanimity rule might be able to handle, voter interests tend to

---

[16] Garmen and Kamien [1968]; Niemi and Weisberg [1968]; DeMeyer and Plott [1970]; Gehrlein and Fishburn [forthcoming]. This literature is reviewed in Niemi [1969]; Riker and Ordeshook [1973, pp. 94–7]; Plott [1976].

coincide, and the probability of a cycle under majority rule will be low. But to the extent the issues to be decided involve redistribution, interests will not coincide, indexes of 'voter antagonism' will be high, and so too will the probability of cycles.

E. Logrolling

For a cycle to take place, issues must be taken up sequentially. X pitted against Y, Y against Z, and Z again against X. When issues are voted on in this way another process may be set in motion, however, one that is usually referred to as logrolling.[17]

To understand the process, consider Table 3.2. Each column gives the utility changes to three voters from an issue's passage; defeat produces no change. If each is decided separately by majority rule, both fail. Voters B and C have much to gain from X and Y's passage, however, and can achieve this if B votes for Y in exchange for C's vote for X. Both issues now pass to B and C's mutual benefit.

Table 3.2

	Issues	
Voters	X	Y
A	-2	-2
B	5	-2
C	-2	5

The existence of beneficial trades requires a non-uniform distribution of intensities. Change the two 5s to 2s and B and C gain nothing by trading. This equal intensity condition is often invoked in arguments in favor of simple (without trading) majority rule, and will be taken up later when we consider the normative case for majority rule.

[17] The seminal discussions of this topic are by Downs [1957], Tullock [1959], and most extensively Buchanan and Tullock [1962]. In political science the classic reference is Bentley [1907].

The trade between B and C can be said to have improved the welfare of the community of 3 votes, if the numbers in Table 3.2 are treated as cardinal, interpersonally comparable utilities. Without trading, the majority tyrannizes over the relatively more intense minority on each issue. Through vote trading, these minorities express the intensity of their preferences, just as trading in private goods does, and improve the total welfare change of the community. With trading there is a net gain of 2 for the community, without a net loss of 2.

An obvious condition for an improvement in community welfare through the changes in outcomes vote trading brings about is that the cumulative potential utility changes for the (losing) minority members exceed the cumulative potential utility changes for the winning majority members on the issues involved. Change the 5s to 3s or the -2s of A to -4s and the same trades emerge as before, since the pattern of trades depends only on the *relative* intensities of preferences of the voters. The sum of utilities for the community with trading is then negative, however. An exchange of votes increases the likelihood of the participants winning on their relatively more important issues. It *tends*, therefore, to increase their realized gains. These increases *can* increase the utility gain for the entire community. Trading also imposes externalities (utility losses) on the non-traders who would have been better off in the absence of trading,[18] however, and, if these are negative and large, they can outweigh the gains to the traders, lowering the community's net welfare. Critics of logrolling have typically envisaged situations such as these. They assume that the cumulative potential gains of the majority exceed those of the minority. Vote trading which reverses some of the outcomes of simple majority rule lowers collective welfare when this is true.

Gordon Tullock's [1959] argument that majority rule *with trading* can lead to too much government spending is of this type. Let A, B, and C, be 3 farmers, and X be a road of use only to farmer B, Y a road of use to only C. If the gross gains to a farmer from the access road are 7 and the cost is 6 which is shared equally,

18 See Taylor [1971, p. 344], and Riker and Brams [1973].

we have the figures of Table 3.2. With these costs and benefits, total welfare is improved by logrolling. But a bill promising a gross gain of 5 at a cost of 6, equally shared, also passes. Such a bill lowers community welfare, by excessively constructing new roads, roads whose total benefits are less than their total costs. Again, the problem arises because majority rule can involve both allocation and redistribution at the same time. The two bills involve both the construction of roads with gross benefits of 5 and costs of 6, and the redistribution of wealth from A to B and C, and the latter can be sufficient to pass the bills.

An important difference separating logrolling's critics and proponents is their views as to whether voting is a positive or negative (at best zero) sum game. If the latter, the game is obviously bad to begin with, and anything which improves its efficiency can only worsen the final outcome. The numerical examples Riker and Brams [1973] present in their attack on logrolling are all examples of this type, and the examples they cite of tariff bills, tax loop-holes, and pork barrel public works, are all illustrations of bills for which a minority benefits, largely from the redistributive aspects of the bill, and the accumulative losses of the majority can be expected to be large.[19] The worst examples of logrolling cited in the literature are always issues of this type in which private or local public goods are added to the agenda for redistribution purposes to be financed out of public budgets at a higher level of aggregation than is appropriate [Schwartz, 1975]. The best the community can hope for is the defeat of all of these issues. Riker and Brams [1973] logically recommend reforms to eliminate logrolling opportunities.

A private good or a very local public good will of course be of great interest to a few and little interest to the majority. The conditions necessary for logrolling are likely to be satisfied, therefore, through the incorporation of these goods into the community's agenda. But, preference intensities can also vary considerably across individuals on what are truly pure public

---

[19] See, also Schattschneider [1935]; McConnell [1966]; Lowi [1969].

goods, e.g. defense, education and the environment. On issues such as these vote trading can be a superior way for revealing individual preference intensities over the public goods.

One of the most positive and influential discussions of vote trading's potential has been presented by James Coleman.[20] He depicts the members of the committee or legislature as entering into logrolling agreements on all public good issues. Each voter forms agreements to swap votes with other voters of the type described above. Each voter increases his ability to *control* those *events* (issues) about which he feels most intense in exchange for a loss of control over those events about which he cares little. A form of *ex ante* Pareto optimum is reached in which no voter feels he can increase his expected utility by agreeing to exchange another vote. This equilibrium is the optimum of Coleman's social welfare function.

Table 3.3

Voters	Issues		
	X	Y	Z
A	-1	-2	-3
B	5	-2	6
C	-2	5	-1

Unfortunately, the outcomes under the vote trading process as Coleman describes it may be neither stable equilibria, nor free from strategic misrepresentation of preferences. Indeed, the same preference orderings that can produce a logrolling situation, can produce the paradox of voting.[21] Table 3.3 presents preferences

---

20 [1966*b*]. See also Coleman [1966*a*, 1970].
21 See Park [1967]; Kadane [1972]; Bernholz [1973, 1974*a*, 1975]; Riker and Brams [1973]; Koehler [1973].

Somewhat of a debate has developed over just what kinds of logrolling situations lead to what kinds of cyclic preference orderings. For a useful review of this issue see Nicholas Miller [1977].

for issues X and Y, which are almost identical to those of Table 3.2. The only difference is that voter A is now no longer indifferent between issues X and Y. If trading is allowed, voters B and C still will choose to trade on issues X and Y. If Z is now added to the list of issues an intransitive social ordering under simple majority rule exists $(X > Y > Z > X)$. The only condition under which a potential logrolling situation is certain not to create the potential for a cycle is when a unanimity rule is imposed [Bernholz, 1973].

Just how serious this problem is is not clear, however. For a cycle actually to occur over X, Y and Z these 3 issues must be treated as mutually exclusive events. Z must defeat Y, Y defeat X, and X defeat Z. But B and C would never agree to swap votes on issues X and Y if they thought that they would appear as *alternatives* on the agenda. The purpose in their trading votes is to produce the simultaneous victory of *both* X and Y. The usual assumption made in the logrolling literature is that the issues are independent outcomes, all of which could pass or fail simultaneously. Under this assumption, the relationship between logrolling and cyclic preference orderings has a different interpretation. The existence of a logrolling situation will then imply the existence of several possible winning coalitions that can emerge under logrolling, all of which are capable of defeating the outcomes from sincere voting under majority rule on the individual issues. Which set of outcomes actually emerges depends somewhat arbitrarily on the particular coalitions that form [Oppenheimer, 1975]. This element of arbitrariness need not worsen the outcome of the voting process, however. We have already considered a situation in which the summation of utility changes was higher with logrolling than when the issues were decided independently by majority rule. It is possible that all of the possible outcomes under logrolling will be superior to those under majority rule without logrolling. Which process yields the preferred outcomes still depends on the nature of the issues to be decided, i.e. whether the committee is playing positive or negative sum games, and the particular coalitions that do in fact form.

When vote trades are parts of only informal agreements, and

take place in sequence, voters have incentives both to misstate their preferences at the time an agreement is formed, and violate the agreement after it is made. A voter who would benefit from X might pretend to oppose it and secure support for some other issue he favors in 'exchange' for his positive vote for X. If successful, he wins on both X and the other issue. But the other 'trader' might be bluffing too, and the end-results of trading become indeterminate [Mueller, 1967].

Even when bluffing is not a problem cheating may be. When issues are taken up *seriatim*, there is an obvious and strong incentive for the second trader to renege on his part of the bargain. We have here another example of a prisoners' dilemma [Bernholz, 1977*b*]. Matrix 3.1 depicts the strategic options for voters B and C,

Matrix 3.1

		Voter C	
		Vote for X and Y	Vote for Y and against X
Voter B	Vote for X and Y	1 (+3, +3)	2 (−2, +5)
	Vote for X, and against Y	3 (+5, −2)	4 (−2, −2)

when issues X and Y must be decided as before. Both voters are better off with the trade (square 1) than without it (square 4), but the incentive to cheat is present. If issue X is decided before issue Y, and voter C lives up to his part of the bargain by voting for X, the outcomes in column 2 becomes infeasible. Voter B must choose between squares 1 and 3 and his choice is obvious, if there is no possibility for voter C to retaliate.

As we have seen in Chapter 2, the cooperative solution to the prisoners' dilemma emerges only if one player thinks that his choice of the cooperative strategy is likely to induce the corresponding strategy choice of the other player. If the strategy options are played in sequence, and the game is played but once, the first player has no means by which to influence the second player's decision at the time the latter is made. Thus, one would not expect vote trading to take place over issues decided sequentially, among coalitions that form but a single time. A stable, cooperative vote-trading game can be expected only when the issues on which votes are traded are all decided simultaneously, say as part of an omnibus highway bill; or when the same constellations of issues come up time and time again, and a prisoners' dilemma supergame emerges. Peter Bernholz [1977a] has recently discussed the latter possibility. Under the assumption that the same types of issues do arise again and again, he shows that the likelihood of a stable prisoners' dilemma supergame emerging is positively related to both the net potential gains from cooperation, and the probability that the same players reappear in each successive game. As Bernholz notes, the depiction of logrolling situations as single plays of a prisoners' dilemma supergame is plausible for a legislative assembly, whose members continually represent the same interests and have reasonably long tenure. Parties, with their party whips, and interest groups can be seen as devices for further reinforcing cooperative behavior among coalition members.

An alternative way of avoiding the instabilities and uncertainties that arise from informal vote trading on sequentially decided issues is to force voters literally to trade votes by setting up 'markets' for the votes on each issue.[22] Each voter could be given an equal number of divisible votes on every issue, and actual trading take place via a Walrasian tâtonnement process in formal vote markets. As in a Walrasian exchange economy all issues would be effectively decided together, and the problem of cycles eliminated. Voters would be prevented from violating trading

[22] Mueller [1967]; Wilson [1971a, b].

agreements by being forced actually to give votes on one issue to obtain those on another. The relative interest of each voter on each issue would be revealed through these trades and would not require any, potentially misleading prediscussion of voter intentions. Simulation of such a vote-trading model in which each voter has a *positive* and *equal* potential utility change from the set of outcomes of the collective choice process indicate that an explicit vote-trading process can come close to achieving the maximum possible gains under collective action [Mueller, Philpotts, and Vanek, 1972].

The explicit vote-trading model is the logical extension of the simple logrolling model, and its logical equivalents, simple majority rule with full-side payments [Buchanan and Tullock, 1962, pp. 152–88] and point voting. Point voting is the simplest and in many ways most attractive procedure for revealing relative intensities on issues.[23] Each voter is given an equal stock of vote-points which he can divide any way he chooses, and asked to allocate them across the issue set in proportion to the relative importance he attaches to each issue. If each voter allocates his vote points sincerely, and if the initial issue set were chosen so that the integral of possible utility changes over the entire issue set were the same for all voters, point voting would achieve the maximum utility gain possible under collective action. These two assumptions are crucial to the argument that vote trading, and point voting schemes improve the collective decision outcomes. We noted above that it is necessary for an improvement in results to come about through vote trading, for the combined utility changes of the minority to exceed those of the majority on those outcomes which are changed under vote trading. This condition will be met, and the outcomes improved if the integral of utilities for each voter over all issues is the same, i.e. each voter has an 'equal stake' in the collective choice process [Mueller, 1971], and voters trade away votes on relatively less important issues for those on relatively more important issues.

[23] Musgrave [1959, pp. 130–1]; Coleman [1970]; Mueller [1973].

The equal stake and honest preference revelation assumptions are also contained in Michael Intriligator's [1973] probabilistic variant on point voting.[24] Intriligator's procedure gives each voter the same number of *probability* points and asks him to allocate these according to his relative intensities over the entire issue set. The *social* probabilities of picking each issue are then obtained by aggregating the individual probabilities over all issues. The social choice is then made by a random drawing from an urn in which each issue is represented in proportion to its social probability. While the assumption that the elements of a probability vector sum to 1.0 may seem more reasonable than the assumption that different voter utility integrals are equal, they amount to the same thing and are equally strong. Each voter's preferences over the entire issues set are given equal weight in the social choice process. The need for voters to vote honestly is again present in Intriligator's probabilistic social choice process.[25]

The equal stake criterion underlying the arguments for vote trading and point voting, and the implicit equal stake criterion contained in Intriligator's probabilistic voting model raise again the importance of the issue selection process. This is obviously also true when logrolling takes place over time as issues are taken up *seriatim*. If logrolling cycles are to be avoided the agenda must be carefully planned and controlled.[26] We have noted above the potential importance of the chairman or agenda setter under simple majority rule. Since logrolling involves the use of majority rule, and is plagued by all the other problems associated with this

[24] See, also Nitzan [1975].
[25] Intriligator presents an *Independence* axiom for his voting procedure. 'The social probability of choosing one alternative depends only on the individual probabilities of choosing that alternative; it is independent of all other individual probabilities' [1973, p. 556]. He notes immediately that this axiom is not the same as Arrow's independence axiom. Nor does it accomplish the same objective. While Arrow's independence axiom protects the social choice from strategic behavior, Intriligator's does not. A change in any of the other issues in the issue set, which affects the probability that an individual attaches to a given issue, will change the probability that this issue is the social choice.
[26] For an interesting discussion of the procedures employed by Congress to control cyclic and logrolling situations see Sullivan [1976].

rule, it is not surprising that the chairman's role is also important in determining the properties of outcomes under vote trading procedures.

The interdependence among all of the outcomes under logrolling and vote-trading-type procedures makes them vulnerable to strategic behavior.[27] By changing his stated or revealed preferences toward one issue, a voter can affect the outcome on another. Under certain conditions it will increase a voter's expected utility to misstate the relative intensities of his preferences by his trading or point-vote allocation decisions. In an explicit vote-trading process, if each individual follows a sophisticated strategy of allowing for the trading behavior of others, when deciding his own trades, final outcomes can be worse with full, enforceable trading than without it [Philpotts, 1972]. Similar problems may arise under point voting. The potential attractiveness of vote trading, as more obviously of point voting, depends upon an absence of this type of strategic behavior on the part of voters. Robert Wilson's proof that, under certain assumptions, a citizen's optimal vote-trading strategy is 'sincere' voting is somewhat comforting in this regard.[28]

F. **A comparison of majority rule with some of its alternatives**

Several variations on or alternatives to the majority rule have been proposed down through the years. A few of the newest and most complicated of these are taken up in the next chapter. In this section we briefly discuss some of the simpler proposals that have been made.

Unlike the logrolling and vote trading schemes just discussed, or

[27] Even majority rule without trading can be plagued by strategy problems, however. A voter who knew or thought that a sincere casting of votes on all issues would produce a stable, and for him undesirable, majority winner, might misstate his preferences to produce a cycle, trusting to chance, or perhaps a known procedure over which he exercises some control, to break the cycle in a more favorable way [Taylor, 1968; Farquharson, 1969; Riker and Ordeshook, 1973, pp. 97–9].

[28] The particular assumptions Wilson imposes (e.g. that a voter's valuation of the votes he acquires on an issue does not depend on their price, and that all bills have the same equilibrium prices), however, make his result more relevant to the case of point voting [1969].

the procedures described in the next chapter, the voting procedures to be discussed in this section are usually not discussed as means for revealing preferences on a public good issue; instead they are usually described as procedures for choosing a candidate for a given office. Thus, unlike in the logrolling examples just discussed, all issues cannot simultaneously be chosen. Only one of them can be. Although such choices are perhaps most easily envisaged by thinking of a list of candidates for a vacant public office, the procedures might be thought of as being applied to a choice from among any set of mutually exclusive alternatives – as for example points along the Pareto possibility frontier.

The seminal discussion of these rules is Duncan Black's [1958, pp. 55–75], and we shall follow it. The problem is to choose *one* from a list of m candidates, where m is greater than 3. We first briefly list the alternative procedures including majority rule, and then discuss their properties.

Majority rule. Choose that candidate who is ranked first by more than half of the voters.

Plurality rule. Choose that candidate who is ranked first by the largest number of voters.

Condorcet criterion. Choose that candidate who defeats all others in pairwise elections using majority rule. This procedure is named after the Marquis de Condorcet who discussed it in 1785 (see bibliographical discussion by Black [1958, pp. 159–80].

Borda count. Give each of the m proposals a score of from 1 to m based on its ranking in a voter's preference ordering: i.e. the proposal he ranks first receives m points, the proposal he ranks second $m - 1$, . . ., the proposal he ranks last one point. Add the points for each proposal over all voters. Declare the proposal with the highest number of points the winner. This procedure was proposed by Jean-Charles de Borda in 1781.[29]

---

[29] See, again Black [1958, pp. 156–9, 178–80]. Black also describes an adjusted Borda count in which the above procedure is adjusted to take into account ties in rankings (pp. 61–4), but this will not concern us here. Simply assume that tied candidates received the average of the sum of the scores they would get if they occupied the same positions in the voter's preference ordering but were not tied.

Exhaustive voting. Ask each voter to indicate the candidate he ranks *lowest* from the list of m candidates. Remove that candidate who is ranked lowest by the most voters from the list. Ask each voter to indicate the candidate from the remaining list of $(m - 1)$ candidates, he ranks lowest. Remove the candidate ranked lowest by most voters from this list. Repeat the process until a single candidate is left. Declare him the winner.

To this list we shall add a procedure not discussed by Black, but recently explored by Brams and Fishburn [1977].

Approval voting. Each voter casts a vote for all of the candidates on the list of m of whom he approves. The candidate with the most votes wins.

A serious problem with majority rule when there are more than 2 candidates is, of course, that no candidate may be ranked first by more than half the voters. There may be no winner.

There will always be a winner under plurality voting, but the winner may have little to be said on his behalf if the candidates' votes are widely and evenly divided. Consider the following set of voter rankings over 4 candidates (Table 3.3). There is no majority

Table 3.4

V_1	V_2	V_3	V_4	V_5
X	X	Y	Z	W
Y	Y	Z	Y	Y
Z	Z	W	W	Z
W	W	X	X	X

winner. X is the winner under the plurality rule. But Y obviously has a lot to recommend it as the 'best' choice from among this list of candidates for it stands relatively high on all voter preference scales. The potential difficulty or objection with the plurality rule is that it, like majority rule, takes into account only information about the voters' *first* preferences, how the other candidates stand in their preference orderings is not revealed.

Each of the other 4 voting procedures takes into account more information about the voters' preference orderings, and whatever advantage (or disadvantage) they have over the other procedures comes from this property. In the example presented in Table 3.3, Y is the Condorcet winner. It defeats Z and W in pairwise elections, 4 to 1; and defeats X, the plurality winner, 3 to 2. Indeed, Y is the winner by any of the other 3 voting procedures which take into account more information about voter preferences.

The Condorcet criterion has the possible disadvantage against the other three in that it, like majority rule, may not choose a winner. Whenever a majority rule cycle can occur over 3 or more issues, the possibility exists that these candidates form a set of 'top' candidates capable of beating all others, but that no winner from among these can be chosen.

Even when a Condorcet winner exists there may be something more to be said for the winner chosen by one of the other three voting procedures. Consider Table 3.4. X is both a Condorcet and

Table 3.5

V_1	V_2	V_3	V_4	V_5
X	X	X	Y	Y
Y	Y	Y	Z	Z
Z	Z	Z	X	X

a majority rule winner. But clearly this voting situation is one which has some characteristics of a 'tyranny of the majority'. Under either the Condorcet or majority rule procedures, the first 3 voters are able to impose their candidate on the other 2, who rank him last. Y, on the other hand, is more of a 'compromise' candidate, who ranks *relatively* high on all preference scales, and for this reason Y might be the 'best' choice from among the three candidates, given the preference orderings of Table 3.4. Y is the winner using the Borda count procedure.

Y is the winner in the situation depicted in Table 3.4, because it stands highest *on average* in the voters' preference orderings.[30] This property of the Borda count procedure gives its outcomes a certain degree of stability or consistency, which may be deemed desirable in and of itself.[31] John Smith [1973], and H. P. Young [1974] have demonstrated formally that the Borda count procedure has the following consistency property, and 3 others we shall not review here, and that any voting procedure having these 4 properties is equivalent to the Borda count:

Consistency. Let N_1 and N_2 be two groups of voters who are to select an alternative from the set A. Let C_1 and C_2 be the respective sets of alternatives which the two groups select using voting procedure B. Then if C_1 and C_2 have any elements in common (i.e. $C_1 \cap C_2$ is not empty), then the winning issue under procedure B when these two subgroups are brought together ($N_T = N_1 \cup N_2$) is contained in this common set of elements ($C_T = C_1 \cap C_2$).

This consistency property has obvious intuitive appeal. If two groups of voters agree on an alternative when choosing separately from a set of alternatives, they should agree on the same alternative when they are combined.

The greater consistency or stability inherent in the Borda count and other procedures relying on more information about voter preference orderings than majority rule or the plurality rule has

---

[30] In a different way the Condorcet criterion also yields an outcome which is *on average* more preferred than all others. Black begins his discussion of the various voting procedures with the normative postulate 'that the candidate who ought to be elected is the one who stands highest on the average on the elector's schedules of preferences' (p. 56). See also his justification [1958, pp. 55–7].

[31] See, also C. Plott [1976, pp. 560–3]. The Borda count, Condorcet criterion and the other procedures that rely in one way or another on information about the complete preference orderings of all voters are, like point voting and logrolling, vulnerable to strategizing on the part of individual voters, or disruptive coalition formations (see Prassanta Pattanaik [1974]). It should be noted that point voting could easily be adapted to decide mutually exclusive issues, if one wanted to weigh voter evaluations of the cardinal utility differences among the candidates, rather than just take account of their ordinal evaluations as the Borda procedure does.

been demonstrated in simulated elections, and in at least one actual election outcome. William Ludwin [1976] has simulated the outcomes from 3 candidate elections assuming the percentages of the population holding each of the 6 possible orderings (ties are not considered) are drawn randomly from a rectangular probability distribution. His main results are reproduced in Table 3.5 (with the runoff method, the candidate receiving the lowest number of votes is eliminated until a majority rule winner is found). The percentages of the cases in which the 4 procedures relying on more complete information disagree are all close together, falling in the range 13–18 percent. All of these procedures are clearly differentiated from the plurality rule procedure, with which they all disagree from 24 to 34 % of the time.

Table 3.6. *Disagreement table: All cases (10,000 cases) per cent*

	Borda	Plurality	Runoff	Exhaustive
Condorcet	18	31	13	13
Borda		24	17	17
Plurality			24	34
Runoff				16

Simulations of election outcomes by Fishburn and Gehrlein [1976a, b] have indicated a high propensity for the approval voting rule to select the Condorcet winner, when one exists. Approval voting is a potentially attractive voting procedure when voters tend to group candidates into two or three preference sets, the 'good guys' and the 'bad guys'. Suppose, for example, the first 3 voters, whose preferences are depicted in Table 3.4, although preferring X to Y, would accept either X or Y's victory rather than have Z win, i.e. the gap in their preference ordering between X and Y is much smaller than between Y and Z. These voters might then cast a vote for X and Y under the approval voting rule. If they did, Y would emerge the winner under this rule, as it did under the Borda count. The closeness of Y to X in the first 3 voters' preference orderings, as indicated by their votes for both Y and X, plus Y's top ranking in V_4's and V_5's preference orderings gives Y a certain amount of intuitive legitimacy as the election winner.

Brams and Fishburn [1977] have proven (Theorem 4) that when voter preferences are such that the list of candidates can be divided for each voter into two subsets, such that the voter is indifferent between all candidates within a subset, then approval voting is the only voting system that is strategy proof for every possible set of preferences. That is, regardless of what he assumes about the voting strategies of other voters, a voter's best own strategy is to vote for all members of his top ranked subset of candidates under approval voting. This (and the sincerity property for trichotomous preferences) would appear to be important advantages of the approval system over its competitors. But the significance of this result must depend on the realism of the assumption that voters will group a list of m candidates into 2 or 3 subsets. Here it might be noted that if voters did group all candidates into two subsets, and were indifferent among the members of any subset, *and assigned all members of a subset the same rank under the Borda procedure*, it would achieve the same outcome as under approval voting.

The agreement among the Borda count, Condorcet criterion and other more complete information procedures as to the choice of winner comes about because these 'criteria are an attempt to pick out the candidate who stands highest on average on the schedules of the electors and each tends to act against candidates who have a low ranking in the estimate of a substantial fraction of the voters; they tend to eliminate candidates who are viewed as extremists of one kind or another' [Black, 1958, p. 75]. The practical significance of this property is revealed in Richard Joslyn's study of the 1972 Democratic presidential primary results [1976]. Primary elections in the US are run under the plurality rule. Joslyn argues that in 1972 this rule favored extremist candidate George McGovern, who was the first choice of a plurality of voters in many states but was ranked relatively low by many other voters, over 'middle-of-the-road' Edmund Muskie, who was ranked relatively high by a large number of voters. Joslyn's most striking result is his recalculation of final delegate counts under the various voting rules presented in Table 3.6 (double election is a two-step runoff procedure). The interesting feature of this table is the dramatic increase in Muskie's delegate strength under any of the voting procedures other than the plurality rule.

Table 3.7*. *Delegate totals under various decision rules*

Candidate	Plurality rule	Double election	Condorcet choice	Borda count	Adjusted Borda count
McGovern	1,307	766	766	766	584
Muskie	271	788	869	869	869

* Adapted from Joslyn [1976, Table 5, p. 12].

One might *argue* that Muskie *should* have been the Democratic Party's nominee in 1972, and that, therefore, one of the other voting procedures is preferable to the plurality rule. Muskie would have had a better chance to defeat Nixon than McGovern, and McGovern's supporters would probably have preferred a Muskie victory to a McGovern defeat in the final runoff against Nixon. And, with the infinite wisdom of hindsight, one can argue that 'the country' would have been better off with a Muskie victory over Nixon.

But all of this is loaded with value judgements. As a *practical* matter one might argue that a party should always field its strongest candidate against the other party (i.e. maximize its probability of success), in which case one would reject the plurality rule. But to argue normatively that a party should always do so is to argue again that a party should nominate candidates that are ranked on *average* higher than other candidates, *should* adopt consistent voting rules, should adopt voting rules that eliminate the extremist candidates. While there is some intuitive justification for these norms, it does not seem to stand on as firm a ground as some of the other normative criteria we shall discuss, like the Pareto postulate, or Nondictatorship.

Whatever their normative justification, the practical implications of adopting the Condorcet criterion, Borda count, or exhaustive voting method are clear. They will eliminate the extremist candidates.

G. Direct democracy when the number of voters is large

One reason direct democracy has given way to representative democracy is because town meeting assemblies become impossible with large numbers of voters [Dahl, 1970]. Modern advances in communications (e.g. the computer and coaxial cable) open up the possibility for direct democracy (with vote trading, or point voting, too, if desired) with almost unlimited numbers of participants [Miller, III, 1969]. Alternatively, the use of rapid communications' technology could allow individual voters to maintain continual contact with their representatives, 'recall' these representatives instantaneously in cases of disagreement, or transfer votes from one representative to another. Thus, direct citizen participation in the democratic process at all levels of decisionmaking is a real possibility for the not-too-distant-future. In addition to increasing the individual citizen's direct participation in the democratic process, such schemes have the advantage of reducing the scope for strategic behavior to its bare minimum, by expanding the number of players of the game, and literally 'isolating' each of them from one another.

But direct democracy at all levels may have its drawbacks. To the extent that democratic decisions evolve out of the informed debate of the participants in the process, participation via the intermediary of the coaxial cable, and instant referenda may worsen the quality of the decisions made. 'Time lags in the political process are precisely the critical periods needed to enable other influences to modify the instantaneous response of an unpremeditating voter' [Shubik, 1970, p. 82]. Shubik's comment raises in turn the question of whether the average citizen has the time, incentive, or expertise to make his participation in the democratic process improve its results. But, this is an old question, and we shall have to encounter it again when we take up representative democracy in Chapter 6.

4

Some new processes for revealing preferences on public goods

The dilemma posed by Samuelson [1954] in his classic paper on public goods has plagued the public choice literature throughout its existence: how to get individuals to reveal their preferences of varying intensities for a good all of necessity consume in equal quantity so as to satisfy the efficiency conditions set out in the Samuelson paper. Traditional voting schemes seem vulnerable to the transaction costs and strategic incentives inherent in the unanimity rule, or the paucity of information and onus of compulsion characterizing less than unanimity rules, as most notably the majority rule. This dilemma has led several writers to pursue new, more sophisticated preference revelation mechanisms, which have the desirable properties sought by Wicksell [1896], Lindahl [1920], and Musgrave [1939, 1959] in the development of the 'voluntary exchange' approach, but involve more plausible incentive structures for revealing individual preferences honestly than seem inherent in the traditional voting mechanisms. In this chapter we describe 3 such proposals, proceeding in a more-or-less chronological order. Given their novelty and complexity, we shall devote relatively more space to them than we have to other topics of equal importance.

A. **Preference revelation through the purchase of insurance**

Earl Thompson [1966] has devised a scheme by which individuals reveal their preferences for public goods through the purchase of insurance against the victory of their least favored issue. To see how the procedure works consider the following example.

The government announces a new proposal, P, to replace the existing elementary school with a new one. The proposal includes both a description of the new school, and of the additional taxes needed to finance it. Should the new proposal fail, the existing school will be kept along with the existing tax system. This alternative is called the *status quo* proposal, S. The government announces on the basis of a sampling of public opinion that the probability of P's victory is p. It then declares itself willing to sell insurance against the victory of P at a price of p per dollar of insurance, and against the victory of S at a price of $(1 - p)$ per dollar.

Assuming individuals are risk averse, each is motivated to purchase insurance against the defeat of his preferred alternative. Thus, if individual j expects to be the equivalent of W dollars better off under the victory of P than he would be if S won, he will purchase W dollars of insurance against S's victory, *if he believes the government's probability estimate*. If all voters believe these estimates and act rationally in the light of this information, the total compensations to be paid in the event of each proposal's victory will equal the aggregate over all voters of the dollar gains foregone through the other proposal's defeat.

The government's rule for declaring a winner is obvious. It chooses that proposal for which the dollar compensation to the losers is smallest. This insures the government of a surplus in its insurance selling operation. To see this assume that ΣV_i must be paid out if P wins, and ΣW_j if S wins, Government gross revenue from selling insurance then equals

$$R = p\Sigma V_i + (1 - p)\,\Sigma W_j$$

Now if $\Sigma V_i > \Sigma W_j$, S is declared the winner and ΣW_j must be paid out to those favoring P. Thus, the government's net revenue equals:

$$NR = p \, \Sigma V_i + (1 - p) \, \Sigma W_j - \Sigma W_j$$
$$= p(\Sigma V_i - \Sigma W_j) > 0$$

and if $\Sigma W_j > \Sigma V_i$, then

$$NR = p \, \Sigma V_i + (1 - p) \, \Sigma W_j - \Sigma V_i$$
$$= (1 - p) \, \Sigma W_j - (1 - p) \, \Sigma V_i > 0$$

The outcome chosen under the decision rule is Pareto optimal. Those who favor the winning proposal receive benefits exceeding their outlays for insurance against the other alternative. Those who opposed the winning proposal are fully compensated for the loss they experience. What is more, the government has a surplus $|\Sigma V_i - \Sigma W_j|$, which it can distribute on a lump sum basis to all citizens, thus ensuring that everyone is strictly better off under the procedure.

The winning proposal in the contest of P against S can be pitted against some new proposal P', and the entire process repeated. In principle this could continue until a proposal defeating all others emerged as the *status quo* winner. To be able to move on from one proposal to the next in this way, however, an additional, rather strong assumption is needed. The marginal rate of substitution between government projects and money must remain constant, even though an individual's income is changing. Although this assumption is reasonable if only a few iterations of the procedure are contemplated, it is less so if a long sequence is envisaged, so that substantial changes in income might cumulate.

The possibility of a long sequence of applications of the procedure resulting in a large cumulative impact on individual incomes also raises the question of how new proposals are selected. To see the importance of this question, suppose that the new proposal P is one which makes a subset of the voters much worse off than under the *status quo*. This group insures itself heavily against P, and the *status quo* triumphs. Now suppose that the next proposal also would make the same group much worse off. Again they would have an incentive to insure against the new proposal, and again they might win. But if a long sequence of similar proposals arose, this group might go bankrupt trying to insure against the defeat of the *status quo* issue.

This example illustrates two additional assumptions implicit in any *normative* justification for this procedure: (1) the original distribution of income and wealth is fair, thus warranting general acceptance of the outcomes emerging from the aggregation of individual decisions to purchase insurance that result from this initial distribution of income, and (2) the issue proposal process is impartial in its distribution of the gains of collective action.

Despite these and other,[1] rather stringent assumptions underlying the procedure, it remains an interesting early attempt to solve the preference revelation problem. And, of the procedures considered here, it has the strongest incentives to induce an individual to *both* reveal his honest preferences, *and go through the trouble of taking part in the process*. For regardless of the impact of his individual insurance purchase on the total amount of insurance bought and thus on the collective choice itself, the impact of an individual's decision on his own economic position is potentially large. Indeed, the more important the government decision is to him, independent of his influence on it, the greater is his incentive to reveal his preferences through the purchase of insurance. This property makes the procedure an attractive first candidate for solving the preference revelation problem.

---

[1] In addition to the assumptions already listed, the key ones underlying the process are (1) that all individuals believe the government's probability figures, and (2) that nonparticipants in the process are excluded from the public good's benefits. These assumptions are complementary and together seem rather strong. Suppose, for example, that a proposal for unilateral disarmament was made. Regardless of how low of a positive probability of this proposal's winning the government announced, many people might not believe the proposal stood a chance, and thus refuse to insure against it even though they would be worse off if it passed. Thus, an accurate revelation of preferences would not be forthcoming. But, I do not see how proposal's of this type, and the problems they raise, can be excluded from arising.

B. **The demand-revealing process**

The most important of the new processes to appear seeks to induce individuals to reveal their demand schedules for public goods, or approximations to their demand schedules, by means of certain taxes imposed upon them. This process was first described in detail by William Vickrey in 1961, and thus in some sense precedes Thompson's insurance scheme discussed above. Indeed, Vickrey attributes the idea to 'an interesting suggestion' A. P. Lerner threw out in *Economics of Control* [1944]. But neither Lerner nor Vickrey applied the procedure to the problem of revealing preferences for public goods, and the potential importance of the procedure in this area was not recognized until the appearance of papers by Edward Clarke [1971, 1972], and Theodore Groves [1973]. During the mid 1970s interest in the procedure has skyrocketed.

To understand how the procedure works, consider again the collective choice between the two issues P and S. Assume a committee of 3 with preferences as given in Table 4.1. Voter A

Table 4.1

Voter	Issue		
	P	S	Tax
A	30		20
B		40	0
C	20		10
Totals	50	40	30

expects to be the equivalent of 30 dollars better off from the victory of P, voter C 20 dollars, and voter B prefers the *status quo*, S, by the equivalent of 40 dollars. The procedure for selecting a winner is to first ask each voter to state in dollars the amount of benefits he expects from the victory of his preferred issue, and then add these figures declaring the issue with the most expected benefits the winner. In the present example this is P, since it promises gains of 50 to voters A and C, while S benefits B by only 40.

The voters are induced to declare their true preferences for the issues by announcing that they will be charged a certain tax dependent on the responses they make, and their impact on the final outcome. This tax is calculated in the following way. The dollar votes of all other voters are added up and the outcome determined. The voter-in-question's dollar votes are now added in to see if the outcome is changed. If it is not, he pays no tax. If it is, he pays a tax equal to the *net* gains expected from the victory of the other issue in the absence of his vote. Thus, a voter pays a tax only when his vote is decisive in changing the outcome, and then pays not the amount he has declared, but the amount needed to balance the declared benefits on the two issues. The last column of Table 4.1 presents the taxes on the 3 voters. Without A, there are 40 dollar votes for S and 20 for P. A's vote is decisive in determining the outcome, and imposes a net cost of 20 on the other two voters, and that is A's tax. B's vote does not affect the outcome, and he pays no tax. Without C's vote S would again win, so C pays a tax equal to the net benefits the other voters would have received had he not voted $(40 - 30 = 10)$.

Under the tax each voter has an incentive to reveal his true preferences for the two issues. Any amount of benefits from P that voter A declared equal to or greater than 21 would leave the collective decision, *and his tax* unchanged. If he declared net benefits of less than 20, S would win, and A's tax would fall from 20 to zero, but his benefits of 30 would also disappear. A voter pays a tax only if his vote is decisive, and the tax he pays is always equal to or less than the benefits he receives. Thus, there is no incentive to understate one's gains, for then one risks foregoing a chance to cast the deciding vote at a cost less than the benefits. And, there is no incentive to overstate one's preferences, since this incurs the risk of becoming the decisive vote, and receiving a tax above one's actual benefits albeit less than one's declared benefits. The optimal strategy is honest revelation of preferences.

To maintain this desirable incentive property, the tax revenue raised to induce honest revelation of preferences cannot be returned to the voters in such a way as to affect their voting decision. The safest thing to do with the money to avoid distorting incentives is to waste it. But this implies that the outcome from the procedure will not be Pareto optimal [Groves and Ledyard, 1977*a*, *b*; Loeb, 1977]. The amount by which the procedure falls short of Pareto optimality can be stated explicitly, it is the amount of revenue raised by the incentive-tax. In the example above, this amount is substantial, equaling 3 times the net gains from collective action.

Fortunately, it appears likely that the amount of taxes raised under the demand-revealing procedure declines, at least relatively, as the number of voters increases.[2] To see that this might be so consider Table 4.2, in which the preferences of 3 other voters, *A'*,

Table 4.2

Voter	Issue P	S	Tax
A	30		10
B		40	0
C	20		0
A'	30		10
B'		40	0
C'	20		0
Totals	100	80	20

B', and *C'* identical to *A*, *B* and *C* have been included. The issue *P* still wins, of course, now by a surplus of 20. Voter *C*'s tax has fallen from 20 to 0, however, and *A*'s from 30 to 10. Without voter *C* the net benefits on the two issues over the other voters are zero

[2] See Tideman and Tullock [1976, 1977]. But, Groves and Ledyard claim to be able to construct counter examples in which the surplus is arbitrarily large [1977*c*, p. 140].

(80 for P and 80 for S). Although his vote tips the outcome in favor of P his gain of 20 does not come at the *net* expense of the other voters. So C pays no tax. A still pays a positive tax, but the amount has been reduced, since the net cost of his vote on all other voters has fallen. With the addition of 3 more voters (A'', B'', C'') with preferences identical to A, B and C, the outcome would again not change, and the taxes on all voters would now be zero. Thus, the collective decision of this committee of 9 would be Pareto optimal. Although the procedure does allow for a weighing of intensities in determining the outcome, the effect of any one voter's preferences on the final outcome will dwindle as with other voting procedures as the number of voters increases. Since a voter's tax equals his impact on the other voters, it too dwindles as the group's size increases.

The procedure can reveal individual demand schedules for a public good, from whence its name arises. We follow here the exposition of Tideman and Tullock [1976]. Each individual is asked to report his complete demand schedule for the public good. These schedules are then vertically added to obtain the aggregate demand for the public good. The intersection of this schedule and the supply schedule for the good determines the quantity provided. If each individual has honestly reported his demand schedule, the procedure determines the Pareto-optimal quantity of public good, as defined by Samuelson [1954] and Bowen [1943].

Individuals are again induced to reveal their true preferences via a special tax imposed upon them. In fact, there are two taxes imposed upon the individual, one designed to cover the full costs of producing the public good, the other to ensure honest revelation of preferences. In our first example, the first of these two taxes was implicitly assumed to be part of the proposals P and S. Let us assume that the public good can be supplied at constant unit costs C, and that each voter is assigned a share of these costs, T_j, such that $\sum_{j=1}^{n} T_j = C$. These T_js are the first components of each individual's tax. The other component is computed in a way analogous to that used to assign each individual a tax in the preceding example. Namely, the quantity of public good that would be demanded in the absence of individual i's demand schedule and contribution to the public good's total costs is first determined. The quantity with his demand schedule and contribution is next determined. The difference represents the impact of this individual's preferences on the collective outcome. The cost to the other voters of the shift in quantity recording his preferences brings about is the absolute value of the difference between the costs of producing these extra units and the sum of the individual demand schedules over these units. Thus, if i forces the community to consume more than it would have without his demand-schedule vote, the costs of the extra output will exceed their willingness to pay for it, and i is charged the difference. Conversely, if voter i causes the community to consume less than they would have, their aggregate demand for the extra units of public good will exceed the good's costs, and the difference, the loss in consumer surplus to the other voters, is charged to the ith voter.

The latter possibility is illustrated with the help of Figure 4.1. Omitting i's demand schedule, aggregate demand for the public good is $D - D_i$. Subtracting his preassigned tax share, the public good's cost is $C - T_i$. With i's preferences removed the community would purchase A. With i's preferences included the community purchases Q, the quantity at which aggregate demand and supply are equal. The cost imposed on the other voters of this shift in outcomes is the difference between the amount the other voters would be willing to pay for the extra units $(A - Q)$, and the taxes they would have to pay $(C - T_i)(A - Q)$ for these units, which is the cross-hatched triangle above the line $C - T_i$. This triangle represents the additional tax, above T_iQ, the ith voter must pay.

To see that the ith voter's optimal strategy is to reveal his true demand schedule in the presence of this incentive-tax, we can construct an effective supply schedule of the public good, S_i, to the ith voter, by subtracting the $D - D_i$ schedule from C. The intersection of the individual voter's demand for the public good, D_i, and this S_i schedule is for him the optimal quantity of public good which, of course, is Q. By stating his demand schedule as D_i, voter i forces the community to consume Q instead of A, and

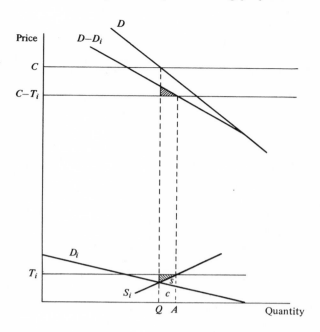

Figure 4.1

thereby saves himself the rectangle $T_i(QA)$ in taxes. He must pay the incentive tax represented by the cross-hatched triangle, which equals the cross-hatched triangle above, and loses the consumer surplus represented by the quadrilateral, c. His net gain from forcing the community to Q rather than leaving it at A is thus the triangle s. That there is nothing to be gained by stating a demand schedule below D_i can be seen by observing that the triangle s vanishes at Q. To the left of Q, i's incentive tax plus consumer surplus loss would exceed his tax saving T_i. If he states any demand schedule above D_i, T_i exceeds his consumer surplus gain and incentive tax saving. The honest revelation of his true demand schedule D_i is i's optimal strategy.

Note that although the quantity selected under the procedure is such that

$$\sum_{j=1}^{n} D_j = C = \sum_{j=1}^{n} T_j$$

at the chosen quantity, it is also generally true that

$$D_j \neq T_j, j = 1, n$$

as is easily seen in Figure 4.1. The independence of an individual's share of the public good's cost from his stated demand schedule is an important element of the procedure. This independence is necessary to ensure the honest revelation of preferences. Only the, probably rather small, incentive tax, represented by the cross-hatched triangle in Figure 4.1 is directly related to the individual's reported demand schedule, and the funds raised here are to be wasted, or at least not returned in any systematic way to the payer.

The idea of a two-part tariff to ensure an efficient allocation of resources in industries characterized by economies of scale, or large fixed costs has been around for some time. The most obvious examples are probably the electric and gas industries (see, e.g., Kahn [1970, pp. 95–100]). The principles underlying these pricing schemes are analogous to those of the demand-revealing process. A proportional charge is made to each customer for his use of the service, and an extra charge is made for the costs on other buyers a customer's demand imposes at the peak (margin) of the system's capacity. Public goods are also characterized by high fixed costs, the joint-supply property, and the demand-revealing process is thus a perhaps not too surprising, if somewhat long-awaited, extension of the idea of the two-part tariff into the public good area.

Green and Laffont [1977] have demonstrated that the class of demand-revealing processes first developed by Groves [1973] in effect defines the full set of procedures of this type, of which the above examples are but one variant, for which honest revelation of preferences is the dominant strategy. That is, regardless of what message the other voters supply to the message gathering agent, it is always an individual's optimal strategy to reveal his true preferences. This property of the procedure is dependent upon an absence of interaction between an individual's fixed tax share, revealed demand schedule, and the revealed demand schedules of the other individuals. There is no way, direct or indirect, by which an individual can influence the tax he pays other than through the immediate effect of his revealed demand schedule. Thus, we have the same assumed independence between the marginal rate of substitution between public goods and money, and the level of income as characterized Thompson's insurance selling scheme. More generally, the procedure as thus described is a purely partial equilibrium approach that abstracts from any interactions among voters via income effects or other means.

Although honest preference revelations, and the Samuelson efficiency conditions are insured under the partial equilibrium variants of the demand-revealing process, budget balance is not, and so Pareto efficiency cannot be presumed. As noted above (p. 74, n. 2), the size of the total tax intake from the incentive-tax is a matter of some controversy, and so too therefore the significance of the Pareto inefficiency property. Groves and Ledyard [1977] have developed a general equilibrium version of the demand-revealing process in which budget balance is achieved. Each individual reports a quadratic approximation to his true demand function of the following form

$$m_i = \beta_i y - \frac{\gamma}{2n} y^2$$

where γ is a constant across all individuals, y is the quantity of public goods, and n is the number of consumers. The individual's tax is given as

$$T_i = a_i y^*(m) + \frac{\gamma}{2} \left[\left(\frac{n-1}{n} \right) \left(m_i - \mu_i \right)^2 - \sigma_i^2 \right]$$

where a_i is a preassigned tax share, $y^*(m)$ is the quantity of public good chosen as a result of the aggregation of all individual messages, μ_i is the mean of all of the *other* voters' messages, and σ_i is the standard error of all of the other voters' messages. Each individual pays a fixed tax share, a_i, and a variable tax that increases with the size of the difference between his proposed quantity and the proposed quantity of all other voters, and decreases in proportion to the amount of dispersion among the other proposals. Thus a voter is again penalized to the extent that his proposed public good quantity differs from that of all other voters, but his penalty is smaller, the more disagreement there is among the other voters over the desired quantity of public good. To supply his optimal message a voter must know his preassigned tax share, the fixed constant, and the mean and standard error of all other voters' messages. Thus, a sequential adjustment procedure is required in which each voter is supplied with the computed mean and standard error of the other voters' messages on the preceding round of calculations to make his calculation on the present one. The present messages then become the data for making new mean and standard error statistics for each voter. The process continues until equilibrium is obtained.[3]

Under the Groves–Ledyard procedure the tax on each individual can be designed to insure budget balance, and if each voter treats the messages of the others as given, each has the incentive to reveal his own preferences honestly, and a Pareto-optimal equilibrium can be established [1977a, pp. 794–806]. But, it may not be in each voter's best interests to treat the messages of all other voters as given. The achievement of budget balance and individual equilibrium via a multistep adjustment process makes each individual's message at one step of the process dependent on the other individuals' messages at the preceding stage. A voter who could deduce the effect of his message on the messages of other voters in subsequent rounds of voting, might have an incentive to manipulate their messages in later rounds via dishonest indication of his own demand schedule in earlier rounds. The proofs of Pareto optimality Groves and Ledyard offer assume essentially Cournot-type behavior: each voter treats the messages of the other voters as fixed at each stage of the adjustment process. Once voters begin to take the reactions of other voters into account, Stackleberg-type behavior may be individually optimal, and both the honest-

---

[3] Groves and Loeb first discussed the possibility of achieving budget balance when the consumer's, in this case a firm, demand schedule is a quadratic function of the form given above [1975].

revelation and Pareto efficiency properties of the mechanism may be lost [1977*b*, pp. 118–20].

Although honest revelation of individual preferences is not the dominant strategy under the Groves–Ledyard balanced budget variant of the demand revealing procedure, it is a Nash equilibrium. That is, given that all other individuals honestly reveal their preferences at each step in the process, it is in each voter's best interest to do so. The significance of this property of the procedure rests heavily on whether it is reasonable to expect voters to adopt a Cournot-type frame of mind when sending messages, at least when the number of voters is fairly large. This issue cannot be settled on the basis of *a priori argument*.[4] Experimental work conducted by Vernon Smith using a variant of the Groves–Ledyard process, albeit one without the budget balance constraint, indicated a fairly fast convergence of the process on the Lindahl equilibrium [1976]. Smith also obtained encouraging results using an 'auction process' with properties analogous to the demand-revealing process. Thus, the vulnerability to individual strategizing of processes requiring sequential adjustment mechanisms may not be serious.

Of the many criticisms and caveats that have been raised about the demand-revealing process, the most serious would appear to be the failure of the various partial equilibrium variants to allow for income effects, i.e. the amount of money being collected from an individual is assumed to be too small to affect his stated demand schedule.[5] This is obviously an extreme assumption and one not typically found in other economic models enjoying widespread acceptance, although it was also present in the preference-revelation insurance scheme discussed in the preceding section.[6] Once income effects are allowed, we move into the general equilibrium framework explored by Groves and Ledyard [1977*a*];

---

[4] The basic result is established by Groves and Ledyard [1977*a*]. For a discussion of its significance see Greenberg, Mackay, and Tideman [1977]; Groves and Ledyard [1977*c*].

[5] For further discussion see Groves and Ledyard [1977*b*].

[6] For a defense of this assumption see Tideman and Tullock [1977*a*].

the dominance property of honest preference revelation vanishes; strategizing becomes potentially attractive.[7]

The remaining difficulties of the process are shared by most if not all other voting processes:

Information incentives: To the extent that the size of the incentive-tax levied on any individual falls as the number of voters increases, the incentive to provide information conscientiously dwindles.[8] Thus, the demand-revealing process is caught in a form of numerical dilemma. If the numbers involved are small, the incentive-taxes may be large, but so too, then, is the potential Pareto inefficiency arising out of the existence of this unutilized tax revenue. If the numbers are large, the Pareto inefficiency may be relatively small, but so too is the incentive to supply the needed information. The information forthcoming from the process could be largely inaccurate, although not systematically dishonest. Clarke [1977], Green and Laffont [1977], and Tullock [1977*a*] have discussed ways to circumvent this problem by relying on representative systems or sampling techniques. These in turn raise the following problem.

Coalitions: a coalition of voters who felt they would be 100 better off from the victory of *P* could increase the chances of *P*'s winning significantly by all agreeing to claim that they were 200 better off under *P*'s victory. So long as *P* won by more than 200, or less than 100 they would be better off under the coalition than acting independently. If *P* lost anyway, they are no worse off. Only if *P* won by between 100 and 200, an unlikely event if the coalition is very large, would a voter be worse off under the outcome with the coalition, than without it. Thus, incentives to form coalitions to manipulate outcomes exists under the demand revealing process [Bennett and Conn, 1977].

Gordon Tullock is undoubtedly correct in arguing that the problem of coalition formation is unlikely to be serious if the number of voters is large and voting is by secret ballot [1977*c*]. For

---

[7] For the most general discussion of this problem see Hurwicz [1975].
[8] See Clarke [1971, 1977]; Tideman and Tullock [1976]; Tullock [1977*a*].

then, the same incentives to free-ride will exist within the coalition as exist now and thwart the functioning of a pure voluntary-exchange voting mechanism. A single voter's optimal strategy is to urge the formation of a 200 vote coalition, and then vote 100, himself. If all voters follow this strategy we are left with honest preference revelation.

But with small numbers of voters, and publicly recorded votes, as in a representative body, the conditions for coalition formation are more favorable. This is particularly true, because we usually elect representatives as members of parties, which are natural coalition partners. Again we find ourselves confronted by a numerical dilemma: in a large numbers, direct democracy no one has an incentive to gather information *or* join a coalition; in small committees of representatives, incentives exist to gather information about not only one's own preferences, but also those of others who may be potential coalition members.

Bankruptcy: Under the demand-revealing process it is possible for an outcome to emerge in which the entire private wealth of an individual is confiscated [Groves and Ledyard, 1977*b*, pp. 116–18]. This is true of almost any voting procedure other than the unanimity rule, however, and is probably not a serious, practical problem. It does point up the need to view the process as taking place within some sort of system of constitutional guarantees, and constraints upon the types of issues that come before the committee.[9]

Thus, the demand-revealing process is very much in the spirit of the Wicksellian approach to collective choice. Collective decisionmaking is *within* a system of prescribed property rights, and *upon* a just distribution of income. The goal of collective action is the improvement of allocative efficiency not the achievement of distributive justice. Such redistribution as will take place is of the Pareto-optimal variety, and is more appropriately viewed as part of the 'allocation branch' of the public weal than of the

---

[9] For further discussion of the bankruptcy issue, see Tullock [1977*a*]; Tideman and Tullock [1977]; Groves and Ledyard [1977*b*, *c*].

'distribution branch'.[10]

We shall discuss some of these points further in the final section of this chapter, but first we review another procedure that shares many of the Wicksellian attributes of the demand-revealing processes.

C. Voting by veto

The chief shortcomings of the unanimity rule for revealing preferences on a decision of potential benefit to all citizens are that (1) the time taken to formulate a proposal benefiting all may be too long, (2) even when formulated, a proposal benefiting all may be strategically 'vetoed' by those seeking a greater share of the gains from collective action, and (3) the *status quo* is unduly favored. Each of these difficulties can be attributed to the unlimited number of effective vetoes allowed each voter under the unanimity rule, and the lack of responsibility for making proposals placed on the participants implicit in most committee procedures.

The voting-by-veto procedure attempts to solve these problems by charging each voter with the responsibility for making one proposal, and limiting each to a single veto of another proposal.[11] The voting process proceeds in two steps. Each voter first adds a proposal to the issue set. Proposals might take any form, but most typically are probably a public good expenditure and tax to finance it. The issue set is then made up of the n proposals of the n committee members, and a *status quo* issue. A table of random numbers is then used to determine an order of veto voting. The sequence is announced to all voters, and the voting proceeds with each voter removing one proposal from the issue set. The proposal remaining is the winner.

To see how the procedure works consider the following example. A piece of land in the public domain is to be put to some

---

[10] Tullock [1977*d*] has explored the redistributive potential of the process and claims somewhat more for it. On the distinction between Pareto optimal redistribution, and other kinds see [Hochman and Rogers, 1969, 1970].

[11] This procedure was first discussed in [Mueller, 1978].

collective use. A committee of 3 is to decide what this use is to be. *T* favors the construction of tennis courts, *G* a garden, *F* a football field. The *status quo* possibility, *S*, is to leave the field vacant, at zero cost and zero benefit to all concerned. *T* will of course want to propose that the field be used to make tennis courts. He can veto one of the other two voters' proposals. But for his proposal to win the other two voters must reject the remaining proposal and the *status quo*. This requires that *T*'s proposal promise greater benefits to at least one voter than the *status quo*, and greater benefits to the other than the remaining issue. But, since *T* knows neither his own position in the voting sequence nor those of the other two voters at the time he makes his proposal, his safest strategy for securing his most favored outcome is to propose greater benefits to both other voters than either the *status quo* or the other proposals contain.

To see this more clearly assume that the 3 proposals and *status quo* promise the following net benefits

$$F\ (10, 10, 50),\ G\ (15, 25, 15),\ T\ (25, 20, 20),\ S\ (0, 0, 0)$$

where the voters are aligned (T, G, F). Suppose the order of voting selected via the random draw is FGT. Although *F* votes first, there is no way he can bring about the victory of his favored proposal, since both remaining voters will reject his proposal over either of the other two. The best *F* can do is secure the victory of *T*'s proposal, since it promises him higher benefits than *G*'s. *F* can achieve this by rejecting *G*'s proposal. *G* will now reject either *S* or *F*, and *T*'s proposal will go on to become the winner. An analysis of the other possible permutations of these 3 voters would indicate that the proposal of *T*, the one promising the highest benefits to the two voters other than *T* himself, would win in 5 of the 6 possible orderings. And as the number of voters increases, the probability of the proposal with the most benefits for the other voters winning approaches 1.0 [Mueller, 1978].

If the committee met but once to decide one set of issues, a voter might try and provide as much benefits for himself, while just exceeding the benefits for the other voters promised on the other proposals. But if the committee meets again and again, there will be a tendency for the committee members to compete against one another by sharing the benefits assigned to themselves, and increasing those assigned to others. In the long run, one expects the winning proposal to promise equal benefits to all voters. This outcome is a Nash equilibrium under the procedure.

T will have an advantage getting his proposal through, if both G and F also enjoy tennis. In the reverse case, T must offer lower tax shares to G and F or even subsidies to secure their support. Nevertheless, should T favor the construction of tennis courts strongly enough, he could always propose some formulation of the issue attractive enough to the other voters to bring about the issue's victory. Thus, there is a tendency under the procedure for both the issue proposal with the largest total benefits to win, and for the winning proposal to contain an equal sharing of benefits.

Voting-by-veto requires each voter to engage in an interpersonal utility comparison in which he evaluates not only the benefits to all other voters under his proposal, but also the benefits to other voters he envisages the other proposals will contain. Procedures requiring interpersonal utility comparisons have generally not been popular among economists. But voting by veto seems to introduce these comparisons in a most innocuous and democratic way. Each individual gets to eliminate a proposal he finds particularly objectionable, and the procedure thereby selects as a winner that proposal providing the least objectionable set of interpersonal utility comparisons of those made.

Voting-by-veto suffers from some of the same shortcomings as other procedures. As the number of participants grows, the incentive to participate declines. The process is also vulnerable to coalitions. If two of the three committee members in the above example could agree on the use of the land, they could both offer the same proposal, perhaps even requiring that the third member pay all of the proposal's costs. The excluded member could veto but one of the proposals, and the other would win. As with other voting rules, however, the coalition problem will be less important the larger the number of voters.

We shall review the other features of the process as we compare the 3 procedures that have been discussed in this chapter.

D. **A comparison of the three procedures**

As Theodore Groves observed in opening a recent paper on the demand-revealing process, 'The concept of a "quid pro quo" is fundamental to an economic theory of exchange' [1976, p. 1]. With the exception of the logrolling models, the idea of a *quid pro quo* has not been part of either theoretical or real world democratic processes, explaining perhaps their limited success at achieving Wicksell's goal of a *voluntary* exchange process of government. In most democratic procedures votes are distributed as essentially free goods, with the only real constraints on their use being the ticking of the clock.

The three procedures discussed in this chapter all break with this tradition in a fundamental way. The insurance-purchase and demand-revealing processes link the act of voting or preference revelation directly to a financial transaction: the purchase of insurance or levying of a tax. Under veto-voting, votes are no longer free goods. Each individual has one proposal to make, and one veto to cast.

Each of the procedures is also in the Wicksellian tradition in that they assume a just distribution of income exists. Indeed, whatever normative properties the 3 procedures possess rest heavily on the assumed justness in the underlying distribution of income.[12] Given this just starting point, the goal of collective action is to increase the welfare of all, and the purpose of the collective decision process is to indicate those situations where that is possible. The proposals differ, however, as to how the gains from collective action are distributed. Under the insurance scheme, all of the gains go to the winners, to those in the 'financial majority', the others are simply compensated for the defeat of their proposal, plus given a pro rata share of the surplus left in the insurance pool. The demand-revealing process tends to move individuals out along

---

[12] For a discussion of this in the context of the demand revealing process, see Tideman [1977].

their demand or offer curves, and to maximize the sum of consumer surpluses across individuals. The Lindahl equilibrium looms as a sort of center of gravity toward which the outcomes move. The normative properties of these processes are contained in the normative properties of the Lindahl equilibrium and the notion of a maximum aggregate consumer surplus.[13] With voting-by-veto the analogy is with the cake cutting exercise, as brought about by the random determination of an order of veto voting. The gains from collective action will tend to be equal across individuals, and the process's normative characteristic is set by this egalitarian property.

The Wicksellian voluntary exchange approach is ineluctably tied to philosophical individualism [Buchanan, 1949]. Each individual enters the collective choice process to improve his own welfare, and the process is established so that all may benefit. Implicit here are a set of constitutional guarantees or constraints upon the collective decision process, and, I believe, an assumption that coalitions of one group *against* another do not form. Each man strives *for* himself, but, as in the market, does not strive, collectively at least, against any other. The three proposals here all assume some form of constitutional constraints on the issues coming before the committee, and explicitly rule out coalitions. Under the insurance scheme, the individual is further able to protect himself against the actions of the collective by the direct purchase of insurance. Compensation must be paid to those injured. Under the demand-revealing process, the tax charged an individual is exactly equal to the cost his participation in the process imposes on all others. Under voting-by-veto an individual can protect himself against a discriminate threat to his well-being by any other voter's proposal through the veto he possesses.

In addition to the inherently individualistic orientation of these 3 proposals, they also resemble one another in the demands they place upon the individual who participates in the process. A simple yes or no will not do. The individual must evaluate in dollars his

---

[13] Gordon Tullock has elaborated on the normative properties of the demand-revealing process [1977*b*].

benefits under various possible alternatives, and, in the case of voting-by-veto, also the benefits for other voters. This task is made easier by another Wicksellian characteristic of the procedures; each assumes that an expenditure issue and the tax to finance it are tied together. Although this latter feature might actually make the voter's decision task easier, the kind of information required of him under the 3 procedures is far more sophisticated than obtained under present voting systems. It is also more sophisticated than one might expect 'the average voter' to be capable of supplying, at least if one accepts the image of him gleaned from the typical survey data regarding his knowledge of candidates and issues. To many the information required of voters will constitute a significant shortcoming of these processes. In my own mind it does not. If we have learned one thing from the sea of work that has emerged following the classic contributions on public goods and democratic choice by Samuelson and Arrow, it is that the task of preference revelation in collective decisions is not an easy one. If we must further assume that the individuals whose preferences we seek to reveal are only capable of yes or no responses, the task is hopeless from the start.

Although each has its weak points, the three procedures reviewed in this chapter give promise that the knotty problem of preference revelation in collective choice can be resolved as both a theoretical and practical matter. Whether the optimal solution will be a variant on one of these processes, or an as yet to be discovered process cannot at this point be ascertained. But the basic similarities running across these three processes are so strong, despite the inherently different procedural mechanics by which they operate, that one is led to suspect that these same characteristics will be a part of any 'ultimate' solution to the preference revelation problem. And, if this is true, it further highlights Knut Wicksell's fundamental insight into the collective choice process.

5

General fund financing

Most of the public choice literature has, often implicitly, assumed that the quantities of public goods are decided in Wicksellian fashion by presenting voters with each public good separately, coupled to a tax to finance it. But this method of financing public expenditures was neither in Wicksell's day nor is it in our own the dominant method for financing public expenditures. Much of government expenditures come out of 'general revenues' and these, in turn, are raised by general taxes on the population. This two-part division of the fiscal process complicates the voter's decision greatly, and leads to uncertainty over whether proposed tax increases, say, will lead to increased expenditures which he favors, or whether proposed budget cuts will reduce his tax burden [Buchanan, 1967, p. 73]. More generally, the use of general fund financing techniques can create a 'fiscal illusion' on the part of voters that they are under- or over-taxed leading to an over- or under-expansion of the fisc.

The concept of 'fiscal illusion' was first put forward and developed into a theory by Amilcare Puviani [1897, 1903]. Puviani views the state as being controlled by a 'ruling class', which seeks to extract as much revenue as possible from the ruled class. The creation of fiscal illusion is thus a deliberate strategy of the state (ruling class) for increasing its revenues and exploiting the ruled.[1] Puviani's hypothesis would seem to have empirical support in some recent work by Richard Wagner [1976]. He posited that fiscal illusion would be greater the more dispersed a government's sources of tax revenue. This hypothesis was supported by a finding of an inverse relationship between the level of local government expenditures and the degree of concentration of their tax revenue on a few (visible) tax sources. It might be noted in contrast, however, that Wicksell, who admittedly held a more benign view of the state than Puviani and Wagner, felt that government expenditures would be larger if each expenditure was tied to its own tax, which is presumably the most visible method of taxation of all [1896, p. 73].

Even if we ignore the uncertainties and illusions general fund financing may cause, and assume each voter knows precisely his tax burden under the two alternatives, there are problems involved in the use of general fund financing schemes. Leif Johansen [1963] and Martin McGuire and Henry Aaron [1969] have shown that the use of general fund financing results in non-Pareto-efficient outcomes. Following Johansen, we assume two public goods, G, and S, and a single private good X. Let Y_A and Y_B be the incomes of two individuals, X_A and X_B their consumptions of X, and $U_A(X_A, G, S)$ and $U_B(X_B, G, S)$ their utility functions. Maximization of U_A and U_B subject to the budget constraints

$$Y_A = X_A + h(G + S)$$

$$Y_B = X_B + (1 - h)(G + S)$$

(5.1)

yields the following first order conditions

$$\frac{\partial U_A}{\partial G} = \frac{\partial U_A}{\partial S} = h \frac{\partial U_A}{\partial X_A}$$

$$\frac{\partial U_B}{\partial G} = \frac{\partial U_B}{\partial S} = (1-h) \frac{\partial U_B}{\partial X_B}$$

(5.2)

---

[1] Puviani's theory is discussed and extended by Buchanan [1967, pp. 126–43].

See also the model of Brennan and Buchanan [1977], also discussed in ch. 8.

There are six equations in (5.1) and (5.2) and 5 unknowns (G, S, X_A, X_B, h). The system is overdetermined, and no tax share, h, satisfying (5.1) and (5.2) is likely to exist. The constraint that G and S be financed by taxing the two individuals at the same rate, h, leads to inefficiency. Both individuals could be made better off (and thus would unanimously approve) some alternative combination of G and S financed under separate taxes. Thus, if g is A's tax share for G, and s his tax share for S, the first order conditions become

$$\frac{\partial U_A}{\partial G} = g \frac{\partial U_A}{\partial X_A} \qquad \frac{\partial U_A}{\partial S} = s \frac{\partial U_A}{\partial X_A}$$

$$\frac{\partial U_B}{\partial G} = (1-g) \frac{\partial U_B}{\partial X_B} \qquad \frac{\partial U_B}{\partial S} = (1-s) \frac{\partial U_B}{\partial X_B} \tag{5.3}$$

along with the budget constraints

$$Y_A = X_A + gG + sS \tag{5.4}$$

$$Y_B = X_B + (1-g)G + (1-s)S$$

There are six equations and six unknowns and the system can be solved for the optimal (G, S, X_A, X_B, g, s). Rearranging (5.3) we obtain the Samuelsonian conditions for a Pareto efficient allocation of a public good

$$\frac{\partial U_A/\partial G}{\partial U_A/\partial X_A} + \frac{\partial U_B/\partial G}{\partial U_B/\partial X_B} = 1 = \frac{\partial U_A/\partial S}{\partial U_A/\partial X_A} + \frac{\partial U_B/\partial S}{\partial U_B/\partial X_B} \tag{5.5}$$

The Wicksellian convention of tying a separate tax to each public good is a necessary condition for Pareto optimality.

The use of majority rule to decide the quantities of public goods or the levels of taxes under general fund financing can lead to 'perverse' relationships between voters' preferences, and the outcomes of the collective choice process.[2] To understand the prob-

---

[2] J. M. Buchanan was the first to compare the properties of general fund and earmarked tax schemes in a collective choice setting [1963]. His work has been extended by C. J. Goetz [1968], Goetz and C. R. McKnew, Jr [1972], and E. K. Browning [1975].

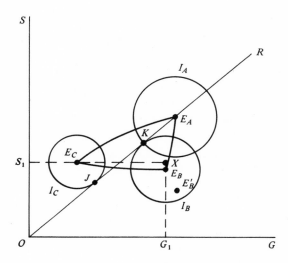

Figure 5.1

lem, consider Figure 5.1.[3] G and S are two public goods to be supplied to a community of three. The circles I_A, I_B, and I_C represent indifference contours derived from the 3 individuals' utility functions, *assuming given tax shares for each individual* summing to the total cost of each public good (the contours need not be perfect circles). Implicit in each combination of G and S for each individual is a bundle of private goods left as a residual from the individual's budget constraint, and his preassigned shares of the costs of G and S. Change his income or his tax shares and the contours shift. The indifference contours have properties similar to those of indifference curves. Each individual is at the same utility level at each point on a circle, given the consumption of private goods implied in these points and his budget constraint. E_A, E_B, and E_C are the three utility maxima for the individuals, under their preassigned incomes and tax shares. Circles nearer these optima represent higher utility levels.

Now consider the determination of the quantities of G and S

---

[3] This figure and the discussion of it follow Browning [1975]. See also Buchanan [1968, pp. 101–25].

through separate votes on each under majority rule. Each voter favors the quantity of public good given by his utility maximum (E_A, E_B, E_C). Each voter's preferences are single peaked in the single dimensions defined over different quantities of the separate public goods. Under majority rule the preferences of the median voter decide. Voter B is the median voter for public good G, and his most preferred quantity of this good G_1 is chosen. Voter C is the median voter for S, and S_1 is selected. Separate decisions on the quantity of each public good result in the choice of $X(G_1, S_1)$.

Assume next that instead of this method of deciding the issues, the following two-step procedure is employed: first the proportion of the general budget to be spent on S is decided, second the size of the total budget. Assume first that each voter votes honestly at both steps. Each will then favor that ratio of S to G implied by the ray passing through the origin, and his maximum utility point. Voter A is the median voter with respect to the choice of ratio between S and G, and OR is chosen under majority rule. Once it is chosen each voter must choose the size of budget, point on OR, he prefers. Voter C favors point J, voter B favors K, and voter A naturally favors E_A. K is the median budget size and it is selected under majority rule. Note that the quantity of one of the public goods, S, is increased by a switch from earmarked to general fund financing, the quantity of the other, G, is decreased. Thus, nothing can be said about the likely impact on the quantity of public goods chosen from a switch from one financing scheme to the other without specific information or assumptions about the nature and distribution of preference functions.

Under earmarked taxes (each good financed separately), an increase in one voter's preferences for a public good must either increase or leave unchanged the quantity of the public good chosen. An increase in the demand for the public good by all voters must increase the quantity chosen. The same is not true under general fund financing. If B's optimum quantities of G and S shifted from E_B to E_B', the quantity of G chosen would *decrease* under general fund financing. The point of tangency between B's indifference contour closest to E_B' (highest utility level) and OR is lower than K along OR. If G were financed out of an earmarked tax, however, the increase in B's desire for G implied in the shift of E_B to E_B' would result in an increase in the quantity of G provided to the community. Browning [1975] presents an example in which the preferences of *all* voters for a public good increase and the quantity chosen under general fund financing declines.

These somewhat paradoxical results come about because the outcomes under majority rule are dependent on the median voter's preferences. There is no reason for the median voter on one issue to be the median voter on another, of course. Under earmarked tax financing the issue to be decided is the quantity of a single public good given its tax price. Under general fund financing the issue to be decided is first of all the *ratio* of public good quantities, and then the size of this bundle. The issues differ, so may the median voters, and so may the outcomes.

It might be noted that the outcome K, under general fund financing, is Pareto optimal, *given* the preassigned tax prices for each individual and their initial incomes. A and C are better off at K than under the earmarked tax outcome, X. Voter B is worse off. A and C could be expected to favor general fund financing, at least for this pair of issues, B earmarked taxes. Normatively, the choice of procedure must rest on the weights assigned to each individual's welfare. A positive analysis of the choice of tax formula would examine the relative strengths of different groups in influencing the choice of formula. Buchanan [1963] has analysed the effects of a shift from earmarked to general fund financing in terms of the elasticities of demand for the public goods. Groups favoring public goods with relatively elastic demands tend to gain more from general fund financing than those supporting goods with relatively inelastic demand. Again redistribution, now of the 'taxpayers' surplus' under the various financing formulae, is involved, and the redistributional aspects of these formulae can dominate their allocational efficiency characteristics.

It should be noted once again that the outcome at K is likely to be inefficient. There is no reason to expect the marginal rates of substitution between the public and private goods for A, B and C

to satisfy the Samuelsonian efficiency conditions. Imposing an additional constraint on a maximization problem will generally produce a dominated outcome.[4] All individuals might be better off if they were free of the initially imposed tax share prices on G and S, and were able to determine both the quantities of public goods and private goods, and the separate tax shares.

By definition general fund financing involves more than one good and voting decision. It is, therefore, vulnerable to logrolling and strategizing.[5] Both voters A and B are better off at some point within the lens formed by I_A and I_B than at K. Voter A might propose a flatter S/G ratio than OR, therefore, in exchange for B's choice of an S/G ratio within the lens $(I_A I_B)$. But a lens also exists between voters A and C, and C might make a counter proposal. And if logrolling can occur so too can a cycle. General fund financing can exhibit all of the undesirable properties deciding separate issues serially or in groups do as discussed above in Chapter 3. The choice between earmarked taxes and general fund financing cannot rest on one's superiority over the other in this area.

Thus, neither the voter's nor the public choice analyst's tasks appear either easy or rewarding under general fund financing. The adoption of Wicksell's 'New Principle' would result in an improvement in welfare for all concerned.

---

[4] We have already encountered this problem in our discussion of cycling, and S. Slutsky's procedure for obtaining a majority rule equilibrium via a dimensionally constrained voting procedure. For a general and rigorous demonstration, see Slutsky [1977*b*].

[5] See Buchanan [1963]; Goetz [1968]; Browning [1975].

6

Public choice in a representative democracy

As we noted at the close of Chapter 3, with large numbers of voters and issues direct democracy is impossible. Even in polities sufficiently small so that all individuals can literally come together to debate and decide issues, say 500, it is impossible for each individual to present his own views, even rather briefly, on every issue. The 'chairman's problem' arises of selecting individuals to represent the various positions most members of the polity are likely to hold [de Jouvenal, 1961]. When the polity is too large to assemble together representatives must by some means be selected.

The public choice literature has focused on three aspects of representative democracy: the behavior of representatives both during the campaign to be elected, and while in office; the behavior of voters in choosing representatives; and the characteristics of the outcomes under representative democracy. The public choice approach assumes that representatives, like voters, are rational, economic men bent on maximizing their utilities. While it is natural to assume that voters' utilities are functions of the baskets of public goods and services they consume, the 'natural assumption' of what maximizes a representative's utility is not as easily made. Anthony Downs made 'the fundamental hypothesis of [his] model: parties formulate policies in order to win elections, rather than win elections in order to formulate policies' [1957, p.

28]. His study was the first to explore systematically the implications of this assumption, and the literature has developed around and from the framework he laid. Only recently has this assumption been seriously challenged [Wittman, 1973], but this criticism has yet to be developed into a model that would rival the Downsian model.

The dominant importance of representative democracy as the mode of political expression has centered much of the interest within the public choice and political science literatures around it. While many of the issues discussed in these literatures have been described here in the context of a model of direct democracy or committees, the committees in mind are often assemblies of representatives, the coalitions, parties. Many of the problems and results already discussed carry over almost directly into the representative democracy area. Thus, the reader will perhaps not be surprised to find the median outcome, cycling, and logrolling all reappearing.

A. Outcomes under two-party democracy

Harold Hotelling first presented the median voter theorem as an outcome of two-party representative democracy in 1929, and this paper is a clear intellectual antecedent to both Downs' and, more indirectly, Black's work. Indeed, it could be regarded as *the* pioneering paper in public choice, for it is the first direct attempt to use economics to analyze a political process.

In the Hotelling–Downs model political opinion is depicted as lying along a single liberal–conservative (left–right) dimension. Each voter is assumed to have a most preferred position along the spectrum for his candidate or party[1] to take. The further the candidate is from this position, the less desirable his election is to the voter, thus the Hotelling–Downs model assumes single-peaked preferences. Figure 6.1a depicts a frequency distribution of most preferred candidate positions. We assume first that this frequency

---

[1] The words candidate or party can be used interchangeably here, for the implicit assumption when discussing parties is that they take a single position in the voter's eyes.

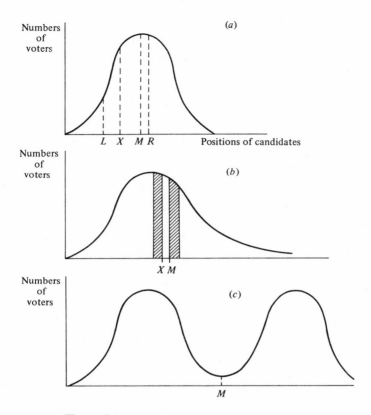

Figure 6.1

distribution is unimodal and symmetric. If every voter votes, and votes for the candidate closest to the voter's most preferred position, L receives all the votes of individuals lying to the left of X, the midpoint of the segment LR. R receives all votes to the right of X. If L and R are the positions the two candidates take, R wins. L can increase his vote total by moving toward R, shifting X to the right, as can R. Both candidates are thus driven towards the position favored by the median voter. The logic of the argument is the same as that demonstrating the victory of the *issue* favored by the median voter, for in the Hotelling–Downs model there is only one issue to be decided, how far to the left or right the winning candidate will be.

The assumptions underlying this initial result are so unrealistic (one issue dimension; a unimodal, symmetric preference distribution; all individuals vote; two candidates), that it naturally led to extensive examination of the consequences of relaxing them. So long as all voters vote, the median outcome holds regardless of the distribution of preferences. As long as all voters vote, the voters lying between a candidate's position and the furthest extreme on his side of the other candidate are 'trapped' into voting for him. Thus, a candidate can 'go after' the votes of the other candidate by 'invading his territory', and both continue to move toward the median.

Arthur Smithies pointed out in an early extension of Hotelling's model, however, that voters might leave a candidate as he moved away from them either to support another (third) candidate, or by simply not voting at all [1941]. Two reasonable assumptions about abstentions are that (1) candidate positions can be too close together to make voting worthwhile (indifference), and (2) the nearest candidate may still be too far away to make voting attractive (alienation). If the probability that a voter does not vote is an increasing function of the closeness of two candidates' positions, a movement toward the center of a symmetric distribution of preferences has a symmetric effect on the two candidates' vote totals. The pull of the median remains, and the equilibrium is again at the median. Indifference does not affect this result. If the probability a voter abstains is an increasing function of a candidate's distance from him, the candidate is pulled toward the mode of the distribution. If the distribution is symmetric and unimodal, the median and mode coincide, however, and again the median voter result is not upset. Thus, neither indifference nor alienation, nor the two combined will affect the tendency of two candidates to converge on the position most favored by the median voter when the frequency distribution of voter preferences is symmetric and unimodal [Davis, Hinich, and Ordeshook, 1970].

The median voter result can be upset, however, if the distribution of voter preferences is either asymmetric or multimodal. If the distribution is asymmetric, but unimodal, the optimal position for each candidate is pulled toward the mode if voters become alienated as candidates move away from them [Comanor, 1976]. This can be seen by considering Figure 4.1*b*. Suppose both candidates are at *M*, the median of the distribution. A move of one to *X* decreases the probability that the voters in the cross-hatched region to the right of *M* vote for him. The move also increases the probability by the same amount that the voters in the cross-hatched region to the left of *X* vote for him (the two cross-hatched areas having equal bases). Since there are more voters in the region to the left of *X* than in the region to the right of *M*, the net effect of a move toward the mode taking account only the effect of alienation, must be to increase a candidate's expected vote. But, since *M* is the median, the same number of voters must lie to the left and right of this point, and the effect of alienation on the candidate's vote must dominate for small moves from *M*. As Comanor [1976] has shown, however, the distance between the median and mode is not likely to be great enough to cause a significant shift in candidate positions due to alienation away from those predicted under the median voter hypothesis.

Figure 6.1*c* depicts a bimodal symmetric distribution. As one might expect, the presence of alienation *can*, via the logic just discussed, lead the candidate away from the median toward the two modes [Downs, 1957, pp. 118–22]. But it need not. If weak, alienation can leave the median outcome unchanged, or produce no stable set of strategies at all, such is the strength of the pull toward the middle in a two-party, winner take all system [Davis, Hinich, and Ordeshook, 1970].

A spreading out of candidates may occur, if elections are in two steps: competition for nomination within parties, competition among parties. To win the party's nomination, the candidate is pulled toward the *party* median; the need to win the election pulls him back toward the *population* median. If he treats the other candidate's position as fixed, a Cournot strategy game results with equilibria generally falling between the party and population medians [Coleman, 1971, 1972; Aranson and Ordeshook, 1972].

In Chapter 3 we noted that single-peakedness will ensure a majority rule equilibrium in general only when issues are defined over a single dimension. When this occurs, single-peakedness ensures that Plott's perfect balance criterion is met for an outcome at the peak preference of the median voter. But, the single-peakedness condition breaks down as we move to more than one dimension. The reader will not be surprised to learn, therefore, that the results concerning the instability of majority rule equilibria in a multidimensional world carry over directly for the literature on representative democracy.[2] The problem a candidate faces in choosing a multidimensional platform which defeats all other platforms is, under majority rule, the same as finding an issue, in multidimensional space, which defeats all other issues. To establish such equilibrium strategies one must again introduce assumptions of single-peakedness of the shapes of the distributions. And when these assumptions do suffice to ensure that equilibria exist, they are at the mean [Davis, Hinich, and Ordershook, 1970, pp. 439–43].

One can combine the assumptions of multi-modal distributions and alienation, and envisage a candidate presenting a platform of extreme positions on several issues and winning the support of a sufficient number of minorities to defeat another candidate taking median positions on all. When this happens, a minority, which supports a candidate for the position he takes on a couple of key issues, regardless of his position on others, is essentially trading away its votes on the other issues to those minorities feeling strongly about these other issues.[3]

Unfortunately, the possibility of logrolling to produce cycles persists. Consider the voter preferences in Table 6.1. Suppose that two candidates vie for election on three issues. If the first takes a

---

[2] For surveys of this literature, see Taylor [1971]; Riker and Ordeshook [1973, ch. 12].

[3] Downs [1957, pp. 132–7]; Tullock [1967, pp. 57–61]; Breton [1974, pp. 153–5]. Note that this form of logrolling is even easier to envisage when issues are arranged in more than one dimension. When this occurs, one need not assumed alienation to get a dominant logrolling strategy.

Table 6.1

Issue	Voter		
	I	II	III
A	4	−2	−1
B	−2	−1	4
C	−1	4	−2

position in favor of all three, the outcome that maximizes the net utility gains for all voters, he can be defeated by a candidate favoring any two issues and opposing the third, say (PPF), since two of the three voters always benefit from an issue's defeat. PPF can be defeated by PFF, however, and PFF by FFF. But all three voters favor PPP over FFF, and the cycle is complete. Every platform can be defeated.

In a single election candidates cannot rotate through several platforms, and cycling is not likely to be evidenced. Over time it can be. To the extent incumbents' actions in office commit them to the initial platform choice, challengers have the advantage of choosing the second, winning platform. Cycling in a two-party system appears as the continual defeat of incumbents.[4]

Edwin Haefele [1971] has argued that two-party representative democracy both avoids cycles and maximizes voter utility gains. He depicts representative democracy as strategic maneuvers between two essentially monolithic parties. Their search for an optimal platform is described by a set of rules, which essentially seeks out the maximum possible utility gain, and not by a strategy of simply winning a majority of votes. Haefele is thus led to conclude, from a matrix similar to Table 6.1, that the PPP outcome is a stable solution under representative democracy (pp. 358–62). I cannot see, however, why a party seeking victory would not

---

[4] Downs [1957, pp. 54–62]. Of course, one of the advantages of being an incumbent is that one can rewrite the election laws to favor the incumbents.

choose PPF in response to the other's PPP platform under majority rule.

Haefele justifies the set of rules that underlie his results and the assumptions about party goals and leadership in part by the following quote from Bagehot:

> the principle of Parliament is obedience to leaders . . . The penalty of not doing so is the penalty of impotence. It is not that you will not be able to do any good, but *that you will not be able to do anything at all*. If everybody does what he thinks right, there will be 657 amendments to every motion, and none of them will be carried or the motion either [1905, p. 141].

It is interesting to contrast this quote with Samuel Brittan's observation that 'Bagehot's Introduction to the Second Edition of *The English Constitution* [the same book Haefele quotes], written after the 1867 Reform Bill, is full of gloomy forebodings about the effects of enfranchising an ignorant and greedy electorate [1975, p. 146]. In contrast to the rather optimistic predictions of Haefele, Brittan's essay is itself a set of gloomy forebodings about the future of democratic society. On the next page he cites Schumpeter [1950].

> Another vital condition put forward by Schumpeter for the success of a competitive vote-bidding system was *tolerance and democratic self-control*. All groups must be willing to accept legislation on the statute book. Political warfare must be kept within certain limits; and this involves the cabinet and shadow cabinet being followed by their supporters and not being pushed from behind. Political action is to be left to politicians without too much back-seat driving, let alone direct action. We cannot expect to see these conditions met unless the main interests are agreed on the broad structure of society. If the electorate is divided into two or more deeply hostile camps, or there are rival ideals on which no compromise is possible, these restraints will cease to function and democracy may wither [1975, p. 147].

The bulk of Brittan's essay contains a development of the argument that this and the other conditions necessary for democratic society are not, today, met. Back-seat driving abounds, violating the party discipline assumption Haefele's model requires. More fundamentally, the assumption that the electorate is 'ignorant and greedy' underlies much of the public choice literature. This may further help to explain why Haefele's optimistic conclusions are at variance with those of the rest of this literature. But these issues are too broad to be pursued further here.

In closing this section we note that, in addition to the criticisms of the Downsian model already discussed, the whole spatial approach to political issues has been challenged on methodological grounds, most forcefully by Donald Stokes [1963]. The focus of Stokes' attack is on the unrealism of assuming or attempting to depict the voter and politician decisions in spatial terms. Some issues, like legalized abortion, provide candidates with only a couple of distinct 'positions' which they can take. And it is difficult to think of candidates as moving toward, by degrees, the position of the other candidate. To economists, used to thinking in spatial or vector terms, Stokes' criticisms may be difficult to appreciate. Indeed, much of his criticism of the spatial model seems reminiscent of early debates in economics over whether profit maximization (or some other) assumption is reasonable. Unfortunately, the defense used for profit maximization, 'the theory is good if it predicts well', is even less applicable here, because of the difficulty in determining whether candidates are at the position of the 'median voter' or not.[5] And this is, of course, part of Stokes' criticism.[6]

The median voter result has also figured in some of the empirical work in public choice to which we now turn.

[5] John Aldrich uses survey data on voter evaluations of candidate positions based on a 1 to 7 scale (e.g. 1 = dove and 7 = hawk) to predict voting behavior with some success [1975]. One disturbing result of Aldrich's study, given the results linking abstentions due to alienation and equilibrium strategies, is that abstentions were unrelated to the 'distances' between the candidate's and the voter's positions on issues.

[6] The spatial approach is admirably reviewed and partially defended by Peter Ordeshook [1974].

B. **Empirical testing of median voter models**

Most, if not all, *normative* theories of redistribution imply that redistribution *ought* to be from the rich to the poor. More cynically, one would expect that redistribution would be to those in 'power', the rich, members of a particular geographic, or ethnic group, or so on. The public choice literature just discussed argues that it is the median voter who is in power, and thus one might expect that redistribution will be toward the middle of the income distribution. The hypothesis that redistribution in a democracy is from the tails of the income distribution to the center has come to be known as 'Director's Law', after Aaron Director who first suggested it, and has been further developed by George Stigler [1970], and Gordon Tullock [1971]. Werner Pommerehne [1975] has incorporated the hypothesis into a testable model, and tested it against the 'altruistic' hypothesis that redistribution is from the rich to the poor, and against what he calls the 'New Left' hypothesis that redistribution is from the poor to the rich. He finds that the results of most existing studies, as well as his empirical work based on data from the Swiss canton of Baselland, strongly support the median-voter-model hypothesis that redistribution is to the middle of the income distribution. Further evidence that party competition constrains outcomes to the choice of the median voter is claimed by Hirschel Kasper [1971], who finds a greater dispersion in income maintenance programs in 'one party' states, than in states with viable two-party competition.

One of the potentially more important empirical applications of public choice is to improve the specification of models to explain local public expenditures. The traditional approach has been to make the level of government expenditures dependent on an index of urbanization, population size and density, mean community income, and perhaps several other socio-economic variables depending on the good in question.[7] The public choice approach breaks with this tradition in two important respects: First, it attempts to specify a *demand* equation for a local public good, and

---

[7] For a survey of this literature see Edward Gramlich [1970].

thus includes a price variable, or proxy thereof. Second, it assumes the demand for a public good is directly dependent on the income and tax share of the median voter.

The latter assumption is obviously taken from the results of the Black–Bowen–Downs–Hotelling model. The application of this result to the empirical estimation of public good demand functions requires several additional, strong assumptions, however. The median voter outcome of the Bowen–Black models pertains to the quantity of a public good demanded from a vote by a committee or town-meeting on a single issue. Most studies to date, however, have estimated their demand equations using data on local government expenditures determined typically by representative governments voting on several issues simultaneously. We have seen, however, that the median voter result does not generally hold when issues are defined over more than one dimension, or several issues are decided simultaneously. The employment of median voter characteristics in the demand functions for local public goods thus assumes that these instability problems can be brushed aside, and one can treat local public expenditures as if they contained one characteristic, and were each decided separately. It further assumes, when applied to representative democracy, that the Hotelling–Downs results concerning the positions candidates take in elections can be extended to describe the policies governments implement in office.

In the public choice model both the median voter's tax price and median voter income are included to explain local public good expenditures.[8] The inclusion of the tax price variable is a clear improvement over previous studies which have not included tax shares in the demand equation. Its inclusion recognizes that the purchase of public goods is the outcome of some form of collective choice process in which the *cost* of the public good to the voter, as

[8] Barr and Davis [1966] and Davis and Haines, Jr [1966] made the pioneering efforts to apply the median voter model, and their work has been followed up by more sophisticated attempts by Borcherding and Deacon [1972], Bergstrom and Goodman [1973], Peterson [1973, 1975], Clotfelter [1976], Pommerehne and Frey [1976], Deacon [1978], and Pommerehne [1978].

well as its value to him as reflected by socio-economic characteristics, is important.

The good performance of median income in explaining local public expenditures cannot be interpreted so readily as lending support to the public choice approach. As already noted, most existing studies have assumed that local public good demand is related to *mean* incomes, and it would take a rather peculiar model of local public finance to obtain a prediction that these variables were unrelated. The contribution of the public choice approach must be, therefore, to argue that it is *median* voter income which determines public good demand not *mean* voter income. Most studies have not tested this hypothesis. Indeed, it is very difficult to test given the other assumptions needed to test a median voter demand equation using cross-section data. As Bergstrom and Goodman [1973, pp. 286–7] point out, to estimate this equation on cross-section data one must assume a certain *proportionality* between the distributions of voters across local communities to insure that the quantity demanded by the voter with the median income always equals the median quantity of public goods demanded in each community. But, if this proportionality holds, the means of the distributions will also be proportional, the correlation between mean and median income across communities will be perfect, and there will be no way to discriminate between the public-choice-approach demand equation and its rivals on the basis of this variable. The only way for the public choice approach to yield different predictions from other models is if the ratio of median to mean incomes differs across communities, i.e. there are different degrees of skewness across communities, and these differences in skewness are important in determining the demand for public goods.

Pommerehne and Frey [1975] have tested this latter hypothesis. They found that the median income variable did work somewhat better at explaining local public expenditures than mean income did, although the superiority of median income as an explanatory variable was not particularly dramatic. More convincing support for the superiority of median income over mean income was obtained in a follow-up study by Pommerehne [1978]. Pommerehne used data on 111 Swiss municipalities to test the hypothesis. These data have the important, and singular advantage of allowing one to ascertain the effect of having representative democracy, since the sample contains municipalities which make decisions via direct, town-meeting procedures, and those which rely on representative assemblies. Pommerehne found that median income performed significantly better than mean income at explaining public expenditures in cities employing direct democracy. In the cities employing representative democratic procedures, median income led 'to somewhat superior results', but its 'explanatory power is not significantly better in any expenditure category'. Thus, the introduction of representatives into the democratic decision process does seem to introduce a sufficient amount of 'white noise' to disguise or almost disguise the relationship between median voter preferences and final outcomes. This throws a cloud of doubt over the US based estimates, which rely entirely on representative election outcomes. Interestingly enough Pommerehne found that even the existence of an optimal or obligatory referendum on expenditure bills in cities governed by representative assemblies added enough of a constraint on the representatives' behavior to make the median voter model perform perceptively better than for those cities in which representative democracy was able to function unchecked.

Before closing the discussion of these models, it will pay to consider one additional aspect of them. The Borcherding–Deacon, Bergstrom–Goodman, Pommerehne–Frey, and Pommerehne studies all estimate a 'degree of publicness' parameter based on the coefficients of the tax price and population variables. This parameter is defined in such a way that 'if [it] were nearly zero, there would be substantial economies to large city size since in larger cities, more consumers could share in the costs of municipal commodities with only minor crowding effects. Where [it] is about one, the gains from sharing the cost of public commodities among persons are approximately balanced by the disutility of sharing the facility among more persons' [Bergstrom and Goodman, 1973, p.

282]. All four of the studies discussed here find that this parameter is typically close to one. Borcherding and Deacon urge that 'great care should be exercised in interpreting' this coefficient, and in particular note that 'normative conclusions drawn from the finding that the goods appear better classified as private or quasi-private rather than public are highly conjectural' [1972, p. 900]. Nevertheless, the temptation to make these normative conjectures is obviously appealing to many, and more than one writer has succumbed to it.[9] Such conclusions are not warranted, however. The coefficients upon which this degree of publicness parameter is estimated are obtained from cross-section equations for which the observations are drawn from communities of differing sizes each of which supplies these services (assumed homogeneous across communities) collectively to all members. A parameter estimate of one for police protection implies that a citizen living in a city of 2 million is no better off after weighing the reduced costs of spreading additional police protection across more tax payers against the additional costs (crime?) resulting from crowding than a citizen living in a city of one million. It does *not imply* that individuals in the larger city can contract for 'private' police protection as efficiently as municipal police departments can supply it. Since no private-contract police service systems are included in the studies nothing can be said about their costs relative to public police protection. Nor can one even say that citizens in a part of the city of 2 million can efficiently form a club and provide their own police protection. If there are heavy spillovers from one part of a city to another there may be no efficient way to supply police protection to a city of 2 million other than to supply it to all collectively, even though the net benefits from police protection to a citizen in a city of 2 million may be no greater than those to a citizen of a city half as large. The conclusion that the results of these studies imply that police protection is a private good comes from a confusion of the joint supply and nonexclusion characteristics of public goods. The studies cited

---

[9] See, e.g., Niskanen [1975, pp. 632–3]; Borcherding, Bush, and Spann [1977].

above show that the net joint supply benefits of public good provision have generally been exhausted for the range of community sizes considered. Whether subsets of these communities can efficiently be excluded from the benefits of providing these services to other subsets, so that they can be provided via private or local clubs is another, as yet untested, hypothesis.

All of this hopefully underlines the point that caution must be exhibited when interpreting the empirical results from public choice models. As in all areas of economics, the sophistication and elegance of the theoretical models of public choice far exceed the limits placed by the data on the empirical models that can be estimated. In going from the theoretical models to the empirical 'verifications' additional assumptions and compromises must often be made, which further hamper a clear interpretation of the results as constituting direct support for a hypothesis. What one is willing to conclude boldly on the basis of results analytically derived from *assumed* behavioral relationships, one must conclude circumspectly on the basis of estimated behavioral equations.

This same caution must be exercised in drawing the broader conclusion that a given set of results from a public-choice-based model supports the public choice approach. It is common practice in economics to 'test' a hypothesis by checking whether the results are 'consistent' with it without exploring whether they are also consistent with other, conflicting hypotheses. While it is perhaps unfair to hold public choice to higher standards than the other branches of economics, I do not think that this methodology suffices here. To demonstrate that public choice has something useful to contribute to the existing empirical literature on public finance and public policy, its models must be tested against the existing models, which ignore public choice considerations. Unless public choice derived models can out-perform the 'traditional, ad hoc' models against which it competes, the practical relevance of its theories must remain somewhat in doubt. To date, few studies have attempted such comparisons. But there are some. We have discussed two above, Pommerehne and Frey [1976] and Pommerehne [1978]. We return to some others later.

C. **The importance of the election rule to the number of parties**

The analysis of two-party convergence to the position favored by the median voter is based on the assumption that voting takes place in a winner-take-all election. As Downs notes, a voting rule limiting the number of winning candidates to one per district should have a tendency to force minority parties to merge to increase their chances of winning.[10] The hypothesis has received strong empirical support in the work of Douglas Rae [1967], who found the existence of a single-member-district election rules an important determinant of the number of parties in his cross-national comparison of election rules.

The hypothesis that single member representation will produce two-party democracy has some affinity to the Riker hypothesis that multiparty systems converge to two coalitions of equal size.[11] The Riker model is based on the assumption that politics is a zero sum game. Under the Downsian assumption that the politician's only goal is getting elected, a winner-take-all election for office is also a zero sum game. Thus, the assumptions underlying the Downsian model of party competition *for office* are the same as those underlying Riker's model of coalitions.

The Riker model can explain both the merging of small parties and the breakup of large ones. It is not quite clear, however, why a party with more than 50% of the electorate in support of it would voluntarily disintegrate if its only goal were getting elected. Thus, the analogy to the Riker model is better at explaining the disappearance of small parties than it is the break-up of large ones. And the existence of stable 'one party' systems (e.g. the South in the US) is quite often observed in the presence of single member

---

10 [1957, pp. 123–4]. Both the number of candidates and their objectives are likely to be affected by the voting rule. Plurality maximization is the optimal strategy when a single winner is selected from each district, vote maximization when several candidates can be elected from a single district. See Hinich and Ordeshook [1970, p. 360].

11 Riker [1962]; Riker and Ordeshook [1973; p. 335, n. 33]. Bernholz [1974*b*] discusses more general conditions leading to two parties of equal size.

election rules.

Tullock has observed that nations with single member district election rules often have more than two viable parties at the national level [1967, pp. 149–53]. Canada, Great Britain and even the United States, if one defines the Southern Democrats as a separate party, are examples of this. This observation raises at least one important qualification to the hypothesis. The demise of minority parties under winner-take-all election rules can really only be predicted *within* any election district. There is nothing in the logic of the rules to prevent a party which disappears in one election district from winning in another, and the existence of but one or two viable parties per district can be *consistent* with several parties maintaining reasonable representation at the national level. That this is more true of Canada and Great Britain, which do not have winner-take-all presidential elections to help narrow the field of parties, is suggestive of the intuitive appeal of the single-member-district two-party hypothesis. But the linkage between the two has not been exhaustively analyzed, and the case for the hypothesis rests heavily on its intuitive appeal and Rae's rather impressive empirical support.

D. **Multiparty systems**

Electoral systems in which only one candidate wins a seat from each district have the property that voters are often 'represented' by individuals for whom they did not vote. In addition, to the extent that single-member-district representation results in two party competition with candidates clustered at the position of the median voter, even when a voter has voted for the winning candidate, this candidate may not take a position very close to the voter's most preferred position. Thus, the degree to which a voter's *views* are in fact *represented* by 'his representative' under single-member-district representation schemes can be called into question.

A candidate guarantees himself a seat in a single member district by capturing 50% of the vote. This forces candidates to appeal to broad groups of voters and adopt positions near the median. If several representatives can be chosen from a district, candidates can 'win' with fewer votes. Multiple representation thus *allows* for the existence of several parties or candidates, each of which takes distinct positions, and for the *representation* of most or all of the voters by a candidate for whom they have voted.

An early discussion of multiple or proportional representation is contained in John Stuart Mill's *Considerations On Representative Government* first published in 1861. Although this book is more accurately characterized as part of the classical political economy literature than of public choice, it remains an excellent introduction to both proportional representation (PR) and political theory more generally. The modern public choice discussion of PR begins, again, with Downs [1957, ch. 8]. Several variants of PR systems have been suggested and exist in practice.[12] All have roughly the following properties. Instead of only one candidate emerging as the winner from a given district, several candidates are elected simultaneously. In the limit one can consider the entire polity (the city, the nation) a single district and have the voters vote on a list of candidates drawn at large from the polity. If the assembly contains m seats, the m candidates receiving the largest number of votes may be declared elected. This would still leave some voters 'unrepresented' by someone for whom they voted, but presumably relatively few. This could be avoided entirely by having a run-off election with the m highest vote getters running in the second election. This election would determine the relative support for each candidate's platform in the population at large. If each candidate were given votes in the assembly in proportion to his number of supporters, the positions of all voters, to the extent they can be approximated by the m platforms of the candidates, would be proportionally represented. PR systems in which *parties* are given seats in proportion to their vote totals are of this type to the extent that party discipline effectively constrains party members to vote alike.

Intuitively, one expects candidates in a multiparty system to

[12] See, e.g., Tullock [1967, ch. 10]; Miller III [1969]; Mueller, Tollison, and Willett [1975].

spread out and cover most of the spectrum of political opinion, and much of proportional representation's appeal comes from the expectation that it accomplishes this end.[13] If all candidates cluster at the position of the median voter, each has an expected share of the vote of $1/m$. But, a candidate can assure himself of winning over one fourth of the votes, when all other candidates are at the median, by taking a position at one of the quartiles. Thus, if all candidates start at the middle there is certain to be a tendency for them to move toward the poles in a multi-member district. In the absence of multimodal distributions, however, the lure of the center is sufficiently strong, so that the stability of a given set of strategies cannot be demonstrated.[14]

In many parliamentary systems the government, i.e. the cabinet and chief executive, are chosen by the majority party or coalition of parties. Proportional representation systems resulting in multiple parties can theoretically lead to unstable majority coalitions, and 'government instability', and Taylor and Herman [1971] provide evidence that PR is less stable in practice. Many observers interpret this as a weakness of the PR system for representing voter preferences, and an indirect defense of single-member-district representation and the two party systems it is expected to produce. It is not clear, to this observer at least, whether the cabinet–chief executive instability which tends to arise under PR systems casts criticism on the PR mode of representing voter preferences in the legislature, or on the constitutional rule requiring the executive branch to be formed out of the parliament. In the United States and some cantons of Switzerland, where the chief executives are selected in separate winner-take-all, at-large elections, the stability of the executive branch can be maintained independently of the characteristics of the legislature. The question of whether PR is a superior mode of *representing* voter preferences in the parliament should not be confused with the

---

[13] Downs [1957, ch. 8]; Tullock [1967, ch. 10]; Mueller, Tollison, and Willett [1975].

[14] See Hinich and Ordeshook [1970, pp, 785–8]; Lindeen [1970]; Selten [1971].

issue of what form of parliament is best suited to forming stable governments.

Rae's empirical work establishes that multi-member-representative election rules do produce larger numbers of parties in the parliament [1967]. Casual observation suggests that a wider spectrum of positions is represented in the parliament under multiparty systems. (Such observations are obviously dependent on one's sense of 'position' and 'distance' in political space.) But, more empirical work on the characteristics of the various electoral rules is needed.

E. Coalitions of parties – the minimum winning coalition hypothesis

William Riker [1962] hypothesized that all single and multiparty systems converge to two parties, or coalitions of parties of almost equal size. The theory rests on his modeling of politics as a zero sum game. The plausibility of this assumption is best appreciated by thinking of all political issues as involving basically zero sum redistributions of wealth. In such a game, the optimal strategy is to allow the opposing coalition to be as large as possible, while remaining a losing-paying coalition. Under majority rule this implies one minimum-winning coalition, and another, one vote smaller.[15]

The most convincing support for Riker's theory is his own discussion of the rapid break-up of 'grand coalitions' into minimum winning coalitions in US political history. If the only goal of a party were winning the election, there would be no reason for a grand coalition to break up. There is always some risk of losing a vote, and the bigger the coalition the safer its position. But, if the gains from winning must be taken out of the pockets of the losers, the rationale for forcing some members of the grand coalition over to the losing side is established. More exhaustive

---

[15] An interesting question raised by Riker's theory is how majority rule emerged as the dominant decision rule, since it is obviously inferior to its predecessors, oligarchy and monarchy, in terms of its potential rewards to the winners.

empirical work has been undertaken by Taylor and Laver using data on coalition formation in Western Europe [1973]. They find Riker's minimum winning coalition hypothesis inferior to Robert Axelrod's [1970] minimum-connected-winning-coalition hypothesis in explaining the appearance and duration of coalitions in Western Europe. The Axelrod hypothesis argues that parties which have less 'conflict of interest' will join to form coalitions, and continue to do so until a minimum winning coalition is formed.

F. The behavior of candidates
1. *The provision of information*

The tendency for candidates to converge on the midpoint of the voter frequency distribution

> leads parties in a two-party system to becloud their
> policies in a fog of ambiguity. True, their tendency
> towards obscurity is limited by their desire to attract
> voters to the polls, since citizens abstain if all parties seem
> identical or no party makes testable promises.
> Nevertheless, competition forces both parties to be much
> less than perfectly clear about what they stand for
> [Downs, 1957, p. 136].

The incentive for candidates to take ambiguous stands on issues is reinforced by the lack of incentive for voters to become informed on issues. Just as the output of government activity tends to be a pure public good whose benefits to any single individual are independent of his tax contribution, the choice of government via the electoral process is largely independent of the individual voter's actions. Thus, he has little incentive to become informed on most of the issues of a campaign. On some 'issues' of a general and broad nature, the voter will have some information as a result of his general education and news consumption. On these issues the politician can appeal to the voter at relatively low cost, and thus 'each party traditionally produces a large output of sanctimonious platitudes praising the flag, motherhood, and the home' [Downs, 1957, p. 226] to win votes on these basic, general 'issues' on which all voters are well 'informed'. The voter will also typically be well informed on a few issues of *special* interest to him. Each citizen is a specialist in that the bulk of his income comes from a particular source, and he lives in a single, specific location. Legislation promising direct benefits to his occupational group, or his geographic area can have relatively large direct benefits for him, and warrant his investment, or the investment of his 'interest group' in becoming informed as to candidates' positions on this special-interest information. Thus, the probability of a citizen's voting for a candidate who supports issues promising special narrow benefits for him may be much greater than for a candidate who supports 'general interest' legislation with equal total benefits for the citizen [Olson, 1965, pp. 141–3]. This can reinforce the incentives for candidates to form coalitions of minorities, each of which is lured to the poles by promises of legislation with special interest to them [Downs, 1957, chs. 12 and 13].

> The pattern of behavior which this picture of the information held by the voters dictates for the politician is essentially that described by logrolling. If there are any political problems on which there are widely and strongly held opinions, then he should try to follow those opinions. In addition, he should try to find opportunities to do things which will confer a simple, easily perceived benefit on small groups, but whose cost is dispersed and hard to understand [Tullock, 1967, p. 122].

The distinction between the two types of issues upon which candidates campaign corresponds to the distinction between allocational efficiency and redistribution decisions. Public good allocational efficiency decisions are characterized by the prisoners' dilemma situation. Individuals have incentives to free-ride on the provision of these goods, and invest little in gathering specific information about them when they are provided collectively. Politicians can be expected to compete for votes on these issues by taking positions near the median of the distribution of preferences, by shrouding their positions in ambiguity, and by underpinning their positions with broad platitudes, which appeal to all voters. The possibility under majority rule to couple allocational efficiency improvements with redistribution allows candidates to attach to their campaigns promises of specific redistribution benefits to particular occupational groups, or geographic regions. Thus, the characteristics of information provision and gathering reinforce the tendency under majority rule to have legislation appear in the form of general allocational efficiency gains, coupled to specific redistributions, and can lead to overexpenditures on the special interest bills, and underexpenditures on the general interest legislation.[16]

2. *Campaign spending*

Having described the quality of the information political competition provides, we turn to its quantity.

The natural way for a political economist to approach the subject of campaign spending is to view these expenditures as an investment, the return on which is in the form of votes or in the rewards from actually being elected. The closest analogy to campaign spending is probably advertising, and it is perhaps not surprising to find one of the pioneers in the development of the investment approach to advertising, Kristian Palda, pioneering in the estimation of the determinants and effects of campaign expenditures [1973].

In his most complete model of campaign spending, Palda postulates a 3 equation model to explain (*a*) the number of votes for a candidate, (*b*) his public image, and (*c*) his campaign expenditures. Each of these variables is assumed to be a function of the other two, and a set of exogenous variables. Unfortunately, the only equation which seemed to hold up well was the dependency of votes on campaign expenditures.[17] But, if politicians are rational, egoistic men pursuing votes, one would expect a positive

---

[16] See Tullock [1970], and Downs [1960]. For further development of the arguments of this subjection, see Downs [1957, chs. 11–13]; Tullock [1967, chs. 6–9].

[17] William Welch also finds a positive relationship between campaign spending and vote totals [1974]. Although Welch sets up the problem as one involving simultaneous interactions, he does not test for a simultaneous relationship among the variables.

relationship between expenditures and votes to have a feedback effect on the level of campaign spending a candidate undertakes. That this linkage could not be discerned, casts some doubt on the model as specified. But the development of this type of model is obviously in its infancy.

Mark Crain and Robert Tollison also estimate the impact of vote payoffs on the level of expenditures [1976b, chs. 5, 6]. They argue that additional votes in the house (seats) are more important the fewer a party has – a sort of diminishing marginal returns to holding seats – and found some support for the hypothesis in the higher expenditures by minority parties in house races where no incumbent ran, and in races classified as 'doubtful' by the Congressional Quarterly (ch. 6).

They further test for a causal relationship between payoff from election and amount of campaign expenditures using data on gubernatorial races [1975, ch. 5; 1977]. They hypothesize a greater payoff to being elected to a single 4-year term than two successive 2-year terms, due to the greater initial security of the 4-year term. They predict *and find* higher expenditures in campaigns for 4-year terms, than in *pairs* of 2 year-term campaigns, thus knocking down the frequently heard conjecture that lengthened terms of office will reduce campaign spending. They also predict and find higher campaign spending for seats for which reelection is not limited.

G. **Behavior of voters in a representative democracy**

One of the many paradoxes which plague public choice is why voters even vote. We have already reviewed the incentives candidates may have to delay taking a position so as not to be vulnerable to defeat by a preferred platform in a situation where voter preferences are cyclical, to blur and conceal positions should they be close together, and so on. All of this naturally tends to discourage the voter from voting and raises issues about the information content behind his vote when he does. In addition, we have *the paradox of voting* created by the prisoners' dilemma nature of this act. These issues were once again first raised in the pages of Anthony Downs' book [1957, chs. 11–14], and a burgeoning literature now exists investigating the 'voter's calculus'.

Two aspects of voter behavior have received considerable attention: information gathering, and direct participation. The voter's decision function can be represented as follows:

$$R = BP - C + D \qquad (6.1)$$

where R = the voter's action (vote, gather information),

B = the potential benefits from the action,

P = the probability these benefits accrue, if the action is undertaken,

C = the action's cost, and

D = private benefits complementary to the action.[18]

R can represent the simple act of voting, in which case it is either zero (abstains) or one (votes), or R can be a continuous variable measuring the amount of time and/or resources devoted to information gathering or running for office. To explain, say, information gathering, B represents the potential gain from picking the *best* candidate, P the probability that the citizen's choice matters, C the cost of gathering the information, and D its extra benefits (psychic income, status with peer group). Although B and P may change as information is acquired, it is plausible to assume they soon become constant. If D diminishes on the margin, and C increases, then the utility from gathering political information is maximized by equating its marginal entertainment value and cost. Political information's likely impact on election results does not affect its acquisition.[19]

Similar arguments have been made about voting. If P is the probability of a single vote being decisive, then it obviously must be very small in a large constituency. Thus, for most people the outcome of an election is a public good and political participation

---

[18] See Downs [1957, chs. 11–14]; Tullock [1967, pp. 110–14]; Riker and Ordeshook [1968], and for a critique Barry [1970, pp. 13–19].

[19] See Tullock [1967, chs. 6 and 7].

is vulnerable to free-riding [Olson, 1965, pp. 86, 159–67]. To the extent two-party competition brings candidate positions together, elections will be close, raising P but lowering the benefits from the best candidate's winning (B). Thus, B and P vary inversely and their product is probably small, implying that participation's entertainment value and costs should dominate this decision. Some have used this result to explain the greater participation rates of high income and high education groups.[20] White collar and professional groups typically have more flexible work hours, and can more easily take out the time to go to the polls. They are also better read, and can be expected to acquire information about the opposing candidates as part of their leisure time reading and conversation. Thus, the opportunity costs of becoming informed and going to the polls may be higher for the upper income groups with higher education.

The left-hand side variables in equation (6.1) imply that voter participation should be a function of the closeness of the election, and the expected probability of the act of voting affecting the outcome. Riker and Ordeshook [1968] found the closeness of the race an important variable explaining voter turnouts in their initial investigation of this hypothesis, and their results have been supported by subsequent empirical work.[21] Tollison, Crain, and Paulter [1975] argue, however, that it is voter information as provided free by television, or through newspapers, which best explains voter participation. Their results, although questioning the importance of the P variable in the voter calculus equation, still are consistent with the rational voter model, since more information for voters implies lower costs of voting, C, to the extent that these costs include the costs of becoming informed.

The most exhaustive investigation of the subject to date is by Ashenfelter and Kelley, Jr [1975]. They examine survey data on voter attitudes and attempt to explain the large difference in

[20] See the exchange among Frey [1971], Russell, Fraser and Frey [1972], and Tollison and Willett [1973].

[21] See, Barzel and Silberberg [1973], Rosenthal and Sen [1973], and Silberman and Durden [1975].

turnouts in the two US presidential elections of 1960 and 1972 on the basis of them. The two most impressive pieces of support for the rational voter hypothesis are the strong negative effect of the poll tax[22] on voting, and the fact that 'the single most important factor accounting for the decline in turnout . . . is the dramatic shift in voter expectations about the closeness of the race in these two elections'. Nevertheless, Ashenfelter and Kelley go on to conclude that,

> The theory of voting that is best supported by our results is that which posits a sense of duty or obligation as the primary motivation for voting. The variables with the greatest quantitative impact on voting are education, indecision, the dummy variables representing the sense of an obligation to vote, and certain cost variables (p. 724).

It is difficult to share their conclusion, however, that these variables could be important in explaining *differences* in voter turnouts between 1960 and 1972, although they might be important in explaining why large numbers of voters vote in every election. There is no reason to suspect, and no evidence is given by the authors, that voters were significantly more moved by a sense of duty and obligation in 1960 than in 1972. In addition, the two candidates in 1960, Kennedy and Nixon, were generally felt to be 'extremely close together' on the issues, while the 1972 candidates, Nixon and McGovern, offered the voters a 'real choice'. Thus, if there were differences in the amount of indecision among voters, one would expect more indecision in 1960 than in 1972, and thus a lower turnout in 1960. But the reverse was the case. The same can be said for the 1976 results. Although for different reasons, Ford and Carter might easily be expected to be close together in the eyes of many voters, and one might have expected, as many predicted, a low voter turnout due to voter apathy and indecisiveness. Yet, the election brought one of the largest turn-

---

[22] The poll tax is an institution somewhat peculiar to the United States, and within the United States peculiar to the South. To vote, the citizen must pay a modest fee at the polls. Its alleged purpose was to keep low income groups (e.g. blacks in the South) from voting.

outs in one of the closest US presidential elections of this century. Although these observations are admittedly casual, they do not seem to be overturned by either the results or arguments Ashenfelter and Kelley provide.

As in most areas of empirical investigation, there is disagreement among observers over the amount and nature of support for the rational voter model. All studies, and this includes Ashenfelter and Kelley, find evidence that *some* of the variables (cost of voting, closeness of race) in the rational voter model are important, however. The disagreement which exists is over which variables are significant and the magnitude of their impact. This conclusion implies that both the quantity and quality of voter participation is capable of being affected by changes in the incentives to vote. Increasing the importance of a citizen's vote say by decentralizing the functions of government, lowering the costs of gathering information and voting, and other experiments might be tried, if the quality of outcomes under modern democratic institutions is thought to suffer from the quality of inputs [Tollison and Willett, 1973].

So as not to close this section on too optimistic a note, let us pose another paradox presented by the results to date from the rational voter model. Although the probability that a single vote would affect the outcome of the presidential election in 1960 or 1976 was undoubtedly much higher than in 1972, say, it still was infinitesimal. For the change in this probability to explain the higher turnouts in 1960 and 1976, voters must have highly elastic reaction functions to changes in the anticipated closeness of elections. Riker and Ordeshook [1968] noted this, and argued that voters were (over)persuaded as to the importance of their vote by television and newspaper public service advertisements stressing the importance of their vote, a possible explanation of the Tollison–Crain–Paulter [1975] results. But, if voters can be this badly misled by nonpartisan, low-key, get-out-the-vote advertising, what is the effect of the highly partisan, far more intense advertising of the candidates?

It is fitting that we close this section, as we began, with a paradox.

7

Exit, voice and disloyalty

In his book *Exit, Voice, and Loyalty* [1970], Albert Hirschman developed the useful distinction between processes in which individuals express their preferences via entry or exit decisions, and those in which some form of written, verbal, or voice communication is employed. An example of the first would be a market for a private good in which buyers indicate their attitudes toward the price–quality characteristics of the good by increasing or decreasing (entry or exit) their purchases. An example of the exercise of voice to influence a price–cost nexus would be a complaint or commendation of the product delivered to the manufacturer. A necessary condition for the effective use of exit is obviously that the potential users of this option be mobile: and full mobility of both buyers and seller (free entry and exit) is an assumption underlying all demonstrations of market efficiency. In contrast, the literature focusing on voting processes, public choice and political science, has almost exclusively assumed (most often implicitly) that exit is not an option. The boundaries of the polity are predefined and inclusive, the citizenry is fixed. A citizen is at most allowed to abstain from participating in the political process, but he cannot leave the polity to avoid the consequences of its decisions.

Given the assumption of fixed boundaries and citizenry, the characteristics of a pure public good, nonexcludability and joint-

125

ness of supply, require that a collective *voice* or nonmarket decision process be used to reveal individual preferences and achieve Pareto efficiency as Samuelson [1954] emphasized. But many goods are 'pure' public goods in a limited sense only. For these goods the nonexclusion principle and/or the jointness of supply property may not be applicable over the full range of possible distribution and production alternatives. For these quasi- or local public goods the possibility may exist for employing *exit* as an alternative or complement to the *voice* process. These possibilities are reviewed in the present chapter.

We close the chapter by discussing a mechanism for expressing one's preferences when neither the exit nor voice options, as customarily defined, are available.

A. Voting-with-the-feet

We examine first the consequences of relaxing the joint-supply (economies of scale) property. Consider a public good with no production costs: the proportion of tulips in the public square (bulbs are free). If the dimensions of the polity coincide with the population, the preference revelation problem persists. Assume more than one policy can exist, however. Within any polity all must consume the same public good (flower bed), but there are no spillovers between communities. With this *limited* degree of exclusion possible, people can reveal their preferences for a local public good by moving into the community providing the most desirable fraction of tulips. Considering only the whole percentile options, 101 communities suffice to achieve Pareto optimality. No ballots need be cast. All preferences are revealed through the silent voting-with-the-feet of individuals exiting and entering communities, a possibility first noted by Charles Tiebout [1956].

In contrast to the disappointing promise of majority rule, unanimity, and the other traditional voting procedures, and the imposing complexity of the newer, more sophisticated procedures for revealing individual preferences, Tiebout's voting-with-the-feet procedure seems to accomplish the task via the surprisingly simple device of allowing people to sort themselves out into groups of like tastes. Strategizing is eliminated, and the voluntary association principle implicit in much of public choice is operationalized through the assumption of mobility between communities.

The Tiebout model rests on a number of extreme assumptions, however. The example above assumes no economies of scale, and this assumption is quite important to Tiebout's argument as we shall see below. In addition, the most important and questionable assumptions appear to be the following.[1]

1. Full mobility of all citizens
2. Full knowledge of all of the communities' characteristics
3. A full range of community options are available spanning the range of public good possibilities desired by the citizens (101 different polities in the example above)
4. No spillovers across communities
5. No geographical constraints are imposed on individuals with respect to their earnings

Some difficulties with respect to assumption 5 are discussed below. Assumptions 1 and 4 tend to work at cross-purposes. The larger the community, the more costly it is to leave it, and the lower mobility is. Thus, exit is a more reasonable alternative from small than from large communities. On the other hand, the smaller the community the more likely it is that the benefits from the provision of any specific public good spill over onto other communities causing externalities across communities and non-Pareto allocations.

Assumptions 2 and 3 raise complementary issues. The basic argument assumes a full range of possible baskets of public goods available at the start. But how is this spectrum of opportunities established? Two possibilities come to mind: Some central authority or auctioneer could set up different local communities with different baskets of public goods and inform all potential citizens of each community's characteristics. This possibility violates the decentralized spirit of the Tiebout model, however.[2] Alternatively,

---

[1] See Tiebout [1956]; Buchanan and Wagner [1970]; Buchanan and Goetz [1972]; McGuire [1972]; Oates [1972]; Pestieau [1977].

[2] See Pauly [1970] and McGuire [1972].

one can envisage new communities being established by entrepreneurial types, who seek out combinations of public goods not provided elsewhere. This solution seems to require that the entrepreneurial city founders receive a share of the 'profits' generated from hitting upon a desirable package of local public goods. Tiebout speaks of 'city managers' in recognition of their entrepreneurial role, perhaps, but does not elaborate as to how the city manager gets his signals as to what package of public goods to offer, or how he captures his share of the 'profits' generated.

Most city managers are probably mayors, who are elected by the present residents and might be expected to reflect their tastes and not necessarily some potentially optimal combination of public goods in a spectrum of communities. If we assume that the public good offerings of each community reflect in some sense the tastes of the median voter, and further that the distribution of preferences in each community is about the same, then each community might start out offering about the same bundle of public goods, and no incentives for migration would exist. Even when differences across communities exist there is no guarantee that the set of public good offerings reflecting the present distribution of population and preferences will provide the right signals for the migration of individuals into alternative communities. One could easily envisage an unstable process in which individuals migrated to a community expecting a given constellation of public goods, only to find that their migration changes the constellation offered, forcing an additional migration, which again changes the set of offerings, and so on.

An additional problem arises as one expands the number of local public goods. Consider the consequences of introducing a second public good in the example above: the proportion of oaks in the square. This issue's resolution requires the further separation of individuals into groups of identical preferences, now with respect to *both* flowers and trees. The number of communities needed to ensure Pareto optimality leaps to 101 squared. Each additional public good raises the number of polities required to a higher exponent. If the number of public goods is very large, one reaches a solution in which the number of communities equals the size of the population. Each community-individual becomes a polity with a basket of public–private goods (garden, woods) tailored to his own tastes, a possible consequence of the model that Tiebout himself observed.[3]

Voting-with-the-feet achieves Pareto optimality by grouping individuals together in polities of homogeneous tastes. In the extreme, it satisfies G. H. Kramer's severe condition for consistent majority rule decisions, that all individuals have identical indifference maps, through the imposition of a silent unanimity rule.[4] It can realistically be assumed to come close to satisfying this goal, when, relative to the size of the population, (1) the number of public goods is small, and/or (2) the number of distinct preferences for combinations of public goods is small. Since *the* task of public choice is the revelation of (differing) individual preferences for public goods, voting-with-the-feet, in part, solves the public choice problem by significantly limiting its scope.

B. The theory of clubs

Consider now the effects of the joint supply characteristic, without the nonexclusion principle. That is, assume that exclusion is possible, but addition of a new member lowers the average cost of the good to all other members, i.e. there are economies of scale. If average costs fall indefinitely, optimal club size is the entire population, and the traditional public good problem exists. If they eventually rise, either because scale economies are exhausted or from the additional costs of crowding, an optimal club size smaller than the population may exist.

J. M. Buchanan was the first to explore the efficiency properties of voluntary clubs using a model in which individuals have identical tastes for both public and private goods [1965a]. To see what is involved, consider the example Buchanan first employed, the formation of a swimming club. Assume first that the size of the

---

[3] See, also, Pestieau [1977].
[4] [1973]. See, also, McGuire [1974], and on the relationship between voting-with-the-feet and the unanimity rule Pauly [1967, p. 317].

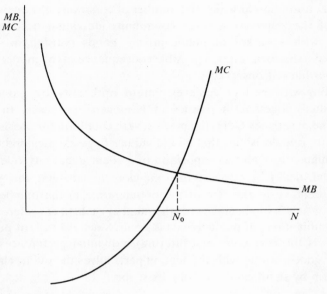

Figure 7.1

pool, and thus its total cost is fixed and the only issue to be decided is the size of the club. Figure 7.1 depicts the marginal benefits and marginal costs from an additional member as seen by any other member. Given identical tastes and incomes it is reasonable to assume equal sharing of the costs. The marginal benefit to the first member from adding the second member to the club is the saving of 1/2 the cost of the pool. The marginal benefit of a third member is the additional saving of 1/3 of the cost of the pool. The additional benefits from adding new members, the savings to the other members from further spreading the fixed costs, continue to fall as the club size (N) increases as depicted by MB in Figure 7.1. The marginal costs of a new member are given by MC. These are psychic costs. If individuals prefer to swim alone, these will be positive over the entire range. If individuals enjoy the company of others in small enough numbers, the marginal costs of additional members will be negative over an initial range of club sizes. Eventually, the positive costs of crowding will dominate, however, and the optimal club size, N_0, is determined where the marginal cost of an additional member from enhanced crowding just equals the reduction in the other members' dues from spreading the fixed costs over one more club member.[5]

Figure 7.1 can also be used to depict the polar cases of pure private and pure public goods. For a pure public good, the addition of one more member to the club never detracts from the enjoyment of the benefits of club membership to the other members. The marginal cost schedule coincides with the horizontal axis. The optimal club size is infinity. For a pure private good, say an apple, crowding begins to take place on the first unit. If a consumer experiences any consumer surplus from the apple, the foregone utility from giving up half of his apple will exceed the gains from sharing its costs and optimal club size is one. Even with such seemingly private goods as apples, however, cooperative consumption may be optimal. If, for example, the unit price of apples is lower when sold by the bushel, the distribution of apples will exhibit joint supply characteristics, and might dictate optimal-sized buying clubs of more than one.

The theory of clubs can be extended to take into account the choice of quantity and other characteristics of the collective consumption good. This extension is, perhaps, most easily undertaken algebraically. Let a representative individual's utility be defined over private good Y, public good X, and N, the club size

$$U = U(Y, X, N) \tag{7.1}$$

Let the production possibility frontier be given by

$$Y = g(X) \tag{7.2}$$

Assuming that the costs of providing the public good are equally shared, each individual's share of these costs can be deducted from his private good income to obtain his net of public good income, $Y - [g(X)/N]$. Substituting this expression into (7.1), we obtain as the objective function

$$O = U\left(Y - \frac{g(X)}{N}, X, N\right) \tag{7.3}$$

[5] See McGuire [1972, pp. 94–7]; Fisch [1975].

to be maximized with respect to the quantity of public good, X, and club size, N. This yields the first order conditions

$$- \frac{\partial U}{\partial Y} \frac{g'(X)}{N} + \frac{\partial U}{\partial X} = 0 \tag{7.4}$$

$$+ \frac{\partial U}{\partial Y} \frac{g(X)}{N^2} + \frac{\partial U}{\partial N} = 0 \tag{7.5}$$

Rearranging (7.4) we obtain the Samuelsonian condition for the efficient consumption of a public good,

$$N \frac{\partial U/\partial X}{\partial U/\partial Y} = g'(X) \tag{7.6}$$

The sum of the marginal rates of substitution over the N (identical) club members must equal the marginal rate of transformation. From (7.5) we get the condition depicted in Figure 7.1,

$$\frac{\partial U}{\partial Y} \frac{g}{N} = - \frac{\partial U}{\partial N} N \tag{7.7}$$

the disutility imposed on the other club members from the addition of one more club member, $(\partial U/\partial N)(N)$, must equal the fraction of the good's costs he pays (g/N), weighted by the marginal utility of private goods to the representative member. Under normal assumptions changes in tastes or technology leading to an increase in the amount of one of the variables will lead to an increase in the other. An increase in public good quantity will increase each individual's share of the costs, raise the marginal utility of private goods $(\partial U/\partial Y)$, and (7.7) will require a larger marginal disutility from additional club membership, and thus a larger club size.[6]

The assumption that individuals have identical tastes and incomes is not as innocuous as it first might appear. As in the Tiebout model, it is inefficient to have individuals of differing tastes in the same club, if this can be avoided. If all individuals are identical except some prefer rectangular pools and others oval

[6] See Buchanan [1965a, pp. 6–10].

ones, then the optimal constellation of clubs will sort out individuals into oval and rectangular pool clubs. The ideal constellation of clubs is one in which all members of any club have identical tastes.[7]

If the number of differing preference functions is small relative to the population size this ideal can be met. An efficient allocation of these quasi-public goods through the voluntary association of individuals into clubs of homogeneous tastes can be envisaged. Pauly compares the rules or charter of the club to a social contract unanimously accepted by all members [1967, p. 317], and the theory of clubs, under these assumptions, is obviously much in the spirit of the contractarian and voluntary exchange approaches to public choice and public finance. Indeed, with large numbers of alternative clubs available, each individual can guarantee himself the equal benefits for an equal share of the costs assumed above, since any effort to discriminate against him will induce his exit into a competing club, or the initiation of a new one. If optimal club sizes are large relative to the population discrimination is possible, however, and stable equilibria may not exist. With an optimal club size of 2/3 of the population, for example, only one such club can exist. If it forms, those not in it have incentives to hire members away by offering disproportionate shares of the benefits gained from expanding the smaller club. But, the remaining members of the larger club have incentives to maintain club size, and can attract new members by offering the full benefits of membership in the big club. And so on. No stable distribution of club sizes and benefits need exist [Pauly, 1967, 1970]. Analytically the problem is identical to the cycling problem confronted earlier. The two farmers forming a winning majority constitute an optimal sized club, but the one farmer left out has an incentive to try and form an optimal club too, and his efforts to form a new club can lead to an unstable equilibrium, a cycle.

Even when stable equilibria are reached, the equal sharing of benefits may no longer occur if the optimal club size is large relative to the number of people having a given preference function. The threat of exit to another club will be weak if an

---

[7] Buchanan [1965*a*], and McGuire [1974].

individual's preferences are such that only a small and relatively inefficient club could be formed by individuals of like tastes. Thus, individuals with 'majority' tastes are in a better position to threaten withdrawal to optimal sized clubs than those with 'minority' tastes, and coalitions with discriminatory sharing of the benefits from cooperation can be anticipated even when stable, Pareto-efficient club sizes are obtained.

We thus are brought to a conclusion similar to the voting-with-the-feet model: The voluntary formation of clubs to allocate public goods is most attractive when the optimal club size is relatively small, i.e. when the quasi-public goods have a limited degree of publicness. Despite this qualification, the voluntary formation of clubs is at least *conceptually* a more promising means for revealing individual preferences for public goods than voting-with-the-feet, for it does not require geographic proximity of club members. In practice, most clubs do provide their benefits to a subset of a local population, as in Buchanan's swimming club example. But even here it is not necessary for members of the local swimming club to join the golf club, and the problems associated with voting-with-the-feet are reduced through the formation of limited membership clubs.

C. **Voting-with-the-feet in the presence of jointness of supply**

When local public goods are produced with economies of scale, it is even more unlikely that individual mobility suffices to achieve Pareto optimality. It is then necessary that there be 'just the right number of individuals' with identical preferences to satisfy the optimality conditions for each public good.

Pareto optimality in a global sense, requires that the incremental change in net benefits to the community an individual joints equal the incremental loss to the community he leaves

$$\sum_{i=1}^{n} \Delta U_A^i = \sum_{i=1}^{m} \Delta U_B^i \qquad (7.8)$$

The change in utility of the nth individual to join community A is his total utility from being in A (U_A^n), just as his loss from leaving B

is his total utility in B, U_B^m. Equation (7.8) can thus be rewritten as

$$U_A^n + \sum_{i=1}^{n-1} \Delta U_A^i = U_B^m + \sum_{i=1}^{m-1} \Delta U_B^i \qquad (7.9)$$

In a world of pure competition, each factor owner's marginal product is the same in all industries and areas. If externalities and other market failures are not present, the welfare of others is unaffected by his location. All ΔU^i are zero except for the moving individual, and he naturally locates in his most favored community. With public goods present, the ΔU^i for individuals in a community are positive for an additional entrant, as the total costs of the public good get spread over a larger number of individuals. A new entrant thus confers positive externalities for a community producing a locally pure public good. Alternatively, a new entrant can produce 'congestion' costs, negative externalities, to a community which has grown beyond the optimal size for its locally provided public goods. In either case, since the moving individual compares only his utility levels in the two communities, and ignores the marginal effects of his move on the others (the ΔU^is in A and B), voting-with-the-feet in general will not produce Pareto optimality in the presence of public goods and externalities.[8]

To see how a non-Pareto efficient equilibrium can emerge, assume that there exist only two communities in which an individual can live, A and B. Each community is identical as are all of the residents. Each community provides a public good, which is optimally provided when 2/3 of the potential residents of the two communities consume it. Thus, there are enough individuals for only one, optimally sized community. The situation is depicted in Figure 7.2. Curve MB_A represents the *average* benefits to a member of community A from membership in the community as a function of community size. These first rise as a result of the economies of scale property of the public good, and then begin to fall as crowding costs begin to outweigh the benefits from cost sharing. The curve MB_A also represents the *marginal* benefits to a

---

[8] See Buchanan and Wagner [1970]; Buchanan and Goetz [1972]; Flatters, Henderson, and Mieszkowski [1974]; Pestieau [1977].

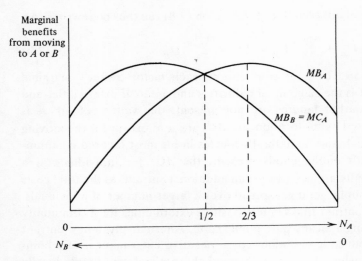

Figure 7.2

member of community B, from migrating to A. MB_B is the mirror image of MB_A defined with respect to the population of B, read from right to left along the horizontal axis, MB_B is also the marginal cost (MC_A) to a citizen of B from migrating to A. As usual, individual equilibrium occurs where marginal cost intersects marginal benefits *from below*. No such intersection exists in the figure. The intersection at an equal division of population is a local minimum. At any distribution in which one community has a higher population than the other, benefits will be higher from membership in the larger community. Migration will be from the smaller to the larger community and this will continue until all of the population enters into one of the communities. If congestion costs rise significantly, MB_A might decline fast enough following its peak to intersect MC_A. This would yield an equilibrium for the larger of the two cities at a size above its optimum, but below that of the entire population. In either case, however, the equilibrium city sizes achieved via voluntary migration are not those which maximize the average utility level of all individuals in the two communities. The latter would occur in this example when the population is equally divided between the two communities. This distribution of population maximizes the *average* benefits from *being* in either community. But, once this point is left, the *marginal* benefits from switching to the larger community will exceed those of staying and population will redistribute itself until the stable, but inefficient equilibrium is obtained.[9]

While the assumption that the optimal sized community is more than half the total population may seem unrealistic when one thinks of an area and population as large as the United States, often the potential migrant may not be considering such a wide spectrum of options. The relevant choice may be staying in small town B or moving to nearby large city A. Within this circumscribed range of choice, the optimal-sized community may be more than 1/2 the combined populations of the two communities and the tendency for overpopulating the central city may be evidenced.

If the optimal sized polity is less than 1/2 the population, the marginal benefits and cost schedules will intersect and yield a stable equilibrium with the population evenly divided between the two communities. This equilibrium does result in a maximization of the potential benefits to each citizen, given the constraint that there be but two communities. When additional communities can be created, and the optimal sized community is small relative to the total population, we return to a Tieboutian world in which free migration and the creation of new fiscal clubs can be envisaged as resulting in a set of communities, each of optimal size.

Additional complications are introduced into the Tieboutian world, however, if individuals earn part of their incomes outside of the community. Assume again two communities with identical production possibilities, and individuals of identical tastes. Within any community each individual receives the same wage, w, from supplying his services to the local production process, and a differential income, $r_i \geqslant 0$, that is tied to him and not to his location. This income can be thought of as coming from dividends, as in Tiebout's example, or as rents on assets peculiar to the individual, e.g. the income of a recording star. We shall refer to this income as simply rental income, covering all non-location-

[9] See Buchanan and Wagner [1970].

specific sources. Now consider two communities with equal numbers of workers, identical production possibility frontiers, and identical tax structures. In equilibrium the total private and public good production in community A must equal the sum of its rental and wage income:

$$\sum_{}^{N_A} Y_i + X = N_A w_A + \sum_{}^{N_A} r_i \tag{7.10}$$

The utility of a resident of A is given by

$$U_i(Y_i, X, N_A) \tag{7.11}$$

as before. Substituting for X from (7.10) into (7.11), we have

$$U_i(Y_i, N_A w_A + \Sigma r_i - \Sigma Y_i, N_A) \tag{7.12}$$

The assumption of identical tax structures implies that the individual can purchase the same bundles of private goods, Y_i, in both communities. With equal populations and production possibilities, N_A and w_A equal N_B and w_B. Assuming the public good is not an inferior good, some of any additional rental income in A will go to increased public good production. Thus, $\Sigma r_i - \Sigma Y_i$ is larger in A than in B if Σr_i is larger in A than in B. Since public goods enter an individual's utility function with a positive sign, an individual is better off joining the community with the higher rents, assuming all other community characteristics are the same.

If the communities have different rental incomes, the same set of tax structures may not be optimal in both communities. Nevertheless, if tastes are the same, an individual always receives a more attractive tax–public good package from the community with higher rental income.

Higher rental incomes thus play the same role in attracting individuals from the other community as larger population in the presence of joint supply characteristics. Indeed, from (7.12) it can be seen that rental income, the wage rate, and the population size all enter the utility function in the same way through the public good term. Thus, any increase in population, the wage rate, or rental income, *ceteris paribus*, increases an individual's utility by increasing the quantity of public goods available. An increase in population also enters the utility function negatively, however, through the congestion effect represented by the third argument in the utility function. Increasing population can also be expected to drive the wage rate down, reducing an individual's command over private goods, and thereby his welfare. In contrast higher rental income has an unambiguous positive impact.

Just as an individual's welfare is higher if he enters the community with the higher rental income, the community's welfare is higher, the higher the rental income of any new entrant. The depressing effect on wages and costs in terms of increased congestion from a new member are identical, but the benefits in terms of increased tax revenue to finance public good provision are obviously greater, the greater the newcomer's rental income.[10] If the community has expanded to the point where the marginal gain from spreading the public good's costs over another taxpayer just equals the marginal cost in terms of reduced wages and congestion, adding another individual who is just a wage earner makes the community worse off. But, if he has a high enough rental income, the additional gains from financing an expansion of public good supply out of this rental income outweigh these costs. Regardless of what the community's size is, an additional member can always increase the welfare of all existing members, if he brings with him a high enough rental income.

In the same way that full mobility between communities may not bring about a Pareto optimal distribution of the population, where economies of scale in public good production are large, full mobility is unlikely to bring about a Pareto optimum distribution of the population in the presence of rents. In the example above, the socially optimal distribution of the population is that which equates the marginal product of a worker in each community. This occurs at equal community sizes. But if the distribution of rents differs between the two communities, migration toward the community with the higher rents will occur. This migration will

---

[10] This effect is particularly apparent in the Flatters, Henderson, and Mieszkowski model in which a golden rule result is obtained in which all rents go to public good production and all wages to private good production [1974, pp. 101–2]. This model is based on different assumptions than the above discussion, however.

continue until the fall in marginal product and rise in congestion costs is large enough to offset the advantage this community has from higher rents, and average utility levels in the two communities are equal.

To achieve the socially optimal distribution of population, taxes and subsidies must be levied on either residence in or movement in and out of a given community. One possibility is to grant a central authority the right to make transfers across communities. Such an authority would then determine what the socially optimum distribution of population was, and levy taxes and subsidies to achieve this optimum distribution. In the general case, the central authority would attempt to achieve the equilibrium condition given in equation (7.9). This requires a tax equal to $\sum_{i=1}^{n} \Delta U_A^i$ on community A, if A is the community which is, or would become, too large, and a subsidy equal to $\sum_{i=1}^{m} \Delta U_B^i$ to community B if it would lose population. If the only difference between the two communities were the level of rental income, the policy would be simple to implement. The central authority would levy a tax on rental income in the community with higher initial rental income, and offer a subsidy to the community with lower rental income to bring about equal rental incomes and populations in both communities.[11]

Alternatively, Pareto optimally can be achieved in a decentralized way, by granting each community the right to tax immigration and emigration. If the externalities for community A from immigration were positive, it could offer a subsidy to new comers equal to $\sum_{i=1}^{n} \Delta U_A^i$ and levy an identical tax on emigration. If B did the same, all individuals would be forced to internalize the external costs their moving entailed and Pareto efficiency would be obtained.[12]

---

[11] Flatters, Henderson, and Mieszkowski [1974], McMillan [1975].
[12] Buchanan [1971]; Buchanan and Goetz [1972].

While these alternatives have identical efficiency outcomes, they differ both in spirit and in their equity properties. The latter weds Tiebout's decentralized voting-with-the-feet with the theory of exclusive clubs to produce a decentralized solution to the population allocation problem. The enaction of such a system of taxes and subsidies by local communities immediately provides communities favored by natural characteristics, population size, income, etc. with a valuable property right, which they exercise by taxing members outside of their community (i.e. those who would have entered in the absence of the tax-subsidy scheme). The centralized solution vests the entire population with a property right in both communities and achieves allocational efficiency by taxing *all* members of the favored community to subsidize the disfavored community.[13]

The difference in policies can be most easily seen by considering again our rent example but assuming that individual rents are not tied to given individuals but are locational rents accruing to all residents of a given community. Granting the right to tax migration into the community with higher rents to its residents would allow them to achieve permanently higher utility levels than in the less-favored community. Those who were lucky enough or quick enough to be born or move into a geographically more desirable area would forever be better off than those left in the less desirable areas. In contrast, the centralized solution would equate utility levels across communities by taxing the higher rent areas and subsidizing the low rent ones.

Even when rental incomes are tied to individuals rather than locations, Tieboutian revelation of preferences coupled with local taxes and subsidies can raise equity issues. As noted above, a community can always be made better off by admitting someone whose rental income is high enough. Once a community has reached its optimal size for sharing the costs of public goods, it might adopt a policy of say, admitting only new members who

---

[13] The discussion of efficiency and equity in a federalist system predates the public choice – Tiebout literature, see, e.g. Buchanan [1950, 1952]; Scott [1950, 1952*a*, *b*], as well as Musgrave [1961].

bring with them a rental income above the average. This can be accomplished by establishing zoning requirements on lot sizes, and apartment dwellings that effectively screen out those with incomes below a given level. The mobile individual on the other hand is better off joining a community with greater rental income than he receives. The intersection of these two strategies could be a sorting out of individuals into communities of equal rental incomes. The identical incomes and preferences assumption Buchanan assumed for convenience in initiating the study of clubs is a plausible outcome to a Tieboutian search for optimum communities.[14]

It also appears to be one which is occurring. Gary Miller [1978] has found an increase between 1950 and 1970 in the degree of homogeneity *within* communities in the Los Angeles area in terms of both their income levels and ethnic composition. At the same time that individual communities were becoming more homogeneous, the differences in income levels and ethnic composition across communities was becoming more pronounced. These homogeneity differences were particularly striking in the new communities formed during these two decades, whose composition is probably most reflective of recent migration decisions. Orbell and Uno [1972] have linked the decision to move directly to dissatisfaction with one's surrounding community. Exit is a direct and frequent response to local conditions. Further support for the Tiebout hypothesis exists in econometric studies linking migration patterns to the levels of local public services and tax rates.[15] Voting-with-the-feet is clearly one of the more practically and politically relevant hypotheses in the public choice field today.

D. **Voluntary association, allocational efficiency, and distributional equity**

Wicksell's voluntary exchange approach achieves allocational efficiency by imposing a unanimity rule on the polity so that each collective decision must benefit all for it to pass. The

---

[14] See, also, Buchanan and Goetz [1972].
[15] See in particular Richard Cebula [1974, 1977], and references cited there.

approach assumes from the beginning that a predefined polity and citizenry exist.

The theory of clubs and voting-with-the-feet seek to determine a Pareto optimal distribution of public goods through the voluntary association of individuals of like tastes. Here the dimensions of the polity and citizenship are outcomes of the 'voting' process. Nevertheless there are issues raised about the limits of the polity, and the rights of citizenship.

When a group of individuals jointly consumes a public good, each one's preferences can, in a meaningful sense, impose costs on the others. If A desires the construction of tennis courts, and B a golf club, then we have seen (with additional voters and issues) that under majority rule a cycle can ensue. Under the unanimity rule an impasse could arise. Even if one of the goods is provided, say tennis, A is likely to be worse off than if B preferred tennis to golf, and was willing to bear a larger share of this sport's costs. If A were incumbent to the community, and B outside, A would clearly prefer that others with preferences closer to his join the community, and, if it were in his power might discriminate in their favor over B.

None of this is very troubling if the public goods are tennis and golf, and the polities private clubs. No one objects too strenuously to a tennis club's restricting membership to those who want to play tennis. But the implications are less comforting for more general definitions of the public goods. When individuals have positive income elasticities of demand for public goods we have seen how an individual can benefit from being in a community with incomes higher on average than his own from the additional units of the public good it provides. Even when each individual is taxed at his marginal evaluation of the public good, i.e. the Lindahl price, an effective redistribution from rich to poor occurs through the egalitarian distribution of the public good that of necessity occurs, when rich and poor consume it together. But, one's income elasticity of demand can be regarded as a sort of 'taste' for a public good. If the incumbent membership of a local polity is free to exclude new members, then, one can expect a sorting out of individuals into local polities of identical tastes *and* incomes, thus thwarting the possibility for this type of redistribution.

Wicksell assumed that voting on allocational issues took place following the determination of a just distribution of income. The same assumption could be made to support a voluntary association solution to the public good problem. But, here it must be recognized that the voluntary association approach is likely to affect the distribution of income, while revealing preferences for public goods. A given distribution of private incomes might be considered just, when individuals reside in communities of heterogeneous income strata, so that the relatively poor benefit from the higher demands for public goods by the relatively well to do. The same distribution of income might be considered unjust if individuals were distributed into communities of similar income, and the relatively poor could consume only those public goods which they themselves could afford to provide.

The latter is the logical outcome of the voting-with-the-feet process, and one which is coming to pass. If the resulting distribution from this process were thought to be unjust, one could correct it by making transfers across communities, but here one runs directly into the issue of the proper bounds of the polity, and the rights of citizenship.

In a federalist system there are two possible ways to view citizenship. Primary citizenship can reside with the local polity, and the central polity can be thought of as a mere union or confederation of the local polities with certain powers delegated to it. Conversely, primary citizenship can reside with the central state, with the local polities being merely administrative branches of the central government, with powers delegated from above. Under the first view of the polity, it would seem that the rights of the local polity to define their own citizenship, and pick and choose entrants would dominate the right of citizenship in the larger confederation to migrate, free of hindrances, to any local polity. Here we see a direct clash between two of the conditions for achieving a decentralized, efficient allocation of public goods: the full mobility assumption, and the right of the local polity to tax and subsidize migration. If primary citizenship lies with the central state, then presumably individuals would be free to enter and exit local communities without incurring locally imposed penalties. Equity issues would be viewed from the perspective of the central polity, and it would be free to engage in intergovernmental transfers.

The issues of the dimensions of the polity and the rights of citizenship in a federalist system have not been resolved in either the fiscal federalism literature or in the political process itself. The United States and much of Western Europe seem to be in transition from having rights reside with the local polity to placing them with the central government. In some countries, e.g. the United States and France, the process is fairly far along. In others, like Yugoslavia, it is just beginning. In still others, e.g. Canada and Great Britain, it may be reversing itself. This is surely an area where theory and practice have much to learn from one another.

E. **The theory of revolution**

When neither the ballot, nor the feet constitute adequate modes of expression, there is still Chairman Mao's barrel of the gun. Given their role in real world politics, one might expect to find more said about revolutions than has been. Gordon Tullock has, however, gotten the discussion underway [1971; 1974]. He proposes to explain a revolutionary's behavior with a model resembling the one used to explain voter behavior. If, R is a potential revolutionary's reaction, B the new government's public good benefits (possibly negative), P the probability that the individual's participation brings about success, D the private gains from participating in the revolution, and C the private costs, we have the same equation as we used to explain the act of voting,

$$R = BP + D - C \tag{7.13}$$

If R is positive he participates in favor of the revolution, if negative, against it. Since R can take on any value, the equation can also be used to explain the degree of participation.

Given the richness of options open to the revolutionary compared to the voter, the terms in (7.13) are more complicated than in the equation to explain voter behavior, and Tullock actually works with more involved equations. P, for example, can vary from individual to individual, and thus a Lenin may choose to participate, the typical man-in-the-street not. D and C include not only the psychic gains and risks from actual participation but also probabilistic personal gains and losses depending on whether the revolution succeeds or fails. The former might, for example, be a position in the new regime, the latter before a firing squad. And, one can weigh the personal gains and risks from participating with the counterrevolutionaries.

As with voting, one assumes that the typical citizen considers the fruits of the revolution as a public good, regards the probability of his affecting the outcome as near zero, and makes his decision on the basis of the private gains and risks of participation. For most, this calculation will lead to apathy or occasional participation in a large rally if it is not too risky and has some entertainment value. For a few, it leads to committed participation with the hope of securing a high position in the new regime.

As Tullock first developed it the public choice theory of revolutions was more a theory of nonrevolution than a theory that would explain and predict the conditions under which revolutions would take place, just as the economic theory of voting offers a better explanation for why people do not vote than for why they do. True the leaders of the revolution can expect large personal gains after its success, and their participation can thus be explained by the usual selfish motives associated with the pursuit of personal power and gain. Indeed, the economic theory of revolution based on the individual maximizing calculus seems much better suited to explaining the *coup d'état*, where the number of actors is small, the odds calculable, and the stakes seemingly large, than it is at explaining 'grass roots' revolutions. Tullock extends his theory to analyze the *coup d'état* in his book, *The Social Dilemma* [1974], and cites the relative importance of coups to 'spontaneous' revolutions as support for his theory.

Silver [1974] has tried to add predictive content to the theory by dissecting some of the factors making up the expected benefits and costs of revolution. He cites examples of revolutions occurring after political reforms and the defeat of the government in foreign wars to indicate that revolutionaries respond to a reduction in the probability of punishment, and increases in the signs that the regime is weakening and lacks resolution. While his examples and those of Tullock are suggestive, the theory is not yet developed to a point and in a manner in which it can be tested against its competitors.

While there are problems in extending the public choice paradigm to the study of revolutions, the theory nevertheless fills an analytic gap in this literature. In a closed polity, an individual is always in danger of being 'exploited' or 'tyrannized' by a majority or minority of his fellow citizens. His choices in such situations are to continue to rely on voice in the hope that the outcomes will change; seek a new polity by migration; create a new one by revolution.

8

The supply of government output

The bulk of the public choice literature is concerned with the positive and normative properties of processes for revealing preferences for public goods (perhaps broadly defined). The implicit assumption in this literature is that the quantity of public good demanded, once collectively chosen, is automatically forthcoming. Several observers have detected some slippage between the lips of the voter and the flow of outputs from the government's cup, however. To understand the reasons for this slippage one must examine the behavior of the government itself. A small, but rapidly growing, stream of the public choice literature has addressed this task. In applying the tools of economics to this subject, this literature has made use of the existing theories of monopoly and the managerial firm.

A. The government as a monopolist

In Albert Breton's [1974] theory of representative democracy, the government is the party in control of the legislature. This theory is thus somewhat more applicable to parliamentary systems as exist in the UK and Canada, where the parliamentary majority is allowed to 'form the government', and includes the executive branch. The governing party has an objective function, which includes the probability of being reelected, but also can include 'variables such as personal pecuniary gains, personal power, his own image in history, the pursuit of lofty personal ideals, his personal view of the common good' (p. 124) and so on.[1] To achieve these goals the governing party takes advantage of its position as a monopoly supplier of certain highly desired public goods, e.g., defense, police and fire protection, highways. A monopolist of a private good can often increase his profits by tying other products, which he does not monopolize, to the monopolized product. So long as the consumer's surplus on the package of tied products exceeds that available on other packages, the consumer will buy the tied products to get the monopolized one. In the same way, the government can often achieve the varied objectives of its members by packaging rather narrowly defined issues that benefit only small groups of voters along with the broadly popular services it monopolizes.

In exploiting its monopoly position the governing party is constrained by the threat of entry by the opposition party or parties (pp. 137–9). To ward off this threat the governing party

> can engage in one or more of four basic activities: it can (1) enact and implement discriminatory policies as well as policies that have the characteristics of pure private goods, including changes in tax rates, basic exemptions, tax credits, loopholes, etc.; (2) discriminatorily adjust the penalties levied against and the probability of apprehending those committing legal offenses; (3) engage in implicit logrolling, combined with full-line supply by combining policies in such a way as to elicit or maintain political support; and (4) seek to alter the preferences of citizens so as to reduce the differences that exist between them and thus make them more homogeneous (p. 143).

Breton's theory of monopoly government is broadly consistent with the Downsian model of representative democracy. Both Downs [1957] and Tullock [1967] predict that majority rule leads to logrolling and the serving of special interests. Tullock [1959] went on to conclude from his initial analysis of logrolling under majority rule, that the size of the government would be too large.

---

[1] See, also, Donald Wittman [1973].

Tullock's conclusion was directly challenged by Downs [1961] himself, however, who argued that the tendency for government to oversupply special interest legislation would be more than offset by the tendency to undersupply general interest (public good) legislation due to the free-rider problem, and the complementary lack of incentives for voters to become informed about this type of legislation.[2]

The Downsian model of majority rule representative democracy was extended by Bernholz [1966] to derive specific predictions as to which special interests are likely to be served: e.g. producers, low profit industries, slow growth and high unemployment districts.[3] This list could easily be joined with Breton's to obtain a predictive theory of representative government.

The Downs–Breton theory of representative government offers one possible explanation for the rapid growth in the size of government that has characterized all Western countries in recent years. Both Downs [1961] and Breton [1974, pp. 192–3] shrink from drawing this conclusion, however. Both would prefer to conclude that some aspects of the government's basket of services are likely to grow too large, but that others are likely at the same time to be too small. A riddled tax structure at a given level of government expenditures is as much a prediction of the Downs–Breton model as an expanded budget and taxes are. Even if the theory falls short of fully explaining the growth of the public sector, however, it helps to explain how some activities that do not fit the textbook definitions of public goods and externalities wind up in the public weal, and why the economist's cherished ideal of horizontal equity in taxes is so flagrantly violated in practice.

B. Empirical investigations of the behavior of governments

Neither Downs nor Breton offers any direct empirical support for their theories. Nevertheless, a still small, but rapidly growing empirical literature has developed that does seem to be

---

[2] For Tullock's reply see [1963].
[3] See, also, Bernholz [1974b].

consistent with the broad implications of the Downs–Breton model.

One of the earliest efforts to formulate an empirically testable model was by Bruno Frey and Lawrence Lau [1968], who assume as in Breton's model that the incumbent party seeks to maximize its utility, which is a function of both ideological variables and its popularity. The latter variable can be considered a proxy for Breton's probability of being re-elected. When a government's popularity is high (expected vote $\geq 52\%$), it pursues its ideological goals; when low, it manipulates the policy variables at its disposal to increase its popularity. The latter were assumed to be the key macroeconomic variables amendable to government intervention. Thus, in the Frey–Lau model the popularity of an incumbent government is linked to the economic health of the economy, and its policies to affect the economy are linked back to its popularity.

In a follow-up work, Frey runs some simulations on this model and finds that the political intervention of the government based on its popularity can have stabilizing or destabilizing effects on the economy depending on the parameters assumed.[4] In a further extension, Frey and Schneider specify and estimate a politico-econometric model in which government popularity is dependent on the price level, unemployment rate, and per capita consumption [1975, forthcoming]. The government's policy variables to affect these macro variables (expenditures, transfers, and government employment) are in turn made dependent on its popularity. They find a significant improvement in the Krelle macro-econometric model of West Germany with the addition of their politico-econometric equations. Follow-up work with this model on data for the United States and United Kingdom has yielded equally successful results [1978*a*, *b*].

Several additional studies have examined the relationship between key macroeconomic variables and either the government's

---

[4] [1974]. See, also, Schneider [1974].

popularity or its election results.[5] One of the best of these is that of Gebhard Kirchgässner.[6] Kirchgässner does a time series analysis of the popularity indexes for the various parties in the UK and West Germany over the post-World War II era. He finds a strong statistical relationship between the unemployment and inflation rates in these countries and the popularity of the *governing parties*. The popularity of the out-of-government parties is not related to these variables. Allan Meltzer and Marc Vellrath [1975] also find the unemployment and inflation rates to be the key explanatory variables in explaining the votes, by state, in 4 recent US presidential elections. They conclude, however, that these economic variables work to the advantage of the Democrats, in or out of office, and do not systematically affect the fortunes of only the incumbent party.

The assumption that government popularity is based on the levels of key economic variables underlies the hypothesis that a 'political business cycle' exists, as already encountered in some of the work of Frey and his associates, and further propounded by William Nordhaus [1975] and Duncan MacRae [1977]. Nordhaus and MacRae postulate voter myopia, which makes them vote for parties offering current, low unemployment levels, when these unemployment levels will later produce unwanted inflation. This myopia coupled with the government's overriding goal of winning the next election leads to an optimal government strategy of raising unemployment levels, thereby reducing inflation, in the politically safe post-election-victory period, and then reducing unemployment going into the election, leaving the resulting inflation to come to roost after the election results are in.

All of the studies reviewed until now in this section assume that governments attempt to affect their probability of being re-elected through the manipulation of macro variables. The Frey models do treat other ideological variables in the government's objective

---

[5] See, e.g., Goodhart and Bhansali [1970]; Kramer [1971]; Frey and Garbers [1972]; Miller and Mackie [1973]; Fair [1978], and for surveys, Frey and Schneider [1975], and Frey [1978].

[6] This paper also contains an excellent review and critique of the empirical work in this area.

function, but these too are thought to be macro-oriented. Left of center parties favor low unemployment rates for ideological reasons, right of center parties low inflation.

This macro-view of the governing party's objectives has been directly challenged. Not surprisingly, the micro-counterattack initiated in Chicago. George Stigler [1973] argues that the unemployed are too few in number and uninfluential to be a major target of government policies, and that rising real income per capita is a basic goal of all political parties. He goes on to question the reliability of Kramer's estimates of the importance of the latter variable in explaining votes for the incumbent party. Having rejected a macro-economic explanation of political behavior, he postulates that 'the economic bases for party affiliation must be sought in [the] area of income redistribution' [1973, p. 167].

Although Stigler did not present any empirical support for this hypothesis, Gavin Wright [1974] has. Wright finds that the volume of income transfers made by Roosevelt's New Deal government does well in explaining party support at the polls. Wright's 'spoils' system of government also fits the view of government underlying the recent work of Crain and Tollison [1976b]. They link the amount of federal expenditures by state to the seniority of its house delegation, using seniority as an index of political power [forthcoming]. This result dovetails nicely with their finding that campaign expenditures, and hence political contributions, are higher for incumbents and increase with their seniority. The more seniority the candidate has the better bet he is to deliver the goods. Other chapters in their book present additional evidence in support of their 'spoils' view of government.

The work of Wright, Crain and Tollison complements Breton's theory of government by suggesting that politicians may seek to be elected as a means to pursuing other, narrow economic goals, via their legislative efforts. Thus, wealth maximization emerges along side of vote maximization as a possible goal of the politician.

This view of the world has been pushed the furthest by William Landes and Richard Posner [1975]. They attempt to explain not only the behavior of legislators within the constitutional rules on the basis of narrow self-interest; but suggest that the choice of rules themselves was also so motivated. They begin by arguing that

> In the economists' version of the interest-group theory of government, legislation is supplied to groups or coalitions that outbid rival seekers of favorable legislation. The price that the winning group bids is determined both by the value of legislative protection to the group's members and the group's ability to overcome the free-rider problems that plague coalitions. Payment takes the form of campaign contributions, votes, implicit promises of future favors, and sometimes outright bribes. In short, legislation is 'sold' by the legislature and 'bought' by the beneficiaries of the legislation (p. 877).

From this behavioral premise they go on to argue that an independent judiciary increases the value of the legislation being sold today, by making it somewhat immune from short-run political pressures that might try to thwart or overturn the intent of this legislation in the future. And this is apparently what the founding fathers had in mind when they established an independent judiciary in the Constitution. In the Landes–Posner theory the First Amendment emerges 'as a form of protective legislation extracted by an interest group consisting of publishers, journalists, pamphleteers, and others who derive pecuniary and non-pecuniary income from publication and advocacy of various sorts' (p. 893). By such fruit has the dismal science earned its reputation.

Despite their obvious differences, the micro- and macro-oriented attempts to explain government behavior have one important characteristic in common: they both focus on income and wealth variables as the major determinants of voter preferences. This common feature allows one to interpret both sets of studies as lending empirical support to the Downs–Breton model of government. For both treat as largely givens the outputs of public goods as traditionally defined, and thus implicitly assume that parties do not compete by taking different positions on these issues, or furthermore that public goods are not part of the ideological variables the government pursues. This interpretation of the goals of government is clearly in conflict with much of the public finance and public choice literature, at least as the latter has been interpreted in the preceding chapters of this book. This literature assumes that the major task of government is providing public goods, and the objective of the voting process is to reveal individual preferences for these goods. To the extent that this empirical literature does succeed in explaining government behavior, it suggests that much of the theory of public finance and public choice is beside the point.

The extent to which this literature does explain government behavior is still a somewhat debatable question, however. There is an old joke about the man who looks for his watch on the corner with a lamp-post, rather than on the corner where he lost it, because he can see better under the lamp-post. One leaves the empirical literature on representative government with a feeling that some of this behavior underlies the work here. It is perhaps all too natural for economists to start testing popularity functions by plugging *economic* variables into their equations. But the behavior of governments in an 'economic' theory of democracy is not necessarily a function of only, or chiefly, narrowly defined economic variables. The public good characteristics of wars, civil rights, corruption, and other 'noneconomic' issues may also play a role. The studies reviewed here have implicitly ruled them out as explanatory factors. Interestingly when political scientist John Aldrich attempts to use the spatial model to predict voting in the 1968 US presidential election, he chooses survey results for the Vietnam War and urban unrest, issues with high saliency scores, but also the only two issues for which he had appropriate data [1975]. Aldrich's spatial model also seems to fit *his data* well on these two, noneconomic issues. And, it is worth noting, 1968 was one of the election years Nordhaus could not explain via his political-business cycle hypothesis [1975].

These observations raise again the point about formulating one's politico-economic model in such a way that it can be tested against alternative theories, and then actually testing it against them. The bulk of studies to date have been content to report results 'consistent with the hypothesis'. How many other hypotheses these results are consistent with is left an open question, and one which, on the basis of the reported R^2s, it is not idle to ask.

The testing of empirical models of public choice is still in its infancy. All empirical studies cited in this section have appeared since 1970. Despite its youth, this area is growing at such a rate that the many questions and gaps left open at this time must soon begin to disappear. It is certainly one of the more exciting subareas of public choice to follow.

C. The budget-maximizing bureaucrat

Once the government, i.e. the legislature and executive, decide what government outputs are to be provided and in what quantities, they must actually be bought. Although some government outputs are bought directly from private industry, most government funds are channeled through a public bureaucracy.

The first, systematic effort to study bureaucracies within a public choice framework is the book by William Niskanen, Jr.[7] Niskanen is critical of our existing understanding of bureaucracies based mostly on analyses by sociologists and political scientists. He 'suspects, our contemporary confusion about bureaucracy derives from the absence of a theory of bureaus that is consistent with an instrument concept of the state, that is, a concept of a state which is only an instrument of the preferences of its constituents' (p. 4). Here we have the fundamental behavioral postulate of economics, and the public choice approach to the study of bureaucracies is characterized by its development of the implications for bureaucratic behavior of this postulate.

---

[7] Niskanen's book [1971] was preceded by two insightful looks at bureaucracy by Gordon Tullock [1965] and Anthony Downs [1967]. Although written by economists, indeed by two of the founding fathers of the public choice field, these earlier works do not attempt to develop a theory or model of bureaucracy from a public choice perspective. Instead, they use the economics methodology to examine various facets of bureaucratic organizations, and cast light on several important issues.

1. *Environment and incentives*

One of the key characteristics of a government bureau is the nonmarket nature of its output [Downs, 1967, pp. 24–5]. Indeed, a bureau does not typically supply a number of units of output as such, but levels of *activities* from which output levels must be inferred [Niskanen, 1971, pp. 24–6]. Thus, the Department of Defense maintains numbers of combat personnel, and weapon systems, although it supplies various degrees (units) of defensive and offensive capabilities. Its budget is defined over the activities it maintains, even though the purchasers, the taxpayers and their representatives, are ultimately interested only in the 'final outputs' of combat capabilities these activities produce. The reason for this is obvious, it is easier to count soldiers and airplanes than it is units of protection. This 'measurement problem', inherent in so many of the goods and services public bureaus provide, creates a monitoring problem for the funding agency. Given the unmeasurable nature of a bureau's outputs, how can the purchaser monitor the efficiency of their production?

The monitoring problem is intensified by the bilateral monopoly nature of the bureau–sponsor relationship [1971, p. 24]. That the buyer of a bureau's output would be a monopsonist follows almost from the nature of the good sold. A public good is by definition consumed by all of the people, and the agent of all of the people is a monopsonist buyer on their behalf. Of course, we have seen that the government may not engage in the supply of only pure public goods, but, nevertheless, it remains the sole agent of whatever interest group it represents in dealing with public bureaucracies. Even if the government acts as sole agent for the population, or an interest group, it is not necessary that it buy from a single source, although this is often as it turns out to be. The usual reason for granting a bureau a monopoly on the provision of a given service is to avoid wasteful duplication. Although there is certainly some validity in this justification, the monopoly nature of most bureaus also frees them from competitive pressure to be efficient, and denies the funding agency an alternative source of information by which to gauge the efficiency of the monopolist bureaus, thus compounding the monitoring problem inherent in the nature of the bureau's output.

Inefficient production of a bureau's services is further induced by the scheme of compensation of bureaucrats. While managers in a private corporation can usually claim a share of the savings (profits) generated by an increase in efficiency, public bureaucrats' salaries are either unrelated or indirectly (and perhaps inversely [Warren, Jr, 1975]) related to improved efficiency. Thus, the public bureau is characterized by weak external control on efficiency and weak internal incentives.

If the bureaucrat has no financial incentive to pursue greater efficiency, what are his goals, and how are they related to efficiency? Niskanen lists the following possible goals of a bureaucrat: 'salary, perquisites of the office, public reputation, power, patronage, output of the bureau, ease of making changes, and ease in managing the bureau'.[8] He then asserts that all but the last two are positively and monotonically related to the size of the budget. Despite the crucial importance of this assumption to his analysis, and its novelty in relationship to the traditional literature on bureaucracy, Niskanen does little to justify this assumption. It is, however, virtually identical to the assumptions made by Penrose [1959], Baumol [1959], and Marris [1964] about the motives of the managers of large corporations. Just as the separation of ownership and control between stockholders and managers creates incentive and monitoring problems for the firm, the nature of the output, and bilateral monopoly setting of a public bureau creates incentive and monitoring problems in this area. The behavioral evidence Penrose, Baumol, and Marris present to justify the use of sales or growth maximization as the objective of the firm's managers, can be used to justify the assumption of budget maximization on the part of the public bureaucrat.[9]

---

[8] [1971, p. 38]. Downs also devotes a good deal of space to the goals of bureaucrats [1967, pp. 81–111].

[9] Relevant here too is the property rights literature that links managerial behavior to the institutional constraints imposed upon it. See Alchian and Kessel [1962], Alchian and Demsetz [1972], and the literature surveyed by Furubotn and Pejovich [1972].

2. *The model*

The bureau receives a budget from its funding agency, say Congress or the Parliament, which is a function of the *perceived* output of the bureau's service

$$B = B(Q), B' > 0, B'' < 0 \tag{8.1}$$

This function may be thought of as a public benefit or utility function. Public benefits are assumed to increase, but at a diminishing rate, with increasing output.

The bureau has a cost function for producing its output that, over the relevant range at least, increases at an increasing rate like a competitive firm's cost schedule

$$C = C(Q), C' > 0, C'' > 0 \tag{8.2}$$

This cost schedule is known only to the bureau's members (or a subset thereof). Thus it is that the monitoring problem arises. The funder knows its total benefit schedule (8.1), but sees only an activity budget from the bureau. It cannot therefore determine whether this output is being supplied Pareto efficiently, i.e. if at the margin public benefits equal public costs. The funder sees only the total output of the bureau and its total budget. This frees the bureau to maximize its budget subject to the constraint that its budget cover the costs of production. If we assume that the bureau does not turn money back to the funder, this constraint is satisfied as an equality; and we get as the funder's objective function

$$O_F = B(Q) + \lambda(B(Q) - C(Q)) \tag{8.3}$$

whose first order conditions yield

$$B'(Q) = \frac{1}{1+\lambda} C'(Q) \tag{8.4}$$

$$B(Q) = C(Q) \tag{8.5}$$

The Lagrangian multiplier λ represents the marginal utility of an expansion of the budget constraint. Were this zero, if the bureaucrat was indifferent to the level of the budget, and maximized the social welfare, the condition for Pareto efficiency would be satisfied, the marginal benefit of an extra unit of output to the funder would equal its marginal cost to the bureau

$$B'(Q) = C'(Q) \tag{8.6}$$

Since the size of the budget provides utility to the bureaucrat, $\lambda > 0$, however, and $B' < C'$. The budget is expanded beyond the point where marginal public benefits equal marginal costs. If B and C are quadratic, B' and C' become straight lines and we have the situation depicted in Figure 8.1, taken from Niskanen [1971, p. 47]. Instead of requesting a budget which would result in the output Q_0, and thereby maximizing the net benefits of the funder, the bureau will request the larger budget consistent with the output Q^*. At Q^* triangle E equals triangle F. All of the consumer surplus gains from the production of the inframarginal units of output up to Q_0 are balanced out against the excess of marginal costs over marginal benefits on the units between Q_0 and Q^*. Note here that Niskanen's description of the public bureaucracy's behavior *vis-à-vis* the government, is quite analogous to Breton's description of the behavior of the government *vis-à-vis* the citizens. The monopoly bureau uses its position to recapture the consumer surplus on its monopolized service, just as the government exploits its monopoly on particular services by tying other outputs to them.

Niskanen also discusses the possibility that the funder's demand schedule would be so far to the right, or inelastic, that the marginal benefit of Q to the funder fell to zero before F grew as large as E. The total budget equals total cost constraint would not be operative then, and the bureau would simply request the output level at which the funder is satiated. This situation is represented by the B'_s and Q_s schedule and quantity in Figure 8.1.

The possibility that a funder might become satiated from a given public good before a bureau had exhausted all of the consumer surplus it is capable of exploiting could lead a budget maximizing bureaucrat to propose other outputs besides the one for which it is solely responsible. This could take the form of radical innovations, or more plausibly infringements of one bureau onto another bureau's domain, or onto the domain of the private market.

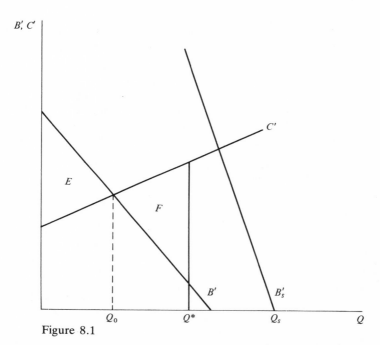

Figure 8.1

Niskanen develops his model of the budget-maximizing bureau to explore this and other cases. He also attempts an integration of his model of the public bureau, and a model of the review process in a representative democracy, based on the median voter model, where the voter in this case is a representative of the citizen-voter [1971, chs. 13–16]. In some cases, the extensions tend to mitigate the tendency for bureaucratic budgets to be too large, in some cases they reinforce them. For example, the practice of choosing as the head of a bureau an individual who was (and/or is likely to become) an executive in companies that sell to this bureau strengthens the bureau's interests in larger budgets. The Congressional practice of appointing representatives of high demand users of a bureau's output (interest groups) to the subcommittees charged with reviewing a bureau's performance weakens the potential for curtailing the expansion of the bureau's budget through this outside monitoring process.

All-in-all one gets the impression from Niskanen's book that the net effect of supplying public outputs by public bureaus is a substantial expansion of the size of government.

3. *Remedies*

Possible reforms to curtail excessive bureaucratic expansion follow directly from the assumptions and logic of the Niskanen model [1971, chs. 18–20].

The introduction of competition among bureaus, although a result initially, perhaps, of bureaucratic efforts to expand, can serve as an aid to limiting the overall growth in bureau size by breaking the monopolies some bureaus have over the provision of certain services, and the concomitant monopolies over the information of the costs of providing these services their monopoly supplier positions grant them. Competition among certain bureaucracies (e.g. the branches of the armed services) has from time to time broken out, and may be said to have always existed at one level of intensity or another. Niskanen's proposals here would serve to institutionalize this practice, and do away with the periodic reorganizations of bureaus that combines all agencies serving a particular need under one bureaucratic administration.

Related to this proposal would be an expansion of the use of private market alternatives to public bureaucracies. Many communities already rely on the private market to supply them with garbage collection, fire protection, hospital, and other services that are often publicly supplied. Studies of the relative efficiency of private and public provision of these goods generally give the nod to the former. Experiments have also been conducted in other areas (e.g. elementary schooling). Further expansion of these alternatives can easily be envisaged.

One of Niskanen's more radical proposals would give bureaucrats an increased incentive to provide services most efficiently by giving them a share of any savings in costs they produced. To avoid the possibility of bureaucrats creating 'artificial' savings, this proposal would have to be coupled with the one of setting up competition among bureaus, and would probably require a reasonably identifiable output. Niskanen discusses several possible ways in which this might be carried out: (*a*) direct shares of cost savings, (*b*) delayed prizes for good performance, and (*c*) limited discretionary control over budget surpluses.

As a way of avoiding the coincidence of interest between the budget-maximizing bureau and its interest-group-representative review committee, Niskanen proposes that committee assignments be rotated and based on a random draw.

As a first pass, Niskanen's proposals for reform are perhaps what one would have expected of an economic approach to the 'bureaucracy problem', even if one did not see the model – more competition, more use of the profit motive. They are useful nonetheless, and more compelling because they follow logically from an analytic investigation of the problem.

D. Extensions of the bureaucratic discretion model

The main assumptions upon which the Niskanen model rests are: (1) that bureaucratic control over information regarding the costs of producing the bureau's output gives the bureaucrats discretion to pursue goals other than the maximization of the sponsor's welfare, and (2) that the reward system and goals of the bureaucrat are most closely associated with the size of the bureau's budget. As noted above, the first assumption is common to all managerial discretion models of the firm. Control over production costs, and investment opportunity information by company managers, and stockholder proclivities toward free-riding in the monitoring of managers gives managers discretion to pursue goals in conflict with stockholder interests. The second assumption, that bureaucrats seek to maximize the budget of their bureau is analogous to the behavioral assumptions underlying the Penrose–Baumol–Marris models of the firm. Although this objective is plausible both for corporate managers and public bureaucrats, other objectives are also plausible and have been advanced to explain managerial behavior. These objectives also have their counterparts for the bureaucrats.

Migué and Bélanger [1974] have pointed out that the relentless use of budget funds to expand the bureau's output would conflict with one of the presumed objectives for having larger budgets – to pursue other goals. Weatherby, Jr [1971] has suggested, *à la* Oliver Williamson [1964], that the expansion of personnel would be one of the additional goals pursued by bureaucrats. Drawing upon the literature on the managerial firm, one can easily expand this list to include the following: leisure, security, emoluments, the staff's racial composition, and all of these may be subsumed under the heading X-inefficiency as coined by Leibenstein [1965], and later applied by him to the firm [1969].

The various conflictual goals of managers or bureaucrats can also be treated in the context of a managerial or bureaucratic utility maximization problem. The basic assumption here is that the manager's or bureaucrat's utility function contains two arguments: Y, the variable his constituents (stockholders or Congressional review committee) seek that he maximize, and X his own, conflictual goal. For the firm, Y is assumed to be either long-run profits, or the present value of the firm's outstanding stock. For the bureau, Y may be defined as the net benefits to the bureau's sponsors from the bureau's supply of services. X can be any of the managerial–bureaucratic goals listed above. The key technological assumption common to all of these models is that, at least after a point, Y decreases with the expansion of X (see Figure 8.2). Both Y and X provide positive utility to the managers or bureaucrats so that we have the familiar convex to the origin indifference contours. Utility maximization must occur at a point along the negative sloped portion of the Y–X opportunity locus. X is produced beyond the point which maximizes stockholder or bureau sponsor's welfare.

None of these behavioral models of bureaucratic behavior have been put to a direct test. Some studies of the growth of government, or the lack of growth of productivity in government have cited Niskanen's and similar hypotheses as being 'consistent' with their findings.[10] Indirect support can be claimed from those studies of the managerial or regulated firm that find that managers do not

[10] See, e.g., Borcherding [1977*b*]; Spann [1977].

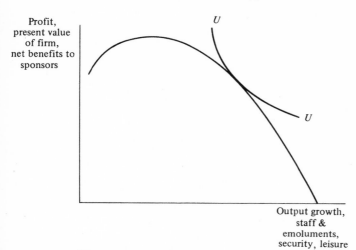

Figure 8.2

maximize profits or minimize costs. More direct evidence that bureaucratic discretion leads to X-inefficiencies of one kind or another is contained in the several studies that have found private production of a quasi-public good to be more efficient than public production.[11]

E. The integration of supply and demand

The Niskanen model is a first and significant step in the direction of redressing the imbalance in the public choice literature between supply and demand considerations. Breton and Wintobe [1975] have pointed out, however, that the Niskanen model goes perhaps too far in its emphasis on the importance of supply factors, to the neglect entirely of the demand side. In the simplest version of the model, the bureaucrat faces a fixed demand schedule and is free to choose any point along it up to the point where all benefits

---

[11] For a survey of these results, which relates them to the literature on bureaucracy, see William Orzechowski [1977].

Cotton Linsday [1976] presents evidence that bureaucrats supply excessive amounts of those characteristics of output that are easiest to measure by the sponsoring agent, and too little of the less tangible characteristics.

(either total or on the margin) from government intervention disappear. This surely casts the demanders of public services in a secondary and nearly impotent role. The proper approach to the problem is undoubtedly an interactive model of supply and demand.

Given the bilateral monopoly nature of the demand and supply interactions between parliamentary review committees and public bureaus, the natural way to approach this question is probably, as by Gary Miller [1977], via game theory. Miller gives the demanders of public services the power to give and withhold rewards, pecuniary and otherwise. The suppliers have the options of high and moderate compliance with sponsor wishes. The options are depicted in Matrix 8.1. Society would be best off if the bureaucrats exhibited high compliance with the wishes of their supervisors.

Matrix 8.1

		Supervisor's strategy options	
		High reward for subordinates	Moderate reward
Subordinate's strategy options	High compliance	A	B
	Moderate compliance	D	C

Source: G. Miller [1977, p. 49].

But, as in the usual prisoners' dilemma game, the link between one player's strategy choice and the other player's choice is too weak in the public sector. The supervisor does not expect the bureaucrat to respond with greater compliance to rewards he gives him; the bureaucrat does not expect to receive rewards should he endeavor to comply more. Both actors choose their preferred strategy on the assumption that it does not affect the other player's choice, and the Pareto-inferior outcome, cell *C,* emerges, as in the prisoners' dilemma game. Readers who have been disappointed by the efficiency, stability, and other normative properties of processes to reveal the demand for public goods the public choice literature has produced, are unlikely to find much solace in these early investigations of the effects of integrating the supply side.

F. Constitutional constraints on a bureaucratic Leviathan

Geoffrey Brennan and James Buchanan have developed a model of citizen voter–government bureaucracy that is radically different from those found in the traditional public finance–public choice literatures, and from the models of public bureaucracy described above [1977]. They take as a postulate that government bureaucracies seek to maximize their expenditures, as hypothesized by Niskanen. Brennan and Buchanan's focus is not upon the annual game of budgetary cat and mouse between the bureaucracy and the congressional review committee, however, but on the long-run constraints placed upon the government by a nation's basic tax laws. They view the basic tax structure as an attempt, in part, to control the tendencies of government to grow without bound.

The key difference between the Brennan–Buchanan model of taxation, and traditional public finance models is in the hypothesized purpose of tax legislation. Traditional analysis assumes that the purpose is to raise a *given amount of revenue* subject to certain efficiency and equity constraints; Brennan and Buchanan assume that citizens seek to impose constraints on the government bureaucracy limiting its revenues to a given amount. To see the difference, consider the familiar problem of how to tax income without discriminating against leisure. Let *AB* in Figure 8.3 represent an individual's opportunity locus in the absence of any tax. An 'ideal tax' would shift the individual's opportunity locus toward the origin without distorting his choice between earning money income and leisure, say to *CD*, by taxing an individual's *capacity* to earn income and not just the income actually earned. If

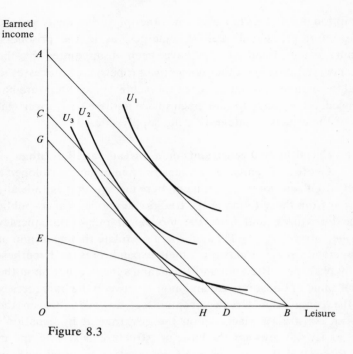

Figure 8.3

the taxing authority is free to raise revenue only by means of a tax on earned income, however, it must raise the equivalent amount of revenue, AC, by imposing a much higher effective tax rate on earned income, as is implicit in the opportunity line, EB. If the amount of tax revenue to be raised were a fixed amount, as the normative literature on optimal taxation assumes, the tax on the more comprehensive tax base would be preferred, since $U_2 > U_3$. But, if the budget-maximizing bureaucrat were free to tax both earned income and leisure, there is no reason to assume he will stop with a tax revenue of AC. If the citizen would tolerate a reduction in utility by the taxing authority to U_3, then the budget-maximizing bureaucrat would push tax rates up sufficiently to raise AG. The difference between a comprehensive definition of income and a restricted definition is not the level of utility of the voter–taxpayer for a given tax revenue, but the amount of tax revenue taken at a given utility level, under the grasping Leviathan view of government.

If the voter always finished up at the same utility level regardless of what the definition of the tax base was, he would be indifferent to the resolution of this question. Brennan and Buchanan assume, however, that there are physical and institutional limits to how high nominal tax rates on a given revenue base can be raised. Given such limits, the bureaucracy's capacity to tax the citizenry is weaker under a narrow definition of the tax base, than under a broad one. A citizen who expected bureaucrats to maximize their budgets would constrain their ability to do so, by constitutionally restricting the kinds of income and wealth that could be taxed.

The Brennan–Buchanan model turns the standard analysis of excess burden in taxation on its head. With the amount of revenue to be raised by taxation fixed, the optimal tax is the one which induces the minimum amount of distortion, which falls on the most inelastic sources of revenue. With the amount of revenue to be raised the maximand, the citizen seeks to limit the government to more elastic tax bases, and shelter parts of his income and wealth from taxation entirely.

When Brennan and Buchanan apply their analysis to other aspects of taxation they sometimes reach conclusions analogous to those existing in the normative tax literature, but the underlying logic is quite different. We have seen from the Downs–Breton model that the government will introduce special tax concessions favoring narrowly-defined interest groups in pursuit of its own objectives. A citizen writing a tax constitution to constrain Leviathan would require that the government impose tax schedules that are uniform across persons to limit the government's capacity to engage in tax-price discrimination as a means of expanding its revenue. Thus, 'horizontal equity' would be favored at the constitutional stage because it limits the government's degrees of freedom, and not for any other ethical reasons. Similar logic leads in general to a preference for progressive over regressive taxes: less revenue can typically be raised by tax schedules imposing high marginal rates than by schedules imposing low ones.

In closing this chapter it is perhaps useful to contrast the views of constitutional government of Brennan and Buchanan with those of Landes and Posner [1975] encountered earlier in this chapter. Both assume the existence of a government with substantial discretionary power and interests that conflict with those of the citizens. In the Brennan–Buchanan theory the citizens are on occasion, as say following a revolution, able to rise up and tame the Leviathan, or at least place some constraints upon it, before they sink back into passive subservience. In the Landes–Posner theory the citizens are forever pawns of the state. Even the constitution is dictated by self-serving interest groups. Although neither view of government is particularly happy, the difference between them is important and worth following up and testing empirically.

We shall encounter some happier views of the constitutional process in Part II of this study, which follows.

PART II

Normative public choice

9

Real valued social welfare functions

While one can speak of *the* positive theory of public choice, based upon economic man assumptions, one must think of normative *theories* of public choice. For there are many views of what the goals of the state *should be*, and how to achieve them. This potential multiplicity has been the focus of much criticism by the positivists, who have argued for a 'value free' discipline. For the bulk of economics, it might be legitimate to focus on explanation and prediction, and leave to politics the explication of the goals of the society. For the study of politics itself, *in toto*, to take this position is less legitimate, thus the interest in how the basic values of society are or can be expressed through the political process. The challenge normative theory faces is to develop theorems about the expression and realization of values, based on generally accepted postulates, in the same way positive theory has developed explanatory and predictive theorems from the postulates of rational egoistic behavior. Part II reviews some efforts to take up this challenge.

The traditional means for representing the values of the community in economics is with a social welfare function. The seminal paper on social welfare functions is by Abram Bergson [1938], with the most significant further explication by Paul Samuelson [1947, ch. 8]. The Bergson–Samuelson social welfare function can be written as follows:

$$W = W(z_1, z_2, \ldots, z_n)$$

where W is a real valued function of all variables, the z_is, that might affect social welfare. The z_is and W are chosen to represent the ethical values of the society, or of the individuals in it [1947, p. 221]. The objective is to define a W, and set of z_is, and the constraints thereon to yield meaningful first and second order conditions for a maximum W. Although in principle any variables might be included in the social welfare function that are related to a society's well-being (e.g. crime statistics, weather data, years of schooling), economists have focused on economic variables. Thus, the social welfare function literature has adopted the same assumptions about consumers, production functions, etc., that underlie the bulk of economics and public choice, and has made these the focal point of its analysis.

The only value postulate upon which general agreement has been possible has been the Pareto postulate. This postulate suffices to bring about a set of *necessary* conditions for the maximization of W, which limit social choices to points along the generalized Pareto frontier. The proof is analogous to the demonstration that movement from off the contract curve to points on it can be Pareto improvements, and the necessary conditions are also analogous. With respect to production these conditions are

$$\frac{\partial X_i/\partial V_{1i}}{\partial X_k/\partial V_{1k}} = \cdots = \frac{\partial X_i/\partial V_{mi}}{\partial X_k/\partial V_{mk}} = \frac{T_{x_k}}{T_{x_i}} \qquad (9.1)$$

where $\partial X_i/\partial V_{mi}$ is the marginal product of factor V_m in the production of output X_i, and T is the transformation function defined over all products and inputs [Samuelson, 1947, pp. 230–3].

> In words this takes the form: *productive factors are correctly allocated if the marginal productivity of a given factor in one line is to the marginal productivity of the same factor in a second line as the marginal productivity of any other factor in the first line is to its marginal productivity in*

the second line. The value of the common factor of proportionality can be shown to be equal to the marginal cost of the first good in terms of the (displaced amount of the) second good [Samuelson, 1947, p. 233, italics in original].

These conditions insure that the economy is operating on the production possibility frontier. If these conditions were not met it would be possible to transfer factors of production from one process to another and obtain more of one product without giving up any amounts of another. Such possibilities are ruled out by the Pareto principle.

The necessary conditions for consumption require that the marginal rate of substitution between any two private goods, i and j, be the same for all consumers

$$\frac{\partial U^1/\partial X_i}{\partial U^1/\partial X_j} = \frac{\partial U^2/\partial X_i}{\partial U^2/\partial X_j} = \cdots = \frac{\partial U^s/\partial X_i}{\partial U^s/\partial X_j} \qquad (9.2)$$

where $(\partial U^k/\partial X_i)/(\partial U^k/\partial X_j)$ is voter k's marginal rate of substitution between i and j [Samuelson, 1947, pp. 236–8]. If (9.2) were not fulfilled, gains from trade would exist again violating the Pareto postulate. Thus, choice is limited to points along the production possibility frontier, and distributions of final products that bring about equality between the marginal rate of transformation of one product into another, and individual marginal rates of substitution [Samuelson, 1947, pp. 238–40].

Through the appropriate set of lump-sum taxes and transfers it is possible to sustain any point along the production possibility frontier as a competitive equilibrium. Thus, the normative issue to be resolved with the help of the social welfare function is which point along the generalized Pareto possibility frontier should be chosen; what set of lump-sum taxes and subsidies is optimal. Both Bergson and Samuelson speak of solving this question with the help of a variant of the social welfare function in which the utility indexes of each individual are direct arguments in the welfare function

$$W = W(U^1, U^2, \ldots, U^s) \qquad (9.3)$$

The issue then arises as to what form W takes, and what the characteristics of the individual utility functions are. In particular, one wants to know whether ordinal utility functions are allowed, or whether cardinal utility indexes are required and if the latter whether interpersonal comparability is required as well. Since the evolution of utility theory over the last century has led to an almost unanimous rejection of cardinal, interpersonally comparable utility functions, the hope is, of course, that they will not be needed. But, alas, that hope is in vain.

To see why this is so consider the following simple example: six apples are to be divided between two individuals. On the basis of knowledge of the positions of the two individuals, their tastes for apples, and the ethical values and norms of the community we believe that social welfare will be maximized with an even division of the apples. The question then is whether an ordinal representation of individuals 1 and 2's preferences can be constructed that always yields this result. Consider first the additive welfare function

$$W = U^1 + U^2 \tag{9.4}$$

We wish to select U^1 and U^2 such that

$$U^1(3) + U^2(3) > U^1(4) + U^2(2) \tag{9.5}$$

Equation (9.5) implies

$$U^2(3) - U^2(2) > U^1(4) - U^1(3) \tag{9.6}$$

If U^1 is an ordinal utility function it can be transformed into an equivalent ordinal function by multiplying it by k. This transformation multiplies the right-hand side of (9.6) by k, however, and given any choice of U^2 which is bounded, a k can always be found which will reverse the inequality in (9.6), assuming $U^1(4) - U^1(3) > 0$.

The same holds if W is multiplicative. We then seek a U^1 and U^2 such that

$$U^1(3) \, . \, U^2(3) > U^1(4) \, . \, U^2(2) \tag{9.7}$$

which is equivalent to

$$\frac{U^2(3)}{U^2(2)} > \frac{U^1(4)}{U^1(3)} \tag{9.8}$$

But, the ordinality of U^2 is not affected by adding a constant to it, so that (9.8) should also hold for

$$\frac{U^2(3)+k}{U^2(2)+k} > \frac{U^1(4)}{U^1(3)} \tag{9.9}$$

But, the left hand side of (9.9) tends toward one as k becomes large, and the inequality will thus reverse for some k sufficiently large, if individual one experiences some positive utility from consuming the fourth apple.

Other algebraic forms of W are possible, but it should be obvious that the pliability of an ordinal utility function is such that these too will be incapable of yielding a maximum at $(3, 3)$ under every transformation. The same arguments could be repeated with respect to a comparison of the distribution $(4, 2)$ with $(5, 1)$, and the distribution $(5, 1)$ and $(6, 0)$. The only way we will get a determinant outcome from a social welfare function whose arguments are ordinal utility indicators is to define it lexicographically. That is, to state that society prefers any increase in 1's utility, however small, to any increase in 2's utility, however large, and have this hold independently of the initial utility levels (distribution of income and goods). Which is to say, that a social welfare function defined over ordinal utility indexes must be dictatorial if it is to select a single outcome consistently. This result has been recently established by Kemp and Ng [1976], and Parks [1976] with proofs that follow the Arrow Impossibility proofs discussed in the next chapter.[1]

The very generality of the ordinal utility function, which makes it attractive for the analysis of *individual* decisions, makes it unsuitable for the analysis of *social* decisions, where trade-offs *across individuals* are envisaged. To make these trade-offs, *either* the relative positions of individuals must be compared directly in terms of the bundles of commodities or command over these

[1] See, also, Hammond [1976].

commodities they enjoy using the ethical norms of the community, or, if utility indexes are employed, these must be defined in such a way as to make cardinal, interpersonal comparisons possible.

All of this would appear to have been known for some time. Although Bergson's initial exposition of the social welfare function seems to have led to some confusion over the need for cardinal utilities and interpersonal comparisons,[2] this need was emphasized by Lerner [1944, ch. 3], and clearly addressed by Samuelson in his initial exploration of the social welfare function.

> An infinity of such positions [points along the generalized contract locus] exists ranging from a situation in which all of the advantage is enjoyed by one individual, through some sort of compromise position, to one in which another individual has all the advantage. Without a well-defined W function, i.e., without assumptions concerning interpersonal comparisons of utility, it is impossible to decide which of these points is best. In terms

---

[2] At several places Bergson emphasizes that only ordinal utility indexes are required when deriving the optimality conditions for the social welfare function, and he states directly that 'In my opinion the utility calculus introduced by the Cambridge economists [i.e. cardinality] is not a useful tool for welfare economics' [1938, p. 20]. From these statements undoubtedly arises the view that Bergson claimed that welfare judgements could be based on ordinal utility indicators. Thus, for example we have Arrow stating, 'It is the great merit of Bergson's 1938 paper to have carried the same principle [Leibnitz's principle of the identity of indiscernibles] into the analysis of social welfare. The social welfare function was to depend only on indifference maps; in other words, welfare judgements were to be based only on interpersonally observable behavior' [1963, p. 110]. But the clauses preceding and following 'in other words' are not equivalent. And, in fact, Bergson goes on following his attack on the Cambridge economists' use of cardinal utility to argue not for the use of ordinal utility indexes or 'interpersonally observable *behavior*', but for interpersonal comparisons of 'relative economic positions' and 'different commodities'. Thus, in rejecting cardinal utility, Bergson opts not for a W defined over ordinal Us but for W defined over the actual physical units, i.e. $W(z_1, z_2, \ldots, z_n)$. This leaves the status of W defined over individual, ordinal utility indexes indeterminate, at best.

In his discussion of Arrow's theorem in 1954, Bergson states quite clearly, to my mind, that interpersonal cardinal utility comparisons are required (see in particular his discussion of the distribution of wine and bread on pp. 244–5, and n. 8), but Arrow would not agree [1963, pp. 111–12].

of a given set of ethical notions which define a *Welfare function* the best point on the generalized contract locus can be determined, and only then [1947, p. 244, italics in original].

And we have Samuelson's subsequent proof that cardinality alone will not suffice, i.e. cardinality *and* interpersonal comparability are required.[3] The issue of whether the arguments of the social welfare function can be ordinal utility indexes would seem to be finally closed with the appearance of the Kemp and Ng, and Parks papers cited above, were it not that these articles have sparked a controversy over precisely the cardinality–ordinality issue involving perhaps surprisingly Paul Samuelson (and indirectly Bergson also). Given the personages involved and the issues at debate it is perhaps useful to pause and examine their arguments.

The main purpose of Samuelson's [1977] attack on the Kemp–Ng and Parks theorems is, as the title of his note states, to reaffirm the existence of 'reasonable' Bergson–Samuelson social welfare functions. And the note is clearly provoked by the claims by Kemp and Ng, and Parks of having established nonexistence or impossibility theorems. In criticizing their theorems Samuelson focuses on the particular form of axiom Kemp and Ng use to capture ordinality in a Bergson–Samuelson social welfare function, an axiom that implies that the social welfare function must be lexicographic. Samuelson is obviously correct in deriding an axiom that makes one individual an 'ethical dictator', but, as Parks' proof perhaps better shows, all Bergson–Samuelson social welfare functions based on ordinal preferences make one individual an ethical dictator.

A careful reading of the Kemp and Ng and Parks papers indicates that they do not claim the nonexistence of *all* reasonable Bergson–Samuelson social welfare functions, but only of those whose arguments are ordinal, individual utility indicators. Interestingly enough Kemp and Ng cite as one of those holding 'the apparently widely held belief that Bergson–Samuelson social

[3] [1967]. See, also, the discussions by Sen [1970a, pp. 123–5] and Harsanyi [1975].

welfare functions can be derived from individual ordinal utilities', Samuelson himself [1976, p. 65]. They cite page 228 of the *Foundations*, the same page, incidently, which Arrow cites to indicate that the social welfare function *is* based on ordinal utilities [1963, p. 10, n.; p. 110, n. 49]. On this page appears the following:

> Of course, if utilities are to be added, one would have to catch hold of them first, but there is no need to add utilities. The cardinal utilities enter into the *W* function as independent variables if assumption (5) [individuals' preferences are to 'count'] is made. But the *W* function is itself only ordinally determinable so that there are an infinity of equally good indicators of it which can be used. Thus, if one of these is written as
>
> $$W = F(U^1, U^2, \ldots),$$
>
> and if we were to change from one set of cardinal indexes of individual utility to another set $(V^1, V^2, \ldots)$, we should simply change the form of the function F so as to leave all social decisions invariant.

This passage clearly states that *W* is ordinal, and seems to imply that the individual utility arguments need not be interpersonally comparable. But the passage appears in the section in which the necessary conditions defining points *along the generalized Pareto possibility frontier* are derived, and is obviously superseded, or amplified by the passage appearing later in the book on p. 244 and quoted above, where Samuelson makes clear that one *must* 'catch hold' of the individual utilities and compare them if a single point out of the Pareto set is to be chosen. Thus, Kemp and Ng, and Parks have proven the impossibility of a social welfare function of a form that Bergson (see n. 2) and Samuelson never posited, i.e. one with ordinal utilities as its arguments. Samuelson's [1977] comment on Kemp and Ng defends not the ordinality of the *arguments* of the social welfare function, but the ordinality or the *welfare function itself* defined over say the full commodity space. Thus, the proper interpretation of *W* based on the original presentations of Bergson and Samuelson and this most recent debate is I believe, (1) that ordinal utility functions are sufficient as arguments of W when deriving the necessary conditions for a Pareto optimum, (2) that cardinal, interpersonally comparable arguments are required to select a single, best point from among the infinity of Pareto optima, and (3) that W is, in any case, ordinally defined.[4]

So we can, I think, safely conclude that all observers agree that the Bergson–Samuelson SWF must be defined over cardinal, interpersonally comparable individual utility indexes or their equivalent, if a single socially preferred allocation is to be determined. The next question is how these cardinal utilities are to be measured, what form is W to take. Surprisingly, these questions have received scant attention in the literature, other than the common recognition that the measurement and comparison of utilities must somehow incorporate the ethical beliefs of the community.[5] Perhaps, this is because the economist's well-developed aversion to cardinal utilities and interpersonal comparisons discourages him from proceeding further once he discovers that these are required to specify fully the social welfare function.

One writer who has not been discouraged from pressing onward, however, is Yew-Kwang Ng [1975]. Ng has presented an existence theorem based on a finite sensibility postulate, i.e. 'the recognition of the fact that human beings are not infinitely discriminative' (p. 545), and a Weak Majority Preference Criterion, which states that if a majority prefers x to y, and all members of the minority are indifferent between x and y, then society prefers x to y. The latter incorporates the ethical values built into the social welfare function. It is obviously a combination of both the Pareto principle and the majority rule principle that is at once significantly weaker than both. In contrast to the Pareto criterion it requires a majority

---

[4] The distinction is clearly brought out in Samuelson's [1977] comment on the Kemp–Ng theorem where he gives an example of a social welfare function that is indeed ordinal, but, as Kemp and Ng [1977] point out in their reply also does involve an implicit comparison of cardinal utilities and/or actual positions.

[5] See Bergson [1938], Samuelson [1947], and Little [1957].

to be better off, rather than just one, to justify a move. And, in contrast to majority rule it allows the majority to be decisive only against an indifferent minority. In spite of this apparent weakness, the postulate nevertheless proves strong enough to support a Benthamite social welfare function made up, of course, of individual cardinal utility indexes

$$W = U^1 + U^2 + \ldots + U^s \qquad (9.10)$$

The one remaining question now, if one accepts Ng's Weak Majority Preference Criterion, is how to measure in practice the individual utilities.

Ng addresses this question also, discussing and citing some of the psychological literature and sensitivity studies.[6] But most of the experiments he discusses seem to involve fairly narrowly defined 'issues', and rather labor intensive measurement techniques, and the question of devising a voting procedure or some surrogate for measuring cardinal preference intensities over the range of public good decisions that must be resolved does not seem to be close to resolution.

If Ng does not succeed in pushing the concept of the social welfare function far enough to make it operational, he at least recognizes that it needs to be moved in that direction, which is more than many do.[7] For the issue of how the community's ethical notions are incorporated into the social welfare function and it in turn is maximized must at some time be addressed, if the concept is to have any practical value. The literature is replete with references to the 'policymaker', the 'ethical observer', and the 'omniscient decisionmaker' who knows the production functions and utility functions of all members of the community, and apparently knows the community's ethical values also, so that he can make its collective choice for it. But the process by which he acquires this knowledge, and how he is chosen and empowered to use it has

---

[6] See, also, Vickrey's [1960] discussion of utility measurement and references to the early and extensive literature on this subject.

[7] For alternative approaches to Ng's that also yield social welfare functions that are cardinal or additive, see DeMeyer and Plott [1971]; Fishburn [1973b].

been left open. This in turn has given rise to the possibility of there being as many ethical observers as individuals in the community, and an equal number of social welfare functions. It is this spectre which has probably caused most contributors to the 'new welfare economies' to stop short of trying to define a social welfare function that selects a unique social optimum, and have confined their attention to deriving necessary conditions for a welfare maximum, to delineating the set of Pareto points. For this reason the literature on real valued social welfare functions remains an introduction to, but apart from, the social choice literature.

10

Axiomatic social welfare functions

The Bergson–Samuelson social welfare function draws an analogy to individual choice. Just as the individual chooses bundles of commodities to maximize his utility, society must choose an allocation of commodities across individuals to maximize its welfare. That consumers make choices to maximize their utility follows almost tautologically from the definition of rationality. In extending the idea of maximizing an objective function to the level of society, however, more is involved than just rationality. Imbedded in the characteristics of the welfare function and the nature of the data fed into it are the value judgements that give the social welfare function its normative content as the discussions of Bergson [1938] and Samuelson [1947, ch. 8] make clear.

An alternative way of analyzing individual behavior from assuming that individuals maximize their utility, is to assume various postulates about individual rationality which suffice to define a preference ordering, and allow one to predict which bundle an individual will choose from any environment. Again by analogy, one can make various postulates about social decisionmaking and analyze society's decisions in terms of social preference orderings. What choice should a society make from any environment? Again, however, in shifting from the individual to the societal level, the postulates change from simply defining rationality to expressing the ethical norms of the community. This is important to keep in

184

mind, because some of the axioms *sound as if* they simply require collective rationality, and some writers have so interpreted them. This is not the course followed here. In discussing each axiom, we emphasize its normative content.

The first and most important attempt to define a social welfare function in terms of a few, basic ethical axioms was by Kenneth Arrow in 1951 [rev. ed. 1963].[1] Although some of Arrow's discussion of the individual axioms seems to mix ethical and rational considerations, the overriding objective of the inquiry is normative and our emphasis on the normative characteristics of the axioms does not seem out of place. Arrow, himself, has accepted the interpretation of these axioms as indicating basic value judgements to be incorporated in the community's social contract or constitution,[2] and this is perhaps the best way to look at them. The question then is this. What ethical norms are we to impose on the social choice process, and what collective choice processes do satisfy these axioms? The answer is disappointing. Given but a few, fairly weak, and ethically uninspiring axioms, no process (voting, the market, or otherwise) exists that satisfies them.

We begin by briefly stating the axioms and sketching the impossibility proof, after which we turn to a more detailed examination of the axioms.

A. Logic of the proof

I follow William Vickrey's [1960] restatement of the postulates and proof, since they are simpler and shorter.

1. Unanimity (The Pareto Postulate). If an individual preference is unopposed by any contrary preference of any other individual, this preference is preserved in the social ordering.

2. Nondictatorship. No individual enjoys a position such that

---

[1] The difference between Arrow's and the Bergson–Samuelson social welfare function has been the subject of much discussion [Arrow, 1963, pp. 23–4, 104–6; Samuelson, 1967; Sen, 1970a, pp. 33–6].

[2] This interpretation was first put forward by Kemp and Asimakopulos [1952], and subsequently endorsed by Arrow [1963, pp. 104–5].

whenever he expresses a preference between any two alternatives and all other individuals express the opposite preference, his preference is always preserved in the social ordering.

3. Transitivity. The social welfare function gives a consistent ordering of all feasible alternatives. That is, $(aPbPc) \rightarrow (aPc)$, and $(aIbIc) \rightarrow (aIc)$.

4. Range. (Unrestricted Domain). There is some 'universal' alternative u such that for every pair of other alternatives x and y and for every individual, each of the six possible strict orderings of u, x and y is contained in some admissible ranking of all alternatives for the individual.

5. Independence of Irrelevant Alternatives. The social choice between any two alternatives must depend on the orderings of individuals over only these two alternatives, and not on their orderings over other alternatives.[3]

Condition 4 perhaps requires an additional word of explanation. The notion of a universal alternative is not crucial here. What is implied by the Range Axiom is that the social choice process presumes that any ordering of the 3 alternatives x, y and u is possible. The process is not established in such a way as to rule out possible orderings.

The theorem states that no social welfare function satisfies these five postulates. To understand the significance of the theorem it is useful to run through the proof, again following Vickrey. We first define a decisive set D.

Definition of Decisive Set. A set of individuals D is decisive, for alternatives x and y in a given social welfare function, if the function yields a social preference for x over y, whenever all individuals in D prefer x to y, and all others prefer y to x.

---

[3] Vickrey states this postulate somewhat differently, but his proof relies on it in this form. This statement of the axiom also differs from Arrow's original statement of it, and others existing in the literature. We shall return to their differences later. For a statement of the axiom in the present way, and impossibility proofs based on it, see Sen [1970a, b].

PROOF:

Step		*Justification*
1.	Let D be a set of individuals decisive for x and y	Assumption
2.	Assume for all members of D $xPyPu$, and for all others (those in C) $yPuPx$	Range
3.	For society xPy	Definition of D
4.	For society yPu	Unanimity
5.	For society xPu	Transitivity
6.	But for only members of D is xPu	Assumption
7.	Society must prefer x to u regardless of changes in rankings of y or any other alternatives	Independence
8.	D is decisive for x and u	Definition
9.	D is decisive for all pairs of alternatives	Repetition of Steps 2–8
10.	D must contain two or more persons	Nondictatorship
11.	Divide D into two nonempty subsets A and B	Assumption
12.	Assume for A $xPyPu$, for B $yPuPx$, for C $uPxPy$	Range
13.	Since for all members of A and B, yPu, for society yPu	Definition of D
14.	If for society yPx, B is decisive for y and x	Definition of D
15.	If for society xPy, then for society xPu	Transitivity
16.	But then A is decisive for x and u	Definition of D

In either case one of the proper subsets of D is decisive for a pair of issues, and therefore by step 9 for all issues. Steps 10–16 can be repeated for this new decisive set, and then continued until the decisive ·set contains but one member, thus contradicting the nondictatorship postulate.[4]

The intuition underlying the proof runs as follows: The unrestricted domain assumption allows any possible constellation of ordinal preferences. When a unanimously preferred alternative does not emerge, some method for choosing among the Pareto preferred alternatives must be found. The independence assumption restricts attention to the ordinal preferences of individuals for any two issues, when deciding those issues. But, as we have seen in our discussions of majority rule, it is all too easy to construct rules which yield choices between two alternatives, but produce a cycle when three successive pairwise choices are made. The transitivity postulate forces a choice among the three, however. The social choice process is not to be left indecisive [Arrow, 1963, p. 120]. But with the information at hand, individual ordinal rankings of issue pairs, there is no method for making such a choice that is not imposed or dictatorial.

B. Relaxing the postulates

To avoid the impossibility result, the postulates must be relaxed. Before doing so, however, let us consider the significance of the theorem as it stands. For its significance stems precisely from the weakness of the postulates as now stated. Although, as we shall see, these axioms are somewhat stronger than they might first appear, they are far weaker than one would wish to impose at the constitutional stage to satisfy reasonable notions of distributional equity. For example, there is nothing in the axioms to preclude one group of individuals, so long as it has more than one member, from tyrannizing over the others, if it stays on the Pareto frontier.[5] Even allowing this and still other violations of our ideas of equity we cannot find a process to choose from among the Pareto optimal set, that satisfies these axioms.

---

[4] This form of 'Chinese boxes' proof to uncover the dictator is replete throughout this literature. For an important variant thereon with infinite numbers of voters, see Kirman and Sondermann [1972].

[5] See Sen's amusing example [1977a, p. 57].

Space precludes a complete review of all modifications of the postulates that have been made to produce either possibility theorems or new impossibility results.[6] Instead, we focus on modifications of particular relevance to public choice.

Relaxing unanimity and nondictatorship seem hardly worth discussing, if the ideals of individualism and citizen sovereignty are to be maintained.[7] These two axioms clearly illustrate that what we are engaged in here is a normative exercise. There is nothing particularly irrational about selecting one indvidual and allowing him to make all decisions for the community, indeed arguments for an omniscient dictator have been around at least since Plato's eloquent defense of this alternative in *The Republic*.[8] But such arguments are inconsistent with our most basic democratic ideals. Of special mention here also is Hobbes' defense of monarchy [1651]. To Hobbes, there was one issue upon which all preferences were identical; life in anarchy was terrible, and inferior to life under a unanimously accepted dictator. If one made the other postulates part of the Hobbesian contract, one might construct a new defense of autocracy. And, of course, in practice the dictatorial solution to the uncertainties and deadlocks of social choice is very popular. Empirically it might be interesting to investigate the frequency with which dictatorial governments replace democratic ones following apparent deadlocks of the latter stemming from voting paradoxes. The other 3 axioms require more detailed discussion.

1. *Transitivity*

Arrow's reasons for requiring that the social choice process produce a consistent social ordering appear to be two:

---

[6] A. K. Sen, P. K. Pattanaik and P. C. Fishburn both survey and extend this literature in important ways [1970a; 1971; 1973]. See, also Riker [1961], Rothenberg [1961]; Arrow [1963, ch. 8]; Taylor [1971], and most recently and exhaustively Plott [1976]; Sen [1977a, b].

[7] But see Little [1952].

[8] Daniel Bell presents the modern version of this position [1973]. After citing Arrow's proof at a number of places to indicate the difficulty purely democratic processes have reaching decisions, he opts for choice by technocratic experts, who form the ruling elite in the Post-Industrial Society.

(1) 'That some social choice be made from any environment' [1963, p. 118], and (2) that this choice be independent of the path to it (p. 120). These are in fact different requirements, and neither of them requires the full force of transitivity.

The requirement that the social choice process be able to make some choice from any environment seems the easiest to defend, deadlocks of democracy being an open invitation to dictatorship. But to achieve this goal one does not have to assume the existence of a social preference ordering defined on the basis of all individual preference orderings. To make choices one needs only a *choice function* that allows one to select a best alternative from any set of feasible alternatives [Sen, 1970a, pp. 47–55; Plott, 1971, 1976]. Transitivity is not required. Either quasi-transitivity or acyclicity will suffice [Sen, 1970a, pp. 47–55]. Both of these conditions are milder than transitivity. Quasi-transitivity requires transitivity of the preference relation, but not of indifference; acyclicity allows x_1 to be only 'at least as good as' x_n, even though $x_1 P x_2, x_2 P x_3, \ldots, x_{n-1} P x_n$. Possibility theorems have been proven by replacing transitivity by either of these and retaining the other Arrow axioms. Gibbard [1969] has shown, however, that requiring a quasi-transitive ordering of the social choice function produces an oligarchy, which can impose its unanimous preference on the rest of the community; and, Brown [1975] has shown that acyclicity gives veto power to *every* member of a subset of the committee which Brown calls a 'collegium'.[9] Thus, as one relaxes the consistency requirement from transitivity to quasi-transitivity, and then to acyclicity, dictatorial power becomes spread and transformed, but does not disappear entirely. Requiring that the social decision process be decisive in some sense, vests one individual or a subset of individuals with the power to decide or at least block any outcome.[10]

Although relaxing the transitivity axiom has some advantage in spreading dictatorial power across a wider group, it incurs the

[9] See, also Blau and Deb [1977].
[10] For further discussion of this point, see Brown [1973], Plott [1976, pp. 543–6], and Sen [1977a, pp. 58–63].

additional cost of introducing a degree of arbitrariness into the process [Sen, 1970a, pp. 47–55]. Under quasi-transitivity, for example, *aIb* and *bIc* can exist along with *aPc*. Then, in a choice between *a* and *b*, society can pick either, but if *c* is added to the set, society must pick only *a*. If *a*, *b*, and *c* are points on the Pareto frontier, there will be distributional consequences to the choice of any one. Those favoured under *b* may question the ethical underpinnings of a process that makes their fate dependent in such a seemingly capricious way on the set of alternatives under consideration.

The gain from relaxing the transitivity axiom is further reduced when one considers the restrictions which must be placed on the patterns of individual preference orderings to ensure that either quasi-transitivity or acyclicity holds. For majority rule, at least, the conditions that are necessary and sufficient for acyclicity are the same as those required for quasi-transitivity, and these in turn will also ensure transitivity when the number of individuals is odd.[11] Thus, if the property of having a choice made from every environment is to be maintained, there appears to be little lost by sticking to the full transitivity requirement.

The intuition behind requiring the final outcome to be independent of the path to it is somewhat different. Here, to begin with, a *path to* the final outcome is obviously assumed. That is, a choice is not made from the full set of all possible candidates, but instead winners are selected from subsets of the full issue set, these in turn are pitted against one another in some manner, and a given path is followed until a final choice set is found. The requirement that the social choice process be path independent amounts to the requirement that the final choice set be independent of how the initial subsets are formed out of the full issue set [Plott, 1973].

Path independence is related to and in fact implies another condition which has received much attention in the literature, Sen's [1969] property *a*. Property *a* states that if *x* is a member of the choice set defined over the full set of alternatives *S*, then *x* is a

---

[11] See Sen and Pattanaik [1969]; Inada [1970]; Sen [1977a].

member of the choice set of any proper subset of S of which it is a member. Property a is one of a group of *contraction-consistent* properties that have been investigated.[12] As the set of alternatives is contracted x must continue to be chosen so long as it is one of the alternatives. The intuitive notion here is perhaps obvious: If x is the best chess player in the world then he is also the best chess player in London. Path independence in this context requires that x's emergence as champion be independent of how the original run-off matches were ordered. This latter requirement is obviously stronger than the former, which explains why path independence implies the a-property, but not the reverse.

Complementary to a and the other contraction-consistent properties are a set of *expansion*-consistent properties such as the β property [Sen, 1969, 1970a, 1977a]. The β property states that if x and y are both members of the choice set for some subset S_1 of the full set S, then x can be a member of the choice set of S if and only if y is. Returning to our chess champion examples, if x and y tie for the chess championship of England, then the β property requires that they be among those who tie for the chess championship of the world. As Sen pointed out, it is quite plausible in examples such as these, for two individuals to tie in a local contest, but one goes on to beat all others and emerge the world champion. Thus, while β may be a reasonable constraint to place on some choice processes, as when contestants are measured in a single dimension like weight, it does not seem as reasonable when the candidates are measured (or compete) in several dimensions. Since issues arising in a social choice context are likely to take the latter form, it is quite possible that a social decision process would violate property β, and still not seem inherently irrational or unfair.

Thus, of the two types of properties, the intuitive support for contraction-consistent or path-independent properties seems much stronger than for expansion-consistent properties of the β type. What we seek is the social choice, or set of choices, that defeats all others. Having found such a choice, it would be

---

[12] See Sen [1977a, pp. 63–71].

comforting to know that its selection was independent of the chance way in which earlier contests were established (path independence), and that it could compete again against any subset of losers and still emerge a winner (a-property). But, unfortunately, it is path independence and the a-properties, even in their weakest forms, which lead to dictatorial or oligarchical social preference orderings; the only possibility theorems that have been proven impose only expansion-consistent properties of the β type.[13]

Let us consider somewhat further what is at stake if we abandon all vestiges of the transitivity axiom. Requiring that the social choice process satisfy this axiom is motivated in part by the desire to avoid the embarrassment of inconsistency and arbitrariness. But this view in turn seems to stem from the belief that, just as it is *irrational* for an individual to exhibit inconsistent preference orderings, it is *wrong* for society to do so. James Buchanan [1954] made an early attack on Arrow's generalization of the concept of individual rationality to collective choice processes focusing precisely on this axiom, and Charles Plott [1972] has extended and generalized this line of criticism. If the transitivity axiom is to earn a place in our constitutional set of constraints on the social choice process, then it must do so by demonstrating that the arbitrary outcomes arising from cyclic preference orderings violate some basic ethical norm. This need not be true. Small committees often resort to random processes such as the flip of a coin, or the drawing of straws to resolve issues of direct conflict. Although obviously arbitrary, the general popularity of random decision procedures to resolve conflictual issues suggests that 'fairness' may be an ethical norm that is more basic than the norm captured by the transitivity axiom for decisions of this sort. One might, then, think of replacing Arrow's notion of collective rationality with the requirement that the social decision process be fair. Transitivity could then be relaxed by simply declaring society indifferent to all choices along the Pareto frontier. Any choice among them will be

---

[13] Plott [1976, pp. 569–75]; Sen [1977a, pp. 71–75].

somewhat arbitrary, but if fair might meet with general acceptance. The winners of chess, tennis and similar elimination tourna-
ments may on occasion be dependent on the particular set of
drawings (paths) occurring. This does not seem to detract from the
widespread acceptability of this form of tournament for determining the 'best' player, however, since the method of determining a
sequence of play is regarded as fair, and the nature of the process
precludes the determination of which of the contests were in fact
path dependent. Thus, it is possible that a social decision process
which was intransitive or path dependent, but had additional
desirable properties, such as fairness perhaps, could be widely
acceptable. If there is more general agreement concerning these
rules, than for transitivity or the other consistency properties, the
Arrow problem is solved [Kemp, 1954].

2. *Unrestricted domain*

The justification for requiring this axiom is something
akin to freedom of choice or expression. Each individual should be
free to have any preference ordering he might select and the
collective choice process should be capable of reflecting these
preferences in accordance with the other axioms. Although freedom of choice strikes a responsive chord, we have seen how
quickly conflict can arise when individuals have different preference orderings even over how a given piece of public land is to be
used. A set of cyclic preferences is quite possible, and if we also
require transitivity, we are well on the way to an impossibility
result. It should be obvious that some preference orderings are
diametrically opposed to one another. This must almost of necessity follow from Axiom 1 which limits consideration to points
along the Pareto frontier, i.e. to pure distributional issues. Establishing a committee procedure to resolve these issues, without
placing any constraints on the preferences the individuals can
express, seems doomed to failure from the start.

There are two ways around this problem. One is to replace
unrestricted domain with other axioms limiting the types of
preference orderings the collective choice process is capable of

reflecting. In the context of public choice, this implies placing constitutional constraints on the types of issues that can come up before the collective. The protection of certain property rights is one example of this type of constraint. Everyone can be a member of the community, but not every preference can be satisfied or necessarily even recorded as part of the collective choice process. The alternative solution is to restrict entry into the community to those having preference orderings that do make collective choices possible.

We have discussed a number of collective choice results that rely on a restricted domain assumption. Single-peakedness ensures that majority rule produces an outcome, namely the median, and single-peakedness along with the other four assumptions produces a social welfare function. In the context of a public choice process, single-peakedness implies strict restrictions on both the selection of issues to be decided and the voters to decide them [Slutsky, 1977b]. Issues must all be of the one dimensional variety; the number of guns, the number of school books. The voters cannot simultaneously consider both the number and kind of books. And their preferences must be single-peaked in this one dimension. If fate provides voters of this type, these kinds of issues can be resolved by majority rule without violating the other axioms, although we are still left with a plethora of multi-dimensional issues to resolve in some other way. If some individuals have multiple peaks, they must somehow be isolated and excluded from the community, or an impossibility result can again emerge.

The single-peakedness condition implicitly introduces a degree of homogeneity of tastes assumption, for there must be a consensus over how things are arranged for single-peakedness to occur.[14] More generally the experimental work on majority rule cycles reviewed above indicates that the probability of a cycle occurring decreases as voter preferences become more 'homogeneous', and increases with increasing voter 'antagonism' [Plott, 1976, p. 532]. These results suggest searching for ways of restricting membership

[14] Arrow [1963, p. 80], and Sen [1970a, pp. 166–71].

in the polity to those with sufficiently homogeneous or complementary preferences to avoid the impossibility result. The
theories of clubs and voting-with-the-feet describe processes by
which groups of homogeneous tastes might form. In the absence of
externalities across clubs (local communities), and perfect mobility, free entry, etc., such a process might avoid the Arrow problem.
But, as we have seen, when spillovers exist some decisions may
have to be made by the aggregate population, and the impossibility
problem will apply here, even when 'solved' in the smaller ones. In
such, likely, circumstances homogeneity of preferences can be
brought about only if individuals adopt, or already have, a
common set of values [Bergson, 1954]. Appeals to reason, *à la*
Kant, or uncertainty, *à la* Rawls and Harsanyi to be discussed
below, are along these lines.

3. *Independence of irrelevant alternatives*

Of all the axioms, this one has been the subject of the
most discussion and criticism. As noted above, Arrow's original
statement of the axiom differs from the one presented here.[15] In
justifying this axiom in 1963 Arrow made the following argument:

> The Condition of Independence of Irrelevant
> Alternative extends the requirement of observability one
> step farther. Given the set of alternatives available for
> society to choose among, it could be expected that ideally,
> one could observe all preferences among the available
> alternatives, but there would be no way to observe
> preferences among alternatives not feasible for society . . .
> clearly, social decision processes which are independent of
> irrelevant alternatives have a strong practical advantage.
> After all, every known electoral system satisfies this
> condition. [1963, p. 110]

---

[15] 'Let $R_1, \ldots, R_n$ and $R_1', \ldots, R_n'$ be two sets of individual orderings and let
$C(S)$ and $C'(S)$ be corresponding social choice functions. If, for all
individuals i and all x and y in a given environment S, xR_iy if and only if
$xR_i'y$, then $C(S)$ and $C'(S)$ are the same (independence of irrelevant
alternatives)' [1963, p. 27].

Here Arrow defends the axiom in terms of limiting attention to feasible alternatives only, and this objective of the axiom has led Plott to restate and rename the axiom specifically in terms of infeasible alternatives [1971, 1976]. But in his original discussion of the axiom, Arrow presents an example using the rank-order or Borda method discussed above, in which candidates are ranked according to their position in each voter's preferences. In the example Arrow gives, x wins from a slate of x, y, z and w, but draws with z when y is dropped from the list (p. 27). Thus, under the Borda method the outcome depends on the nature of the full list of candidates. One of Arrow's objectives for invoking the axiom would appear to be to eliminate procedures like the rank-order so that, 'Knowing the social choices made in pairwise comparisons in turn determines the entire social ordering and therefore the social choice function $C(S)$ for all possible environments' (p. 28). Now this is precisely what the independence axiom stated above (condition 5) achieves, and it does eliminate procedures like the Borda method from consideration. Thus, our use of this form of the independence axiom would appear to be fully consistent with Arrow's objectives in introducing this axiom.[16] The question then is, what is the normative value to limiting the informational content of collective choice processes in this way?

The outcomes under the Borda procedure and similar schemes are dependent upon the specific (and full) set of issues to be decided. Thus, abandonment of the independence axiom raises the importance of the process which selects the issues to be decided, in a way its acceptance does not. When the choice between x and y can be made by considering voter preferences on only x and y the rest of the agenda need not be known. This property of the independence axiom has an appealing economy to it, but it is this

[16] As Plott [1971, 1976] and Ray [1973] have shown, however, Arrow's original statement of the axiom as given in n. 15 does not exclude the Borda procedure limited to outcomes in the feasible set. It does eliminate the Borda procedure when the ranks are assigned over the set of all possible alternatives, feasible and infeasible, and thus does limit some of this procedure's scope for stategic behavior [Plott, 1976]. For additional comment on this axiom see Bergson [1954]; Blau [1971]; Hansson [1973].

property that opens the door to endless cycling over these *other* items in the agenda.

By restricting the choice between two alternatives to information on individual rankings of these two alternatives, the independence axiom excludes all information with which one might cardinalize and interpersonally compare utilities [Sen, 1970a, pp. 89–91]. It was the desire to establish a welfare function that was not based upon interpersonal utility comparisons that first motivated Arrow [1963, pp. 8–11, 109–11]. There would appear to be two distinct justifications for wishing to exclude cardinal utility information from a collective choice process. The first is that the measurement of cardinal utilities is difficult and arbitrary, and any process that was based on combining interpersonally comparable, cardinal utilities would be vulnerable to abuse by those making the cardinal utility measurements. This would appear to be Arrow's chief fear (pp. 8–11). It rests on Arrow's view of the collective choice process as one in which information is gathered by public officials, who make the actual choices for the collective (pp. 106–8). Allowing these officials to engage in cardinal, interpersonal utility comparisons would vest them with a great deal of discretionary power, and might be something to be avoided.

The danger of an abuse of discretionary power does not arise, however, if the cardinal utility information is provided by the voters themselves, as when they take part in the process using the Borda method, vote trading, or point voting. Now a different problem arises, however. These procedures are all vulnerable to strategic misrepresentation of preferences. The independence axiom eliminates not only these strategy-prone procedures, but all voting procedures which are vulnerable to strategizing.[17] When a social choice process is not perversely responsive to an individual's ranking of x and y, and depends on only his and other rankings of x and y, he can do no better than state his true preferences between them. If the outcome on x and y also depends on his ranking

---

[17] Vickrey's speculation that immunity to strategy and the independence axiom are logically equivalent [1960, pp. 517–19], has been rigorously proved by A. Gibbard [1973] and M. A. Satterthwaite [1975].

between y and z, however, he may be able to benefit from misstating one set of preferences, if it increases his chances of winning on the other. This need not worsen the outcome of the social choice process, e.g. as when positive-sum-game logrolling occurs. But it might. And it does introduce an element of uncertainty, and dependency on bargaining abilities that might be considered undesirable. The independence axiom excludes these possibilities, and this characteristic of the axiom is one of the points in its favor.

The question then is how important is it that we do not have a voting procedure that is vulnerable to strategizing? How likely is it that individuals vote strategically rather than sincerely? What are the consequences if they do? Although some work has been done along these lines, the existing literature does not allow us to answer these questions with much confidence. The answers may also be heavily dependent upon the context in which voting is seen taking place. The likelihood that the individual voter, whose 'irrational' presence at the polls seems largely explained by a sense of civic duty, votes insincerely seems fairly low. But a member of a small, parliamentary subcommittee voting by secret ballot might succumb to the temptation. If individuals do vote insincerely, and the consequential outcomes are intolerable, then some strategy-proof voting procedure is required. And this in turn will violate one of the other axioms.

4. *Implications for public choice*

The Arrow theorem is built on 5 axioms of collective choice that appear to be fairly moderate and reasonable restrictions to place on the collective choice process. The theorem states that no process can exist that satisfies all five axioms simultaneously. In designing a collective choice process, writing our political constitution, we must violate one or more of the axioms, although in so doing we may be able to satisfy the others, and still more to be added to the list.

From a public choice perspective there appear to be two promising avenues that might be followed out of the Arrow paradox. One is to drop the transitivity axiom and abandon the search for a *best* alternative, *the* social preference. In its place could then be substituted the requirement that the social choice process be fair or democratic or accord with some other generally held value. Alternatively, if a social ordering must be made, then either the independence axiom or unrestricted domain must be relaxed.

If we continue to interpret these axioms as restrictions on the collective choice process written into the constitution, then these conclusions have the following implications. Axiom 1 limits consideration to points along the Pareto frontier. But a choice from among these involves distributional issues directly, and cycles will occur under any voting process requiring less than full unanimity. Thus, if the majority rule or any other less than unanimity rule is chosen, some fair or otherwise generally accepted way for breaking cycles must be included in the constitution.

Relaxing the unrestricted domain assumption to allow only single-peaked preferences does not seem to be a very promising way out of the paradox, since so few issues can realistically be thought of as unidimensional. More realistically, one can think of designing the constitution in such a way as to allow for the revelation of preferences for public goods via voluntary association in private and local clubs. This solution solves the problem by imposing a form of unanimity condition, but leaves aside all distributional considerations, and the problems of resolving differences of opinion on globally public goods.

Where strategic behavior is not a problem, one of the procedures that gathers information on the voters' preferences over the full set of alternatives, like the Borda procedure or vote trading, can be used. As we noted in our discussion of logrolling in Chapter 3, however, the normative properties of these procedures depend heavily upon what type of issues are allowed into the decision set. Thus, relaxing either the unrestricted domain assumption or independence of irrelevant alternatives raises questions as to what issues are to be decided, who is to decide; of those who decide, which preferences shall be weighed. Such choices directly or indirectly involve interpersonal utility comparisons, and must rest on some additional value postulates, which if explicitly introduced would imply specific interpersonal utility comparisons. The latter cannot be avoided, if a preferred social choice is to be proclaimed.[18]

And so, we close our discussion of the Arrow axiomatic social welfare function at the same point as we were with the Bergson–Samuelson real-valued social welfare function.

C. **The impossibility of a Paretian liberal**

The necessity to engage in interpersonal utility comparisons to resolve the dilemmas of social choice is further illustrated by considering A. K. Sen's theorem on Paretian Liberalism [1970a, b]. This theorem, which first appeared as a 6-page note, has generated a surprisingly large number of further comments, so large a number in fact as to warrant its own individual survey [Sen, 1976], to which the reader is referred for more detailed references to the literature.

Sen set out to find a social decision function that would satisfy the following property:

> Acceptance of personal liberty: there are certain personal matters in which each person should be free to decide what should happen, and in choices over these things whatever he or she thinks is better must be taken to be better for the society as a whole, no matter what others think [1976, p. 217].

He formalizes this condition by allowing each individual to be decisive for the social choice over one pair of alternatives, and shows that this condition, unrestricted domain, and the Pareto principle are sufficent to produce a cyclic social decision function [1970a, b]. The theorem is remarkable, as in the Arrow case, in that it achieves so much from so few constraints. Neither transitivity (only acyclicity) nor the independence of irrelevant alternatives are involved (but see below).

---

[18] Kemp and Asimakopulos [1952]; Hildreth [1953]; Bergson [1954]; Sen [1970a, pp. 123–5, 1974, 1977b].

Sen illustrates his theorem with the following example: A copy of *Lady Chatterly's Lover* is available to be read and the following 3 social states are possible:

> *a. A* reads *Lady Chatterly's Lover*, and *B* does not,
> *b. B* reads *Lady Chatterly's Lover*, and *A* does not,
> *c.* neither reads it.

A, the prude, prefers that no one reads it, but would rather read it himself than have *B* read it. Lascivious *B* prefers most that prudish *A* read the book, but would rather read it himself than see it left unread, i.e.

> for *A* $cPaPb$,   and
> for *B* $aPbPc$

Invoking the liberal rule to allow *B* to choose whether he reads the book or not results in

> bPc

Doing the same for *A* results in

> cPa

But, both *A* and *B* prefer *a* to *b*; thus, by the Pareto principle

> aPb

and we have a cycle.

A certain degree of extra conflict is introduced into the example by assuming that there is but one copy of the book to read. This assumption assures that each individual who is making a choice is choosing between two social states, since if he is free to choose between reading the book or not the other individual cannot be reading it. But this makes somewhat artificial the presentation of this choice to both individuals, since both cannot decide to read the book at the same time. The decision of who reads the book is obviously a collective decision from the start, and cannot be a purely personal matter for both individuals at the same time (see Buchanan [1976*b*]).

This difficulty can be gotten around by assuming that the book is available to both, and redefining the liberalism axiom to require that each individual is decisive over an element pair (whether he reads *Lady Chatterly* or not) in all possible social states, i.e.

Matrix 10.1.

| | | B, the lascivious | |
		Does not read *LCL*	Reads *LCL*
A, the prude	Reads *LCL*	*a*	*d*
	Does not read *LCL*	*c*	*b*

independent of the others.[19] The decision options can now be illustrated by Matrix 10.1 in which the possibility

> *d*. Both *A* and *B* read *Lady Chatterly's Lover*

has been added. While Sen's condition grants *A* the choice of either row, *given that B is constrained to the first column*, the modified liberalism condition gives *A* the choice of row, regardless of what column *B* chooses, and assigns the analogous right to *B* with respect to the choice of column.

Since this new liberalism condition is stronger than Sen's, it obviously does not overturn his theorem. Applying the condition to *A*, we have

$$(c, b)P(a, d)$$

and from *B*'s preference ordering

$$(d, b)P(a, c)$$

The intersection of these two choice sets is *b* which is Pareto inferior to *a*. Notice that Pareto optimal *a* is the only social state ruled out entirely by the application of this modified liberalism principle.

Although this new liberalism principle does not solve the liberal's paradox, it does suggest a way out of it. Matrix 10.1 is the

[19] Bernholz [1974]; Seidl [1975]; Buchanan [1976*b*]; Breyer [1977].

prisoner's dilemma matrix, and the Pareto inferior outcome at *b* comes about from each individual's *independent* decision to exercise his own liberal rights without regard for the externalities this decision inflicts on the other.[20] The way out of the dilemma, as in the case of other externalities, is to invoke another liberal axiom – all individuals are free to engage in mutually beneficial trades – and allow *A* and *B* to form a contract in which *B* agrees not to read the book in exchange for *A*'s reading it [Coase, 1962]. The power to form such contracts requires that the liberalism axiom be redefined to allow an individual either to exercise his assigned right or trade it away, i.e. agree not to exercise it.[21]

If *A* and *B* were next door neighbors who always did their reading in full view in the backyard, and their reading concerned them and only them, we could leave the problem at that. *B*'s appearance with the notorious volume would lead *A* to volunteer to read it, if *B* promised not to buy another copy, and the Pareto-optimal move would be made. But, just as backyard negotiations cannot be relied on to eliminate all externalities, the voluntary exchange of liberal rights cannot be expected to eliminate all 'liberal dilemmas'. When large numbers are involved, the transaction costs of contracting become large, and we are back into a collective choice problem.

Sen's theorem raises in a direct way the distinction between the rights and rules under which a society makes collective decisions, and the collective decisions themselves. If all individuals were like *A* and *B*, and *Lady Chatterly's Lover* the only book that might ever be read, the issues of who should read the book *and* whether individuals are free to read what they choose could never simultaneously arise. Everyone would realize that the reading of this book was a collective choice to be decided as other issues involving public goods and externalities. The dilemma presented by Sen can arise *only if* the liberalism condition has been established *prior to* the emergence of the issue of who reads *Lady Chatterly's Lover*.

---

[20]   Fine [1975]; Buchanan [1976*b*].
[21]   Gibbard [1974]; Kelly [1976]; Buchanan [1976*b*]; Nath [1976]; Breyer [1977].

Such a condition might rationally be imposed if it were thought that for most books and most people, the choice of what book an individual reads is a purely personal matter, and that society is better off in the long run if each individual is free to make this choice himself.

In the presence of such a long-run liberalism condition, books like *Lady Chatterly's Lover* and individuals like *A* and *B* might come along and lead to a short-run conflict between the condition of liberalism and the Pareto postulate. If the Pareto-optimal move cannot be made via a voluntary and unanimous agreement to trade rights, then in the short run at least either the Pareto principle will be violated or liberal rights will have to be set aside. Sen, almost alone against his critics, has argued that it is the Pareto principle that should give way under such circumstances; the preference orderings of 'meddlesome' individuals, which sometimes give rise to Pareto gains from violating long-run liberal rights, should not be given weight in the social decision process.[22]

It may be argued that the long-run decision to establish liberal rights must have been Pareto preferred or it would not have been made, and at this level, therefore, liberalism and the Pareto principle are not in conflict. This may be true, but it raises another problem. To establish a long-run rule allowing each individual to read what he chooses as being socially preferred, the set of all likely books to appear, and all individual preference functions must somehow be envisaged and weighed. Interpersonal utility comparisons are likely to be involved, the independence axiom violated. The Pareto principle and the liberalism axiom, at least as Sen uses them, 'slip in' a form of the independence axiom, since both are defined in terms of issue pairs.[23] More generally, the spirit behind the Sen theorem, as with the Arrow theorem, is to base the social decision on individual ordinal preferences. But, to establish the superiority of the maintenance of long-run liberal

---

[22] [1970a, pp. 83–5; 1976, pp. 235–7]. Rowley and Peacock [1975] are also willing to abandon the Pareto principle in favor of liberalism, although their liberalism axiom differs considerably from Sen's.

[23] Sen [1970a, p. 84]; Blau [1975].

rights in the face of short-run Pareto inefficiencies more information is going to be required.

Our investigation of the Paretian Liberal has brought us to about the same place as we were after the Arrow theorem. Interpersonal utility comparisons are required,[24] the independence axiom must be violated, and some suspicion has now been cast in the direction of the Pareto principle.[25] The subject of constitutional choice has also now arisen, and we must soon turn to it. But, before doing so, we consider a set of additional results from the axiomatic social choice literature.

---

[24] See also on this point Ng [1971].

[25] Placing restrictions on the range of preference orderings is also a possibility. See Sen [1970a, pp. 85–6; 1976, pp. 232–4].

11

The assumptions underlying the majority and unanimity rules

The conditions imposed and their analysis in much of the social choice theory are sufficiently abstract that it is often difficult to relate these axioms directly to actual voting rules. The Arrow theorem says that all voting procedures fail to satisfy the 5 axioms, but presumably each will satisfy some. What are the axioms that are consistent with each voting procedure? What are their advantages and disadvantages?

In this chapter we try to answer some of these questions, and to add a bit of institutional flesh to the bare bones axioms that make up the social choice literature. We do so by returning to the study of actual voting processes, and examining some of the underlying assumptions about how these processes actually work in practice. Given its popularity the logical place to start is the majority rule. We have already discussed the majority rule in Part I, and seen that it is vulnerable to cycles. The focus there was purely positive, however. Here we shall be concerned with the normative assumptions supporting the majority rule.

We begin by discussing Kenneth O. May's [1952] important theorem, which appeared shortly after the publication of Arrow's book, and is in much of the same spirit.

A. **May's theorem on majority rule**

May begins by defining a *group decision* function

$$D = f(D_1, D_2, \ldots, D_n)$$

where n is the number of individuals in the community. Each D_i takes on the value 1, 0, -1 as voter i's preferences for a pair of issues are xP_iy, xI_iy, yP_ix, where P_i represents the strict preference relationship and I indifference. The function f sums the D_i and assigns D a value according to the following rule:

$$\left(\sum_{i=1}^{n} D_i > 0 \right) \rightarrow D = 1$$

$$\left(\sum_{i=1}^{n} D_i = 0 \right) \rightarrow D = 0$$

$$\left(\sum_{i=1}^{n} D_i < 0 \right) \rightarrow D = 1$$

Thus, the D_i serve essentially the function of ballots, and f operates like the majority rule, counting and declaring the candidate with the highest number of favorable ballots the winner. May then defines the following 4 conditions.[1]

Decisiveness: The group decision function is defined and single valued for every possible set of preference orderings.

Anonymity: D is determined only by the values of D_i, and is independent of how they are assigned. Any permutation of these ballots leaves D unchanged.

Neutrality: If x defeats (ties) y for one set of individual preferences, and all individuals have the same, *ordinal* rankings for z and w as for x and y (i.e. $xR_iy \rightarrow zR_iw$, etc.),[2] then z defeats (ties) w.

Positive Responsiveness: If D equals 0 or 1, and one individual changes his vote from -1 to 0 or 1, or from 0 to 1, and all other votes remain unchanged, then $D = 1$.

---

[1] The names and definitions have been changed somewhat to reflect subsequent developments in the literature and to simplify the discussion. In particular, the definition of neutrality follows Sen [1970*a*, p. 72].

[2] $[(xR_iy) \rightarrow (xP_iy \text{ or } xI_iy)]$.

May then proves that a group decision function is the simple majority rule *if and only if* it satisfies these 4 conditions. Note first that we do *not* have an impossibility theorem here, although we could get one by adding majority rule's *bête noire*, transitivity. But without it the theorem states that these 4 conditions do yield the majority rule – that is all it is. What is more, any other voting rule satisfying these 4 conditions, no matter what its mechanics look like, is equivalent to the majority rule.

The next question then is what are the normative implications of each of these conditions. Decisiveness is uncontroversial. If we have a *decision* function we want it to be able to decide at least when confronted with only two issues. Positive responsiveness is also a reasonable property. If the decision process is to reflect each voter's preference, then a switch by one voter from opposition to support ought to break a tie.

The other two axioms are less innocent than they look or their names connote. The neutrality axiom introduces the independence property.[3] In deciding a pair of issues only the ordinal preferences of each voter over this issue pair are considered. Thus, information concerning voter preferences on other issue pairs is ruled out, and thereby one means for weighing intensities is eliminated. It is this axiom that allows Kemp and Ng [1976], and Parks [1976] to prove their impossibility theorems for the Bergson–Samuelson social welfare function. The neutrality axiom requires that the voting rule treat each issue pair alike regardless of the nature of the issues involved. Thus, the issue of whether the lights on this year's community Christmas tree are red or blue gets decided by the same kind of weighing of individual preference orderings as the issue of whether John Doe's property should be confiscated and redistributed among the rest of the community.

While the neutrality axiom guarantees that the voting procedure treats each *issue* alike, anonymity assures that each *voter* is treated alike. On many issues this is probably a desirable property. On the issue of the color of the Christmas lights, a change of one voter's preferences from red to blue, and another from blue to red

[3] Sen [1970*a*, p. 72]; Guha [1972].

probably should not affect the outcome. Implicit here is a judgement that the color of the tree's lights is about as important to one voter as the next. This equal intensity assumption is introduced into the voting procedure by recording each voter's expression of preference, no matter how strong, as a plus or a minus one.

But consider now the issue of whether John Doe's property should be confiscated and distributed to the rest of the community. Suppose John is a generous fellow and votes for the issue and the issue in fact passes. Suppose now John changes his vote to negative, and at the same time his worst enemy, who always votes the opposite of John, now switches to a positive vote. By the anonymity condition the issue still should pass. A voting procedure satisfying this procedure is blind as to whether it is John Doe or his worst enemy who is voting for the confiscation of John Doe's property. In some situations this may obviously be an undesirable property.

B. The Rae–Taylor theorem on majority rule

Although on the surface they seem quite different, May's theorem on majority rule is quite similar in its underlying assumptions to a theorem presented by Douglas Rae [1969] and Michael Taylor [1969].

Rae sets up the problem as one of the choice of an optimal voting rule by an individual who is uncertain over his future position under the voting rule [1969, pp. 43–4]. Thus, the discussion is set in the context of constitutional choice of a voting rule as introduced by Buchanan and Tullock.[4] Politics, as Rae and Taylor depict it, is a game of conflict. Some individuals gain from an issue's passage, some inevitably lose. The representative individual in the constitutional stage seeks to avoid having issues he opposes imposed upon him, and to impose issues he favors on others. He presumes that the gains he will experience from a favorable issue's passage will equal the loss from an unfavorable issue's passage, i.e.

---

[4] [1962, pp. 3–15]. See, also, Buchanan [1966].

that all voters experience equal intensities on each issue.[5] Issues are impartially proposed so that each voter has the same probability of favoring, or opposing any issue proposed. Under these assumptions it is reasonable to assume that the representative voter selects a rule which minimizes the probability of his supporting an issue that is defeated, and opposing an issue that wins. Rae [1969] illustrates and Taylor [1969] proves that majority rule is the only rule which satisfies this criterion.[6]

The full flavor of the theorem can best be obtained by considering an example of Brian Barry [1965, p. 312]. Five people occupy a railroad car which contains no sign either prohibiting or permitting smoking. A decision must be made as to whether those occupants of the car who wish to smoke are to be allowed to do so. If an individual placed himself in the position of one who was uncertain as to whether he would be a smoker or nonsmoker, the natural assumption is that a nonsmoker suffers as much from the smoking of others, as they suffer from being stopped from smoking. The equal intensity assumption seems defensible in this case. With this assumption, and uncertainty over whether one is a smoker or nonsmoker, majority rule is the best decision rule. It maximizes the expected utility of a constitutional decisionmaker.

This example illustrates both the explicit and implicit assumptions underlying the Rae–Taylor theorem on majority rule. First, the situation is obviously one of conflict. The smoker's gain comes at the nonsmoker's expense, or vice versa. Second, the conflictual situation cannot be avoided. The solution to the problem provided by the exit of one category of passenger from the wagon is implicitly denied.[7] Nor does a possibility exist to redefine the issue to removal the conflict and obtain consensus. Each issue is

---

[5] Rae [1969, p. 41, n. 6]. The importance of this equal intensity assumption has been recognized by several writers. Additional references for each assumption are presented in the notes to Table 11.1, where the assumptions are summarized.

[6] The 'only' must be qualified when the committee size, n, is even. With n even, majority rule and the rule $n/2$ share this property. See, Taylor [1969].

[7] Rae stresses this assumption in the implicit defense of majority rule contained in his critique of unanimity [1975].

unidimensional and must be voted up or down as is. Fourth, the issue has been randomly or impartially selected. In this particular example, randomness is effectively introduced through the chance assemblage of individuals in the car. No apparent bias in favor of one outcome has been introduced via the random gathering of individuals in the car. The last assumption contained in the example is the equal intensity assumption.

The importance of each of these assumptions to the argument for majority rule can perhaps best be seen by contrasting them with the assumptions that have typically been made in support of its antithesis, the unanimity rule.

C. Assumptions underlying the unanimity rule

As depicted by Wicksell [1896] and Buchanan and Tullock [1962] politics is a cooperative, positive sum game. The committee's business is the collective satisfaction of needs common to all members. The committee (or community) is a voluntary association of individuals brought together for the purpose of satisfying these common needs.[8] Since the association is voluntary, each member is guaranteed the right to preserve his own interests against those of the other members. This right is preserved by the power contained in the unanimity rule to veto any proposal that runs counter to an individual's interest, or through the option to exit from the community, or both.

Given that the purpose of the committee is the satisfaction of the wants of the committee members, the natural way for issues to come before the committee is from the individuals themselves. Each individual has the right to bring issues before the committee, which will benefit him and he thinks might benefit all. Should an initial proposal fail to command a unanimous majority, it is redefined until it does, or until it is removed from the agenda. Thus, the political *process* implicit in the unanimity rule argument is one of discussion, compromise and amendment continuing until a formulation of the issue is reached benefiting all. The key assumptions underlying this view of politics are both that the game

[8] See, also, Buchanan [1949].

is cooperative and positive sum, i.e. a formulation of the issue benefiting all exists, *and* that the process can be completed in a reasonable amount of time, that the transaction costs of decision-making are not prohibitive.[9]

Let us also illustrate the type of voting process the proponents of unanimity envisage with an example: the provision of fire protection in a small community. A citizen at a town meeting proposes the provision of fire protection through the purchase of a truck and station, and couples his proposal, in Wicksellian fashion, with a tax proposal to finance it. Suppose this initial tax proposal is that each property-owner pay the same fraction of the costs. The citizens with the lowest valued property complain. The expected value of the fire protection (the value of the property times the reduction in the risk of fire) to some property-owners is less than their share of the costs under the lump sum tax formula. Enactment of the proposal would make the poor subsidize the protection of the property of the rich. As an alternative proposal, a proportional tax on property values is offered. The expected benefits to all citizens now exceed their shares of its cost. The proposal passes unanimously.

D. **The assumptions underlying the two rules contrasted**

Fire protection, the elimination of smoke from factories and similar examples used to describe the mutual benefits from collective action are all examples of public goods and externalities – activities in which the market fails to provide a solution

---

[9] Both Wicksell [1896] and Buchanan and Tullock [1962] recognize that decision time costs may be sufficiently high to require abandonment of a full unanimity rule in favor of a near unanimity rule (Wicksell) or some even lower fractional rule. Indeed, much of Buchanan and Tullock's book is devoted to the choice of the optimal 'nonunanimity' rule as discussed here in Part I. Thus, one might question whether they can legitimately be characterized as champions of unanimity. I have chosen them as such, because I think their arguments can be fairly characterized as stating that *were it not for these transaction costs*, unanimity would be the best rule, and, therefore, that some rule approaching unanimity, or at least greater than a simple majority is likely to be the best in many situations. In contrast, Rae [1975] and Barry [1965] both argue that their critique of unanimity is not based solely on the decision cost criterion.

beneficial to all. The provision of these public goods is an improvement in allocative efficiency, a movement from a position off the Pareto frontier to a point on it. Proponents of unanimity have assumed that collective action involves collective decisions of this type.

In contrast, the advocates of majority rule envisage conflictual choices in which no mutually beneficial opportunities are available, as occurs when a community is forced to choose from among a set of Pareto-efficient opportunities. In the fire protection example above, there might be a large number of tax share proposals which would cover the cost of fire protection and leave all better off. All might receive unanimous approval when placed against the alternative of no fire protection. Once one of these proposals has achieved a unanimous majority no other proposal from the Pareto efficient set can achieve unanimity when placed against it. Any other proposal must make one voter worse off (by raising his tax share), causing him to vote against it.

Criticisms of unanimity and defenses of majority rule often involve distributional or property rights issues of this type. In Barry's example, the train car's occupants are in conflict over the right to clean air and the right to smoke; Rae uses the similar example of the smoking factory and the rights of the nearby citizens to clean air, in criticizing the unanimity rule [1975, pp. 1287–97]. In both cases, a property right decision must be made with distributional consequences. If the smokers are given the right to smoke, the seekers of clean air are made worse off. Even in situations in which the latter can be made better off by bribing the smokers to reduce the level of smoke, the nonsmokers are worse off by having to pay the bribe than they would be if the property right had been reversed, and the smokers had to offer the bribe [Rae, 1975]. Buchanan and Tullock discuss this same example [1962, p. 91]. They assume, however, that the initial property rights issue has already been fairly resolved at the constitutional stage. This illustrates another difference between the proponents of unanimity and majority rule. The former typically assume decisionmaking takes place *within* a set of predefined property rights, the latter, as with Barry and Rae, assume that it is the property right decision itself which must be made. In Barry's example it is the *only* decision to be made. Rae's argument is more complicated. He argues that the constitution cannot resolve all property right issues for all time, so that technological and economic changes cause some property rights issues to *drift* into the resolution of public goods and externalities. In either case, however, unanimous agreement on the property right issue of who has the initial claim on the air is obviously unlikely under the egoistic man assumptions all writers are assuming in this discussion. A less than unanimity rule *seems* necessary for resolving these initial property rights distribution issues in an equitable way.

The last statement is qualified, because it requires the other assumptions introduced in the discussion of majority rule: exit is impossible (or expensive); the issue cannot be redefined to make all better off. The need for the first assumption is obvious. If the occupants of the railroad car can move to another car in which smoking is explicitly allowed or prohibited, the conflict disappears, as it does if either the factory or the nearby residents can move costlessly. The importance of the second assumption requires a little elaboration.

Consider again the railway-car-smoking example. Suppose the train is not allowed to proceed unless this car's occupants can decide whether smoking is to be allowed or not. If the unanimity rule were employed, the potential would exist for the type of situation critics of unanimity seem to fear the most – a costly impasse. Out of this impasse, the minority might even be able to force the majority to capitulate, if the benefits to the majority from the train's continuation were high enough. Under these assumptions, majority rule is an attractive alternative to unanimity.

Now change the situation slightly. Suppose that *all passengers of the entire train* must decide the rules regarding smoking before the train may proceed. Since there is undoubtedly some advantage in having the entire train from which to choose a seat rather than only part of it, a rational egoist can be expected to prefer that the entire train be declared an area which accords with his prefer-

Table 11.1. *Assumptions favoring the majority and unanimity rules*

Assumption	Majority rule	Unanimity rule
1. Nature of the game[a]	Conflict, zero sum	Cooperative, positive sum
2. Nature of issues	Redistributions, property rights (some benefit, some lose) Mutually exclusive issues of a single dimension[b]	Allocative efficiency improvements (public goods, externality elimination) Issues with potentially several dimensions and from which all can benefit[c]
3. Intensity	Equal on all issues[d]	No assumption made
4. Method of forming committee	Involuntary. Members are exogenously or randomly brought together[e]	Voluntary. Individuals of common interests and like preferences join[f]
5. Conditions of exit	Blocked, expensive[g]	Free
6. Choice of issues	Exogenously or impartially proposed[h]	Proposed by committee members[j]
7. Amendment of issues	Excluded, or constrained to avoid cycles[j]	Endogenous to committee process[i]

a Buchanan and Tullock [1962, p. 253]; Buchanan [1966, pp. 32–3].

b Barry [1965, pp. 312–14]; Rae [1975, pp. 1286–91].

c Buchanan and Tullock [1962, p. 80]; Wicksell [1896, pp. 87–96].

d Rae [1969, p. 41, n. 6]; Kendall [1941, p. 117]; Buchanan and Tullock [1962, pp. 128–30].

e Rae [1975, pp. 1277–8].

f Wicksell [1896, pp. 87–96]; Buchanan [1949]. This assumption is common to all contractarian theories of the state, of course.

g Rae [1975, p. 1293].

h This assumption is implicit in the impartiality assumed by Rae [1969] and Taylor [1969] in their proofs, and in Barry's example [1965, in particular on p. 313].

i Wicksell [1896]; Kendall [1941, p. 109].

j Implicit.

ences regarding smoking. If majority rule were used to decide the issue, then smoking would either be allowed or prohibited throughout the entire train. But, if a unanimity rule were employed, the train's occupants would be forced to explore other alternatives to having the entire train governed by the same rule. The proposal of allowing smoking in some sections and prohibiting it in others might easily emerge as a 'compromise', and win unanimous approval over having the train remain halted. Members of the majority would be somewhat worse off under this compromise than they would have been had the entire train been designated according to their preferences, but members of the minority would be much better off. An impartial observer might easily prefer the compromise forced on the group by the unanimity rule, to the outcome forthcoming under majority rule.

The arguments in favor of majority rule implicitly assume that such compromise proposals are not possible. The committee is faced with mutually exclusive alternatives.[10] Mutually beneficial alternatives are either assumed to be technologically infeasible, or the voting process is somehow constrained so that these issues cannot come before the committee.

Table 11.1 summarizes the assumptions that have been made in support of the majority and unanimity decision rules. They are not intended to be necessary and sufficient conditions, but are more in the nature of the most favorable conditions under which each decision rule is expected to operate. It is immediately apparent from the table that the assumptions supporting each decision rule are totally opposed to the assumptions made in support of the alternative rule. The crucial importance of these assumptions in determining the normative properties of each rule can be easily seen by considering the consequences of applying each rule to the 'wrong' type of issue.

[10] Buchanan and Tullock [1962, p. 253]; Rae [1969, pp. 52–3].

E. The consequences of applying the rules to the 'wrong' issues

1. *Deciding improvements in allocative efficiency via majority rule*

On an issue that all favor, nearly one half of the votes are 'wasted' under majority rule. A coalition of the committee's members could benefit from this by redefining the issue to increase their benefits at the expense of noncoalition members. In the town-meeting example, one could easily envisage a reverse scenario from that described above. An initial proposal to finance fire protection via a proportional property tax is made. All favor the proposal and it would pass under the unanimity rule. But, the town meeting now makes decisions under majority rule. The town's wealthiest citizens caucus and propose a lump-sum tax on all property owners. This proposal is opposed as regressive by the less well-to-do members of the community, but it manages to secure a majority in its favor when placed against the proportional tax proposal. A majority coalition of the rich has succeeded in combining the provision of fire protection with a regressive tax on the poor. Wicksell's belief that the unanimity rule would favor the poor (p. 95), was probably based on similar considerations.

But there are other ways in which *de facto* redistribution can take place under majority rule. A coalition of the residents of the northside of the town might form and propose that the provision of fire protection for the entire town be combined with the construction of a park, to be built on the northside, both to be financed out of a proportional tax on the entire community.[11] On the assumption that the southsiders do not benefit from the park, this proposal would redistribute income from the southsiders to the northsiders just as clearly as a proposal to lower the taxes of the northsiders and raise the southsiders' taxes would.

Thus, under majority rule, a process of issue proposal and amendment internal to the committee can be expected to convert

---

[11] This example resembles Gordon Tullock's [1959] example in his demonstration that majority rule can lead to *over*expenditure in government as discussed above.

purely positive sum games of achieving allocational efficiency into games which are a combination of an allocational change and a redistribution. As Buchanan and Tullock have shown, when logrolling games are played with money side-payments allowed, the redistribution of wealth for and against any proposal will balance out [1962, pp. 190–2]. In logrolling games where direct side-payments are not allowed, the exact values of the net income transfers are more difficult to measure. Nevertheless, when stable coalitions are not able to form, the dynamic process of issue redefinition under majority rule to produce winning and losing coalitions of nearly equal size and differing composition can be expected to result in essentially zero *net* redistribution in the long run. Riker's assumption that all politics is a zero sum game of pure redistribution, might characterize *the long run redistributive aspects of the outcomes* of the political process under majority rule.[12]

[12] It is perhaps worth pausing here to consider the consequences of combining Riker's assumption that politics is a zero-sum redistributional game, and the equal intensity assumption. If u_w is the utility gain to a member of the winning coalition, and u_l the utility decline to a loser, then equal intensities imply

$$u_w = u_l$$

Riker assumes the money gain to the n_w winners equals loss to the n_l losers

$$G = L$$

If we assume the gains and losses are divided equally among winners and losers, we have

$$u_w \left(\frac{G}{n_w} \right) = u_l \left(\frac{G}{n_l} \right)$$

Since $n_w > n_l$, each winner receives less income than each loser gives up. For the utility change to be equal, the marginal utility of a dollar to the member of the losing coalition must be less than the marginal utility of a dollar to the member of the winning coalition. If we make the frequent assumption that the marginal utility of money declines with income, the equal intensity assumption requires redistribution from the rich to the poor. To summarize, if politics is a zero-sum game of redistribution, as Riker argues, then the equal intensity assumption is equivalent to a quasi-normative postulation that the marginal utility of money declines with increasing income, and a factual assumption that redistribution is from the rich to the poor. Of course, to the extent that Riker's minimum winning coalition proposition holds, $n_w \to n_l + 1$, and the differences in marginal utilities and incomes assumed under the equal intensity assumption approach zero.

We have seen that the redistributive characteristics of majority rule can make stable winning coalitions difficult to maintain, and lead to cycles. If a stable, winning coalition can form, however, the transaction costs of cycling and coalition formation and destruction can be greatly reduced or eliminated. If committee members are free to propose and amend issues, a stable majority coalition can engage in continual redistribution from the losing committee members. This 'tyranny of the majority' outcome may be even more undesirable than a futile, but more or less impartial redistribution emerging under a perpetual cycle [Buchanan, 1954].

Thus, implicit in the arguments supporting majority rule we see the assumption that no stable majority coalition forms to tyrannize over the minority, and a zero transaction costs assumption, analogous to the zero decision time assumption supporting a unanimity rule. The issue proposal process is to be established so that cycles either cannot form or, if they do, they add a purely redistributive component to a set of allocational efficiency decisions that are predetermined or somehow unaffected by the cycling-redistribution process.

2. *Deciding redistribution by unanimity*

Any issue over which there is unavoidable conflict is defeated under a unanimity rule. Redistributions of income and wealth, redefinitions of property rights are all blocked by this rule.

Critics of unanimity have found two consequences of this outcome particularly disturbing. First is the possibility that all progress halts.[13] The train cannot proceed until the five occupants of the car have reached a consensus on the smoking issue. Most technological progress makes some worse off. Indeed, almost any change in the economic or physical environment may make someone worse off.[14] Although in principle each proposed change,

---

[13] See Reimer [1951]; Barry [1965, p. 315]; Rae [1975, pp. 1274, 1282, 1286, 1292–3].

[14] This would appear to be the point behind Rae's arguments with respect to property rights drift in the smoking chimney example [1975, 1287–93]. As Gordon Tullock [1975] points out, however, these criticisms do not suffice as a justification for majority rule to decide this issue. The other assumptions we have discussed are needed.

down to the choice of color of my tie, could be collectively decided with appropriate compensation paid to those injured, the decision costs of deciding these changes under a unanimity rule are obviously prohibitive. The decision costs' objection to the unanimity rule reappears. In addition, as an implicit defense of majority rule, this criticism seems to involve the assumption that technological change, or those changes involving *de facto* redistributions of income and property rights are impartial. The utility gain to any individual favoring a change equals the utility loss to an opponent. And, over time, these gains and losses are impartially distributed over the population. Behind this assumption is another, that the process by which issues come before the committee is so arranged, that issues cannot be amended in such a way as to benefit one group systematically at the expense of the others. Time and the environment cast up issues involving changing property rights and redistribution impartially, and the committee votes these issues up or down as they appear, using majority rule. All benefit in the long run from the efficiency gains inherent in allowing technological progress to continue unencumbered by deadlocks in the collective decision process.

The second important fear of using the unanimity rule to decide redistribution and property rights is that the veto power this rule gives a minority, benefits one particular minority, violating a generally held ethical norm. The abolition of slavery is blocked by the slave owners; the redistribution of income by the rich. If one group achieves a larger than average share of the community's income or wealth via luck, skill, or cunning, the unanimity rule assures that this distribution cannot be upset by collective action of the community. Those who gain from the maintenance of the *status quo*, under the unanimity rule, always succeed in preserving it.[15]

F. Conclusions

A follower of the debate over majority and unanimity rule could easily be forgiven for concluding that there is but one type of

---

[15] Barry [1965, pp. 243–9]; Rae [1975, pp. 1273–6, 1286].

issue to be decided collectively, and one best rule for making collective decisions. Thus, we have from Wicksell:

> If any public expenditure is to be approved . . . it must generally be assumed that this expenditure . . . is intended for an activity useful to the whole of society and so recognized by all classes without exception. If this were not so . . . I, for one, fail to see how the latter can be considered as satisfying a collective need in the proper sense of the word [1896, p. 89].

A similar position is inherent in all contractarian positions, as e.g. in John Locke:

> men . . . enter into society . . . only with an intention in everyone the better to preserve himself, his liberty and property (for no rational creature can be supposed to change his condition with an intention to be worse), the power of the society, or legislative constituted by them, can never be supposed to extend farther than the common good, but is obliged to secure everyone's property.[16]

On the other extreme, we have Brian Barry:

> But a *political* situation is precisely one that arises when the parties are arguing not about mutually useful trades but about the legitimacy of one another's initial position [1965, p. 313, italics in original].

And in a similar vein William Riker:

> most economic activity is viewed as a non-zero-sum game while the most important political activity is often viewed as zero-sum [1962, p. 174].

But, it should now be clear, the collective choice process is confronted with two fundamentally different types of collective decisions to resolve, corresponding to the distinction between allocation and redistribution decisions [Mueller, 1977]. Some

---

[16] [1939, p. 455, §131]. Wilmore Kendall [1941] depicted Locke as a strong defender of majority rule. The only explicit reason Locke gives for using the majority rule in place of unanimity is a sort of transaction cost problem of assembling everyone, analogous to the Wicksell–Buchanan–Tullock decisions cost rule for choosing some less than unanimity rule [p. 422, §98]. In this sense, Locke is a consistent unanimitarian.

important political decisions involve potentially positive-sum-game decisions to provide defense, police and fire protection, education, environmental protection, and so on. These decisions are made neither automatically nor easily. It is similarly obvious that part of political decisionmaking must and should concern itself with the basic questions of distribution and property. The inherent differences between the underlying characteristics of these two types of decisions suggests both that they be treated separately conceptually, and as a practical matter that they be resolved by separate and different collective decision processes.

In some ways, it is an injustice to Wicksell to have quoted him in the present context, for it was one of Wicksell's important insights, and the most influential contribution to the subsequent development of the literature, to have recognized the distinction between allocation and redistribution decisions, and the need to treat these decisions with separate collective decision processes. Indeed, in some ways he was ahead of his modern critics, for he recognized not only that the distribution and allocation issues would have to be decided separately, but also suggested that unanimity would have to give way to majority rule to resolve the distribution issues [1896, p. 109, note *m*]. But, Wicksell did not elaborate on how the majority rule would be used to settle distribution issues, and the entire normative underpinning for the use of the unanimity rule to decide allocation decisions is left to rest on an *assumed* just distribution having been determined prior to the start of collective decisionmaking on allocation issues.

Unfortunately none of the proponents of majority rule has elaborated on how the conditions required to achieve its desirable properties are established either. Somewhat ironically, perhaps, the normative case for using majority rule to settle property rights and distributional issues rests as much on decisions taken *prior to* its application, as the normative case for using the unanimity rule for allocation decisions rests on a prior determined just income distribution. The Rae–Taylor theorem presupposes a process which is impartial, in that each voter has an equal chance of winning on any issue, and an equal expected gain (or loss) from a decision's outcome. Similar assumptions are needed to make a compelling normative case for May's neutrality and anonymity conditions. But what guarantees that these conditions will be met? Certainly they are not met in the parliaments of today, where issue proposals and amendments are offered by the parliamentary members, and the outcomes are some blend of cycles, manipulated agendas, and tyrannous majorities. To realize majority rule's potential for resolving property rights and redistribution issues some new form of parliamentary committee is needed that satisfies the conditions majority rule's proponents have assumed in its defense. A constitutional decision is required.

But what rule is used to establish this new committee? If unanimity is used, those favored by the *status quo* can potentially block the formation of this new committee, whose outcomes, although fair, would run counter to the *status quo*'s interest. But if the majority rule is employed, a minority may dispute both the outcomes of the distribution process, and the procedure by which it was established. What argument does one use to defend the justness of a redistribution decision emerging from a parliamentary committee to a minority, which feels the procedure by which the committee was established was unfair, and voted against it at that time? This query seems as legitimate when raised against a majority rule decision, whose justification rests on the fairness of the issue proposal process, as it is when raised against a unanimity rule, which rests its justification on some distant, unanimous agreement on property rights. At some point, the issue of how fairness is introduced into the decision process, and how it is agreed upon, must be faced.

We have run up against the infinite regress problem. The only satisfactory way out of this maze is to assume that at some point unanimous agreement on a set of rules and procedures was attained.[17] If this agreement established a parliamentary committee to function under the majority rule, then the outcomes from this committee can be defended on the grounds that all at one time

[17] See Buchanan and Tullock [1962, pp. 6–8].

must have agreed that this would be a fair way of resolving those types of issues that are allowed to come before the committee. This interpretation places the majority rule in a secondary position to the unanimity rule at this stage of the analysis, and reopens the question of how unanimous agreement, now limited perhaps to establishing the parliamentary procedures to decide both distributional and allocation efficiency issues, is reached.

We have brushed up against the constitutional or more fundamentally social contract stage at several points, now it is time we turn to it.

12

A just social contract

One of the most influential studies of the prior stages of the social choice process in recent years has been John Rawls' *A Theory of Justice* [1971]. This book is at once a contribution both to moral and to political philosophy. Rawls relies on work and results appearing in various branches of the social sciencies, however, and applies his theory to several of the major issues of the day. For this reason, Rawls' work has been widely read and discussed, and has had a substantial impact on the economics literature in general, and on collective choice in particular.

Rawls' theory differs from those which we have discussed up until now most dramatically in its focus on the *process* or *context* in which decisions are made, as much as if not more so than the outcomes of this process. The goal is to establish a set of just institutions in which collective decisionmaking can take place. No presumption is made that these institutions or the decisions emerging from them will in any sense maximize the social good (pp. 30–1, 586–7). Here we see a clear break with the social welfare function approach. More generally, Rawls challenges the utilitarian philosophy which underlies the social welfare function methodology, and has reigned so dominantly in discussions of these topics over the past two centuries.

Rawls sets out to develop a set of principles to apply to the development of 'the basic structure of society. They are to govern the assignment of rights and duties and regulate the distribution of social and economic advantages' (p. 61). These principles form the foundation of the social contract, and Rawls' theory is clearly one of the major, modern reconstructions of the contractarian argument. The theory is developed in two parts: First, the arguments in favor of the contractarian approach are established. Here the focus is upon the characteristics of the original position from which the contract is drawn. The moral underpinning of the social contract rests on the nature of the decision process taking place within the *original position*, which in turn depends upon the setting in which the original position is cast. The second part of the theoretical argument develops the actual principles embedded in the social contract. Rawls emphasizes the independence of these two arguments. One can accept either part without necessarily committing oneself to the other (pp. 15 ff.). This point is important to keep in mind since the different parts have been attacked in different ways and one might feel more comfortable about one set of arguments than another. This two-part breakdown forms a natural format by which to review Rawls' theory. Following this review, we examine some of the criticisms of the theory that have been made.

A. **The social contract**

Perhaps the easiest way to envisage how the social contract comes about in Rawls' theory is to think of a group of individuals sitting down to draw up a set of rules for a game of chance, say a game of cards, in which they will subsequently participate.[1] Prior to the start of the game, each individual is ignorant of the cards to be dealt to him, and uncertain of his skills relative to those of other players. Thus, each is likely to favor rules that are neutral or fair with respect to the chances of each player, and all might be expected to agree to a single set of fair rules for the game. Here again the incentive 'to get on with the game' can be expected to encourage this unanimous agreement.

---

[1] The analogy between a social contract or constitution and drawing up rules for a parlor game is often used by James Buchanan. See, e.g., Buchanan [1966], Buchanan and Tullock [1962, pp. 79–80].

In Rawls' theory life is a game of chance in which Nature deals out attributes and social positions in a random or accidental way (pp. 15, 72, 102 ff.). Now this natural distribution of attributes and chance determination of social position is neither just nor unjust (p. 102). But it is unjust for society simply to accept these random outcomes, or adopt institutions that perpetuate and exaggerate them (pp. 102–3). Thus, a set of just institutions is one which mitigates the effects of chance on the positions of individuals in the social structure.

To establish such a set of institutions individuals must divorce themselves from knowledge of their own personal attributes and social positions by stepping through a *veil of ignorance* that screens out any facts, which might allow an individual to predict his position and benefits under a given set of principles (pp. 136 ff.). Having passed through the veil of ignorance, all individuals are in an *original position* of total equality in that each possesses the same information about the likely effects of different institutions on his own future position. The *original position* establishes a *status quo* of universal equality from which the social contract is written (pp. 3–10).

Individuals in the *original position* about to choose a set of principles to form a social contract, resemble individuals about to draw up rules for a game of chance, with one important difference. Individuals choosing rules for a game of chance are ignorant of their future positions by necessity, and thus can be expected to adopt fair rules out of self-interest. Individuals in the original position are ignorant of their present and likely future positions, because they consciously suppress this information by voluntarily passing through the veil of ignorance. Although once in the original position they may choose institutions out of self-interest, the act of entering the original position is a moral one, whose ethical content rests on the argument that information about the distribution of certain 'factors [is] arbitrary from a moral point of view' (p. 72). Justice is introduced into the social contract via the impartiality incorporated into the collective decision process through the nature of the information made available to individuals in the original position. Thus emerges the fundamental notion of *justice as fairness.*

What then is the nature of the information screened out by the veil of ignorance? Rawls' views here are rather strict. Not only is knowledge of their natural talents, tastes, social position, income and wealth denied them, but also information about the generation to which they belong, the state of economic and political development of their society, and other fairly general information, which Rawls argues might nevertheless bias an individual's choice in the direction of one set of principles over another. For example, knowledge of the generation in which an individual lives might lead him to favor a particular type of public investment policy, or social discount rate, thereby benefiting his generation at the expense of others. Given the very general nature of the information individuals have in the original position, it is plausible to assume that the principles on which they agree are impartial with respect to the advantages they provide, not only for specific individuals, or individuals in well defined positions, but even for individuals in different generations, and living under different economic and political systems. Since all individuals have access to the same information once they have passed through the veil of ignorance, all will reach the same conclusions as to the set of just principles which ought to be embedded in the social contract. Equality in the original position leads to unanimity over the social contract.

B. The two principles of justice

Given the information available in the original position, Rawls argues that the following two principles will be chosen as the pillars of the just social contract.

First: each person is to have an equal right to the most extensive basic liberty compatible with a similar liberty for others.

Second: social and economic inequalities are to be arranged so that they are both (a) reasonably expected to be to everyone's advantage, and (b) attached to positions and offices open to all (p. 60) . . . [these] two principles

(and this holds for all formulations) are a special case of a
more general conception of justice that can be expressed
as follows. All social values – liberty and opportunity,
income and wealth, and the bases of self-respect – are to
be distributed equally unless an unequal distribution of
any, or all, of these values is to everyone's advantage (p.
62).

It is perhaps intuitively obvious that something like the 'more
general conception of justice' appearing on p. 62 would emerge
from a collective decision process in which the individuals were
ignorant of their future positions and thus induced to act impartially. Indeed, in some ways the setting of the original position
resembles the familiar cake-cutting problem in which one individual divides the cake and the other chooses the first piece. By
analogy with this example, one would expect the principles
emerging from the original position to have an egalitarian tone as
is present in the more general conception. Rawls adds flesh to his
theory, however, by deriving the two, more specific principles
quoted above as part of the *special* conception of justice that is
thought to hold once a society has reached a point of moderate
scarcity, and by further arguing that these two principles will be
chosen in lexicographical order. The first principle always has
precedence over the second (pp. 61 ff., 151 ff., 247–8).

Rawls defends the lexicographical ordering of these two principles as follows:

Now the basis for the priority of liberty is roughly as
follows: as the conditions of civilization improve, the
marginal significance for our good of further economic
and social advantages diminishes relative to the interests
of liberty, which become stronger as the conditions for the
exercise of the equal freedoms are more fully realized.
Beyond some point it becomes and then remains irrational
from the standpoint of the original position to
acknowledge a lesser liberty for the sake of greater
material means and amenities of office. Let us note why
this should be so. First of all, as the general level of

well-being rises (as indicated by the index of primary goods the less favored can expect) only the less urgent wants remain to be satisfied by farther advances, at least insofar as men's wants are not largely created by institutions and social forms. At the same time the obstacles to the exercise of the equal liberties decline and a growing insistence upon the right to pursue our spiritual and cultural interests asserts itself (pp. 542–3).

Thus, Rawls sees society as better able to 'afford' the extension of equal liberties to all citizens as it develops, i.e. he sees liberty as essentially a luxury good in each individual's preference function. With increasing levels of income the priority of liberty over other psychological and material needs rises, until at some level of development it takes complete precedence over all other needs.

The second principle of justice, which Rawls names the Difference Principle, also contains a lexicographic ordering. The welfare of the worst off individual is to be maximized before all others, and the only way inequalities can be justified is if they improve the welfare of this worst off individual or group. By simple extension, given that the worst off is in his best position, the welfare of the second worst off will be maximized and so on. The difference principle produces a lexicographical ordering of the welfare levels of individuals from lowest to highest. It is important to note here that Rawls defines welfare levels not in terms of utility indexes or some such similarly subjective concept, but in terms of primary goods. These are defined as the basic 'rights and liberties, powers and opportunities, income and wealth', which a society has to distribute (p. 62, see also pp. 90–5). Here we have another example of the break which Rawls is trying to establish between his theory and classical utilitarianism. The principles embedded in the social contract must be general. They must apply to all and be understandable by all (p. 132). This requirement places a bound on the complexity that can be allowed to characterize the basic principles of the social contract. The lexicographical nature of the difference principle, and its definition in terms of objectively discernable primary goods make it easy to apply.

The difference principle is closely related to the maximin strategy of decision theory. This strategy dictates that an individual always choose that option with the highest minimum payoff regardless of what the other payoffs are, or the probabilities of obtaining them. The force of the strategy can easily be seen in an example Rawls himself uses when discussing the principle (pp. 157–8). Let W and B be two possible states of the world, say the drawing of a white or black ball from a sack. Let S_1 and S_2 be the strategy options with prizes as given in Table 12.1. The maximin strategy requires that one always pick strategy S_2, regardless of the value of n and regardless of the probability, p, of a white ball being drawn, so long as $n < \infty$, and $p > 0$. One will never pay an amount, however small, to win a prize, however large, no matter what the probability of winning is, so long as it is not a sure thing.

Table 12.1

	W	B
S_1	0	n
S_2	$1/n$	1

Given the conservatism inherent in the maximin decision rule, Rawls goes to great pains to rationalize incorporating this rule into his basic principle of distributive justice. His reasons are three:

> First, since the rule takes no account of the likelihoods of the possible circumstances, there must be some reason for sharply discounting estimates of these probabilities (p. 154) . . . Now, as I have suggested, the original position has been defined so that it is 'a situation in which the maximin applies . . . the veil of ignorance excludes all but the vaguest knowledge of likelihoods. The parties have no basis for determining the probable nature of their society, or their place in it. Thus they have strong reasons for being wary of probability calculations if any other course is open to them. They must also take account of the fact that their choice of principles should seem reasonable to others, in particular their descendants, whose rights will

be deeply affected by it (p. 155).

The second feature that suggests the maximin rule is the following: the person choosing has a conception of the good such that he cares very little, if anything, for what he might gain above the minimum stipend that he can, in fact, be sure of by following the maximin rule. It is not worthwhile for him to take a chance for the sake of a further advantage, especially when it may turn out that he loses much that is important to him. This last provision brings in the third feature, namely, that the rejected alternatives have outcomes that one can hardly accept. The situation involves grave risks (p. 154).

Thus Rawls' arguments for the difference principle rest heavily upon his assumptions about the information available in the original position, and the economic conditions facing society. Society is in a state of 'moderate scarcity', the poor can be made better off without great sacrifice to the rich (pp. 127–8). The assumption of moderate scarcity also plays an important role in justifying the lexicographic priority of the liberty principle over the difference principle as noted above (pp. 247–8). Obviously, situations could be envisaged where an individual would be willing to give up a certain degree of liberty for an increase in material goods, or risk being slightly poorer for a chance to be substantially richer. Rawls assumes, however, that the marginal utility of material gains declines rapidly enough as prosperity increases, and that society is already wealthy enough, so that these trade-offs and gambles at unknown odds are no longer appealing.

C. **Extensions of the theory to other political stages**

Rawls extends his theory to consider the characteristics of subsequent stages in the political process: the constitutional stage, the parliamentary stage, and administrative and judicial stages. In each subsequent stage, the veil of ignorance is lifted to some extent and individuals are given more information with which to make collective decisions. For example, in the constitutional stage, individuals are allowed to know the type of economic system with which they are dealing, the state of economic development, etc. At each subsequent stage, however, knowledge of specific individual positions and preferences is denied to individuals making collective decisions. Impartiality is thus preserved, and the two principles of justice continue on into subsequent stages of the political process in precisely the same form in which they appear in the social contract. Thus, the social contract forms the ethical foundation for all subsequent political stages. As with the social contract stage itself, Rawls does not envisage here actual political processes at work, but rather a form of *Gedankenexperiment* in which individuals reflect upon the principles that *ought* to underlie the social contract, constitution or subsequent stages. In the original position, as defined for the constitutional stage, a hypothetical, just constitution is drafted, in the same way that a hypothetical, just social contract is drafted by individuals at this earlier stage. This just constitution, once drafted or conceptualized, can then be compared with actual constitutions to determine in what respect they are in accord with the ethical principles contained in this hypothetical constitution. Of course, once one has specified the principles underlying a just constitution, and assuming all can agree on them, one would be free to redraft actual constitutions, to conform to these principles. But the leap from hypothetical constitutions formulated introspectively, to actual constitutions written by individuals with real conflicts of interest may be a great one.

D. Critique of the Rawlsian social contract

A Theory of Justice has precipitated so much discussion and critical evaluation that we cannot hope to survey all of this material here. We shall, instead, focus on those issues that are most relevant to the public choice literature. Again the material can be most easily organized around Rawls' arguments in favor of the contractarian approach, and the two principles underlying the contract formed.

1. *The social contract*

Until the appearance of Rawls' book social contract theory had fallen into disrepute. The historical version of the theory had been fully discredited for over a century, and as a purely theoretical account for the existence of the state it was thought by many to be redundant.[2] This latter criticism is certainly valid from a public choice perspective. The theory of public goods, the prisoners' dilemma, externalities, the existence of insurable risks, and a variety of similar concepts suffice to explain why individuals might out of self-interest reach unanimous collective agreements. Now a contract is nothing more than a unanimous collective agreement to the provisions specified in the contract. Thus, any decision that can be explained via the creation of a contract can probably be explained just as well as a unanimous collective decision (vote). Not all public good and prisoners' dilemma situations require the existence of a state, of course. But one does not have to think very long to come up with *some* public goods with sufficiently strong joint supply and non-exclusion properties to require the participation of *all* members of a given geographic area. If such collective goods exist, then we have an explanation for a unanimous agreement to provide them.[3]

We have seen, however, how the provision of public goods is plagued by the free-rider problem; the cooperative solution to the prisoners' dilemma game is dominated. The notion of a social contract, with the connotation of mutual obligations, and rewards and penalties for abiding by the contract, may serve a useful purpose in winning adherence to the provisions of the collective agreement.

Rawls is concerned throughout much of the latter portions of his book with the problem of obtaining a stable, well-ordered, just society (pp. 453–504). To do so, it is necessary that individuals adhere to the principles of justice incorporated in the social contract not only in the original position, but also, by-and-large, in daily life when they are cognizant of their actual positions. One of the important advantages claimed for the principles derived from the original position is that they stand a greater chance of

[2] For a review of this literature, see Gough [1957].
[3] For a reluctant demonstration that this is so for at least one category of public goods, see Robert Nozick [1974].

compliance in the real world than any of their competitors (pp. 175–80). For this to be true, however, it is necessary that the principles be formulated so that all individuals can determine fairly readily what conduct compliance requires, and, of course, all must be compelled by the nature of the arguments for compliance based upon a consensus reached in the original position.

To see that the first condition may be a problem in the Rawlsian system, consider the following example presented by H. L. A. Hart [1973]. The application of Rawls' first principle requires that one liberty be constrained only for the advancement of another (pp. 201–5). This requires that individuals in the original position trade-off the benefits from advancing one liberty against the costs of constraining another. Private property, including the right to own land, is one of the possible freedoms Rawls allows in his system. But the right to own land might be defined to include the right to exclude trespassers, and this in turn would conflict with the right of free movement. Thus, rights to exclude trespassers and rights to free movement are among those that would have to be sorted out at the original position. Now suppose a farmer and a hiker get into conflict over the hiker's right to cross the farmer's field. The priority of liberty principle will do nothing to promote compliance with the social contract if the farmer and hiker, or any two people selected at random, are not likely to agree on whose right is to be preserved upon adopting the reflective frame of mind called for in the original position. But, as defined, the original position does not seem to contain enough information to allow one to sort out the priority of different liberties, and thus compliance with these important stipulations of the social contract cannot be presumed.

It might be possible to resolve this kind of conflict from the original position if more information were available to individuals in this position. If they knew the amount of land available, population densities, the impact of trespassing on agricultural productivity, the alternatives to trespassing and their costs, etc., they might be able to specify whether the right to own property took precedence or not, or even work out mixed cases in which trespassing was prohibited on land smaller than some size, but public pathways were required on larger plots. Allowing this kind of information would effectively allow individuals to make probability calculations, however, and this is precluded from the original position by the characteristics of the veil of ignorance. Thus, at the level of generality at which they are derived, the principles inherent in Rawls' social contract may be an imperfect guide for compliance.

A somewhat similar criticism has been leveled against the difference principle. Rawls bases his argument for greater compliance with his social contract than with a set of principles based on utilitarianism on the proposition that one could not expect compliance from the poor, under any set of principles requiring them to make sacrifices for the rich, as might occur under a set of utilitarian principles (pp. 175–80). But under the difference principle the rich are to be asked to make sacrifices (possibly quite large) for the benefit (possibly quite small) of the poor. This could lead to a problem of noncompliance by the rich.[4] Rawls has responded to this form of criticism by noting that the 'better situated . . . are, after all, more fortunate and enjoy the benefits of that fact; and insofar as they value their situation relatively in comparison with others, they give up much less' [1974, p. 144]. However plausible this argument is in its own right, it does not seem adequate as a part of a defense of the difference principle within the context of Rawls' theoretical framework. The latter would seem to dictate that the appeal for compliance rests on the inherent justness (fairness) of the principle's application, and the proposition that the rich would agree to this principle from behind the veil of ignorance. But here we have a difficulty. The gains to the rich are excluded from consideration under alternative distributions because probability information is barred from the original position. But the exclusion of probability information cannot entirely be defended on the grounds that it would lead to principles favoring one *individual against another*. Knowing the

---

[4] Nagel [1973, p. 13]; Scanlon [1973, pp. 198ff.]; Klevorick [1974]; Mueller, Tollison, and Willett [1974*a*]; Nozick [1974, pp. 189–97].

numbers of rich and poor in the country, and yet not knowing one's own income could still lead one to select a set of rules that were impartial as to one's own future position.[5] But these rules would undoubtedly not include the difference principle. As Rawls' three arguments in defense of the difference principle indicate, in the presence of general knowledge about probabilities something more akin to a utilitarian principle of distribution giving some weight to the interests of rich as well as poor would be selected. Rawls' chief reason for ruling out information about probabilities from the original position would thus appear to be to remove rational calculations of an average utility sort. But, as Thomas Nagel has pointed out [1973, pp. 11–12], the elimination of competing principles is supposed to be a *consequence* of the working out of the justice as fairness concept not a presupposition of the analysis.[6] Note here, also, that Rawls does allow individuals in the original position certain pieces of information that are particularly favorable to the selection of his twin principles, e.g., a period of moderate scarcity reigns, individuals care little for what they receive above the base minimum. A utilitarian might ask that this information be excluded from the original position along with the general probability information that serves to handicap the selection of utilitarian rules. In any event, the construction of the arguments in favor of the difference principle is such that an individual more favorably situated than the worst off individual in the society might question whether his interests have been fairly treated in the original position. If he does we have a compliance problem. Rawls' social contract and his arguments in support (pp. 175–80) seem to be constructed entirely for the purpose of achieving the compliance of only one group, the worst off individuals.

Problems of compliance could also arise among the various candidates for the worst off position [Klevorick, 1974]. As Arrow [1973] and Harsanyi [1975] have noted, these are likely to include the mentally and physically ill and handicapped as well as the very

---

[5] Nagel [1973]; Mueller, Tollison and Willett [1974a]; Harsanyi [1975].
[6] See, also, Hare [1973, pp. 90–1, 102–7]; Lyons [1974, pp. 161 ff.].

poor. But with the set of primary goods defined over several dimensions, individuals in the original position will be forced into the same kind of interpersonal utility comparisons as the type Rawls seeks to avoid [Arrow, 1973]. Should individuals disagree in their rankings, then the problem of noncompliance could again arise, since those who fail to qualify as the worst off under Rawls' difference principle receive no weight whatsoever in the social outcome. If someone truly believed that the affliction he bore was the worst that anyone could possibly bear, it is difficult to see how one could make a convincing argument to him that his position was ignored in the meting out of social justice on the grounds that from an original position in which he did not know he had this affliction he would weigh it below some other. He in fact has it, and the knowledge this imparts to him convinces him that he is the worst off.

Inevitably, in trying to justify an actual implementation of the difference principle and win compliance, one is led to appeal for compliance by one individual by pointing to another who is unquestionably worst off. This resembles Hal Varian's suggestion to define the difference principle in terms of envy; the worst off individual is the one that no one envies [1974, 1976]. Here, of course, we can still have conflicts. The blind may envy those who are paralyzed but can see, and the latter may envy those who can walk but are blind. Even if the envy relationship is, from behind the veil of ignorance, transitive, it risks resulting in the selection of the worst off individual as someone who is very bad off indeed – someone perhaps like the pathetic creature in Trumbo's *When Johnny Comes Marching Home*. Literal application of the procedure to someone in this position could lead to the expenditure of immense resources to achieve a very modest improvement in individual welfare. Arrow is undoubtedly right in arguing that this is the type of special case to which Rawls' principles are not meant to apply [1973]. But the number of special cases is likely to be large, and it is particularly awkward to set aside these often pitiable and ethically difficult cases from the application of the principles of justice, because it is precisely these kinds of cases that one would like an ethical theory to handle.

These problems are all variants on the general problem of compliance raised in the example of the rich and poor. Much of Rawls' discussion of the difference principle seems couched in terms of a comparison of *the* rich and *the* poor, as if there were but two groups to compare and one criterion by which to compare them. But in reality there are many possible groupings of individuals and many possible dimensions over which their welfares can be defined. Thus, a line must be drawn on the basis of some sort of interpersonal utility comparisons, around those who are to be categorized as *the* worst off. Unless fair consensus exists on where this line is to be drawn, compliance with the principles of justice may not be forthcoming [Klevorick, 1974]. For the difference principle treats all of those outside of the line, the rich and the not so rich, as being equally rich. This may lead to compliance problems among the very rich, who have to make great sacrifices for the worst off, and among the fairly poor, who receive no special treatment at all. In this way, a utilitarian principle, which weighed each individual's welfare to some degree might achieve greater compliance than the difference principle, which ignores the welfare of all but a single group [Harsanyi, 1975].

2. *The two principles of justice*

Even if we accept the above criticisms of the social contract aspect of Rawls' theory, it is still possible to consider the two principles of justice based on the justice as fairness argument as candidates for a set of political institutions. The question then is, can the arguments behind these two principles be sustained?

The ethical support for these two principles is derived from the impartiality characterizing the original position, and the unanimity that stems from it. Is, then, the original position truly impartial with respect to all competing principles of justice? If one were there, which principles would one choose? The answer to the latter question obviously depends on one's goals, on the conception of the social good, what it is that makes men happy. Here is a possible area of conflict. Men may differ, even while being impartial with respect to their own future social positions, in their conceptions of the good life. Rawls avoids this possibility for disagreement by assuming that individual conceptions of the good are removed by the veil of ignorance (pp. 173–4).

But does this not possibly bias the selection of principles of justice? An individual's conception of the good is not obviously 'morally irrelevant' information. To deny him knowledge of his own conception of the good is to risk establishing institutions, which, upon lifting the veil of ignorance, are in conflict with his most basic ethical convictions. Furthermore, in setting up the problem as one in which 'free and equal persons' voluntarily assent to principles to govern their lives, liberty receives a prominent position from the start.[7] It is perhaps no surprise, therefore, that liberty is 'chosen' as the top priority principle from the original position.

A similar argument has been made by Robert Nozick [1974] against the difference principle: 'A procedure that founds principles of distributive justice on what rational persons who know nothing about themselves or their histories would agree to *guarantees that end-state principles of justice will be taken as fundamental*' (pp. 198–9, italics in original). Given that people know nothing about the economic structure of society, about how primary goods and the other outcomes of economic and social interaction are produced, they have no choice but to ignore these intermediate steps, and any principles of justice that might govern them, and focus on final outcomes, the end distribution of primary goods. Nozick argues that this conceptualization of the setting for choosing principles of justice excludes consideration of principles that would govern the *process* of economic and social interaction. In particular, it excludes consideration of an *entitlement* principle of distributive justice, in which individuals are entitled to their holdings so long as they came to them via voluntary transfers, exchanges and cooperative productive activity, i.e. by legitimate means (pp. 150–231). To choose such a principle, one would have

---

[7] Nagel [1973, pp. 5–11]. The quoted words are from Rawls [1971, p. 13].

to know something about how the society functions, information unavailable in the original position.

The flavor of Nagel's and Nozick's criticisms can possibly be captured by returning to our rule-making card-game example. In this particular example, it is highly unlikely that the players choose rules to bring about particular end-state distributions. If they did, they would probably agree to have all players wind up with an equal number of chips, or points. But this would destroy much of the purpose of the game, which is presumably to match each player or couple's skill against the other players, given the chance distribution of the cards. The fun of the game is in the playing, and *all* of the rules would govern the *process* by which winners are selected and not the *final positions* of the winners.

My point here is not to argue that life is like a game of cards and thereby defend Nozick's entitlement theory. But it is valid to argue that individuals may want to consider the *context* and *process* by which outcomes are determined, perhaps along with these outcomes, in choosing principles of justice.[8] It is ironic that Rawls' theory, which derives its conception of justice from the process by which principles are chosen, rules out all consideration of principles that deal with the subsequent process of social interaction (except for those contained in the equal liberty principle) [Nozick, 1974, p. 207]. Indeed, the theory based on the notion of justice as fairness seems to exclude the selection of a principle of justice that would give to each individual anything that he had acquired by fair means, a principle that does resemble Nozick's entitlement principle.

Even if we accept Rawls' constraints upon the information available in the original position, and view the problem as one of selecting an end-state distribution principle, it is not clear that the

---

[8] 'The supression of knowledge required to achieve unanimity is not equally fair to all the parties . . . [it is] less useful in implementing views that hold a good life to be readily achievable only in certain well-defined types of social structure, or only in a society that works concertedly for the realization of certain higher human capacities and the suppression of baser ones, or only certain types of economic relations among men' [Nagel, 1973, p. 9].

difference principle is the one which would necessarily be chosen. As Harsanyi [1975] has argued, in the absence of objective probability information, we implicitly and almost instinctively apply subjective probability estimates, or act as if we do, when making decisions. Suppose the prize for correctly identifying the color of the ball drawn from a bag in our previous example is $5, and nothing is paid, or charged, if the color is incorrectly guessed. Since the game is free, even a maximin risk averter will play. If he chooses white he is implicitly assuming that the probability of a white ball being chosen is equal to or greater than 0.5. If he chooses black, the reverse. If he is indifferent between the choice of color and perhaps uses a fair coin to decide, he is implicitly applying the principle of insufficient reason. Harsanyi argues that it is difficult to believe that individuals in the original position will not form probability estimates of this sort, perhaps to eliminate the awkward special cases of physical and mental illness discussed above, and if they do they are unlikely to choose the maximin rule.

Using arguments such as these, several writers have questioned the plausibility of claiming that all would choose the maximin rule from behind the veil of ignorance.[9] More fundamentally, under the assumptions Rawls makes about the original position, utilitarianism is likely to give outcomes rather similar to those of Rawls' system.[10] The assumption that 'the person choosing has a conception of the good such that he cares very little, if anything, for what he might gain above the maximum stipend that he can, in fact, be sure of by following the maximin rule' is equivalent to rapidly diminishing marginal utility of income (primary goods). Incorporated into von Neumann–Morgenstern utility indexes it would imply extreme risk aversion and would undoubtedly lead to fairly egalitarian redistribution rules, although probably not the difference principle so long as individuals do care something for what lies above the minimum. More generally, under the rather favorable economic conditions that exist when the special conception of

[9] Sen [1970a, pp. 135–41]; Arrow [1973]; Hare [1973]; Nagel [1973];
    Mueller, Tollison, and Willett [1974a]; Harsanyi [1975].
[10] Arrow [1973]; Lyons [1974]; Harsanyi [1975].

justice, including the difference principle and the lexicographic ordering of the two principles, is chosen, it is likely that utilitarianism would also favor liberty and redistribution greatly. Arrow [1973] points out that an additive social welfare function will order liberty lexicographically over all other wants, if all individuals do, as they might given enough wealth. Rawls' arguments that utilitarianism would produce significantly different outcomes, e.g. slavery, often seem to rest on the assumption that utilitarianism is operating in the harsher economic environment under which only Rawls' *general* conception of justice applies. But this general conception of justice also allows tradeoffs between liberty and economic gain, and thus resembles utilitarianism to this extent [Lyons, 1974].

As a final example of the close relationship between Rawls' theory and utilitarianism consider a purely utilitarian theory of redistribution, Hochman and Rogers' [1969] theory of Pareto optimal redistribution. In their theory rich Jeff gives to poor Mutt because Mutt's utility is an argument in Jeff's utility function. Assuming that Mutt's utility is positively related to his income, we can write Jeff's utility as a function of both Jeff's and Mutt's incomes

$$U_J = U(Y_J, Y_M)$$

Given such a utility function we can expect rich Jeff to make voluntary transfers to poor Mutt, if the latter figures heavily enough in Jeff's utility function. In a world of more than one Mutt, Jeff will receive the highest marginal utility from giving a dollar to the poorest Mutt. Thus, although the Pareto-optimal approach to redistribution does not fully justify the maximin principle, it does justify a redistribution policy that focuses sole attention on the worst off individual or group [von Furstenberg and Mueller, 1971]. An altruistic utilitarian and a Rawlsian will both consider the welfare of only the worst off individual(s) in society.[11]

---

[11] For still another defense of the difference principle that differs from Rawls', see Buchanan [1976a].

E. Conclusions

The reader is by now weary of these criticisms of Rawls' theory. Renewed admiration and perhaps even enthusiasm for the social contract approach can be obtained, however, by reading Rawls' book. It is a most inspiring and rewarding adventure. Nevertheless, the criticisms raised above and the others in the literature are so numerous and often sufficiently weighty to bring into question whether our quest for a theory of the unanimous agreement to the rules and principles underlying the collective choice process is at an end. Let us proceed, therefore, to some of its competitors.

13

Utilitarian contracts

Within economics and public choice several works have appeared, which bear a resemblance to Rawls' theory in their use both of the idea of impartiality, and of the unanimity rule. John Harsanyi [1953, 1955, 1977] and William Vickrey have used impartiality to derive a social welfare function; James Buchanan and Gordon Tullock [1962], and Harvey Leibenstein [1965] have applied the impartiality notion to the analysis of collective decisionmaking. These works form a bridge between John Rawls' contribution to moral philosophy, and the welfare economics and public choice literatures. We begin with the work of Harsanyi.

A. The just social welfare function

Harsanyi's social welfare function differs from other contributions in this area in that it is based on very individualistic postulates. An organic view of the state never appears, even by implication. Harsanyi distinguishes between an individual's *personal* preferences, and his *moral* or *social* preferences. The first are what he uses to make his day-to-day decisions. The second are used on those more seldom occasions when he makes moral or ethical choices. In making the latter decisions, the individual must weigh the consequences of a given decision on other individuals, and thus must engage in interpersonal utility comparisons. In making his everyday decisions, of course, he simply considers his own preference function.

Building on the work of Fleming [1952], Harsanyi derives a social welfare function on the basis of the following three assumptions:[1]

(1) Individual personal preferences satisfy the von Neumann–Morgenstern–Marschak axioms of choice.

(2) Individual moral preferences satisfy the same axioms.

(3) If two prospects P and Q are indifferent from the standpoint of every individual, they are also indifferent from a social standpoint.

He then uses these 3 postulates to prove the following theorem concerning the form of the social welfare function, W.

Theorem. W is a weighted sum of the individual utilities of the form

$$W = \sum_i a_i U_i$$

where a_i stands for the value that W takes when $U_i = 1$ and $U_j = 0$; for all $j \neq i$ [1955, p. 52].

This is clearly a rather powerful result given the 3 postulates. The additive social welfare function has had, of course, a long and venerable history in economics. But since the work of Bergson [1938] and Samuelson [1947], the idea that *the* social welfare function would *necessarily* take this form has not been popular. Harsanyi's theorem reintroduces the Benthamite conception of social welfare on seemingly weak postulates. As always, when powerful results follow from weak premises one must reexamine these premises to see whether they perhaps contain a wolf in disguise.

The first assumption simply guarantees a form of individual rationality in the face of risk and seems rather innocuous as such. It allows each individual's utility to be expressed as a von Neumann–Morgenstern utility index.

The second assumption extends the concept of rationality from

---

[1] The seminal contributions appeared in 1953 and 1955. The argument has been reviewed and alternative proofs to the theorem presented in Harsanyi's recent book [1977, ch. 4]. The reader is also referred to this source for full statements of the various axioms.

an individual's own personal preferences to his moral preferences. The same rationality axioms apply when an individual makes ethical, interpersonal utility comparisons as apply when he makes selfish intrapersonal ones. This assumption can be criticized in the same way Buchanan [1954] criticized the Arrow postulates, as an illegitimate extension of the notion of individual rationality, and this criticism has been made by Pattanaik [1968, pp. 1164–5], focusing on the transitivity axiom, as did Buchanan. But this objection seems to carry less weight against Harsanyi's generalization of the concept of individual rationality than against Arrow's. Harsanyi is assuming *individual* evaluations in both cases, no aggregate will or organic being is even implicitly involved. The W in Harsanyi's theory is a subjective W in the mind of an individual. If individuals differ in their subjective evaluations there will be different W's for different individuals. A collective W need not exist.

The von Neumann–Morgenstern–Marschak axioms as applied to social choices raise another issue, not raised by the Arrow analysis. The social choice becomes directly dependent on individual attitudes toward risk. Arrow himself raised this criticism prior to Harsanyi's work, but in clear anticipation that the, then, newly invented von Neumann–Morgenstern cardinal utility indexes would be used by someone to create a social welfare function [1951, second ed. 1963, pp. 9–11].

> This [the von Neumann–Morgenstern theorem] is a very useful matter from the point of view of developing the descriptive economic theory of behavior in the presence of random events, but it has nothing to do with welfare considerations, particularly if we are interested primarily in making a social choice among alternative policies in which no random elements enter. To say otherwise would be to assert that the distribution of the social income is to be governed by the tastes of individuals for gambling [1963, p. 10].

More generally, as Sen notes, the use of the von Neumann–Morgenstern–Marschak axioms introduces a degree of arbitrariness as is inherent in all cardinalizations of utilities [1970*a*, p. 97].

Whether social choices *should* depend on individual attitudes toward risk is a knotty question. It raises, also, the more general question of whether certain individual preferences (for pornography, for education) are to be given more or less weight in the social welfare function. The only way this issue can be dodged is if *all* preferences, including those toward risk, are allowed to affect the social choice. The knowledge that an individual would pay X for a p probability of winning Y tells us something about his preferences for X and Y, just as the knowledge he prefers X to Y does. The former knowledge actually contains more information than the latter, and this information does not seem *a priori* inherently inferior to knowledge of simple preference orderings. At least the inferiority of the former sort of information would seem to require further justification.[2]

The third postulate introduces the individualistic values that underlie Harsanyi's social welfare function. It is this postulate that forces an additive characterization onto the social welfare function. That an individualistic social welfare function *ought* to be additive is perhaps intuitive. If each individual's preferences are to count in the social decision, then each's preferences must be introduced independently of one another. A multiplicative function will not do, for example, since then a zero evaluation of a social outcome by one individual would wipe out the preferences of all others. What is remarkable about Harsanyi's theorem is that he has been able to derive the intuitively plausible, additive social welfare function by introducing such a modest amount of individualism as contained in the third posulate.

Knowing that the social welfare function is additive is only the first, even though large, step in determining the social outcome, however. The weights to be placed on each individual's utility index must be decided, and the utility indexes themselves must be

---

[2] For additional criticism and discussion of the role of risk preferences in the Harsanyi social welfare function see Diamond [1967]; Pattanaik [1968]; Sen [1970*a*, pp. 143–5].

evaluated. It is here, that Harsanyi derives the ethical foundation for his social welfare function. He suggests that each individual evaluate the social welfare function at each possible state of the world by placing himself in the position of every other individual and mentally adopting the preferences of the other individuals. To make the selection of a state of the world impartial, each individual is to assume that he has an equal probability of being any other in the society [1955, p. 54].

The selection of a state of the world is to be a lottery with each individual's utility index (evaluated using his own preferences) having an equal probability. 'This implies, however, without any additional ethical postulates that an individual's impersonal preferences, if they are rational, must satisfy Marschak's axioms and consequently must define a cardinal social welfare function equal to the arithmetic mean of the utilities of all individuals in the society' [1955, p. 55]. Thus, the *Gedanken experiment* of assuming one has an equal probability of possessing both the tastes and position of every other person solves both of our problems: the utility functions are evaluated using each individual's own subjective preferences, and the weights assigned to each, the a_i, are all equal. The social welfare function can be written simply as the sum of all individual utilities

$$W = \sum_i U_i$$

Of course, the practical problems of getting people to engage in this form of mental experiment, of evaluating states of the world using other individuals' subjective preferences, remain, and Harsanyi is aware of them [1955, pp. 55–9; 1977, pp. 57–60]. Nevertheless, he holds the view that with enough knowledge of other individuals, people could mentally adopt the preferences of other individuals, and the U_i terms in each individual's evaluation of social welfare would converge. Thus, the mental experiment of adopting other individual's preferences combined with the equiprobability assumption would produce the same kind of homogeneity of ethical preferences, and unanimity as to the best state of the world to choose as Rawls achieves via the veil of ignorance [1955, p. 59]. All individuals would arrive at the same, impartial social welfare function.

The latter conclusion has been challenged by Pattanaik [1968] and Sen [1970a, pp. 141–6]. Even under the assumption that all individuals are able to adopt the subjective preferences of other voters (agree on the values for all U_i), Pattanaik and Sen question whether all individuals will accept a fair gamble at being in everyone else's position.

To see the problem, consider the following example. Let there be two individuals in the community, rich (R) and poor (P), and two possible states of the world, with a progressive tax (T), and without one (W). Table 13.1 gives the possible outcomes in *dollar* incomes.

Table 13.1 *Outcomes in dollars*

State of the world	T	W
Person		
R	60	100
P	40	10

Table 13.2 presents for illustrative purposes the von Neumann–Morgenstern utility indexes for R and P at each level of income scaled in such a way, let us say, to make them interpersonally comparable. R is assumed to have constant marginal utility of income, P diminishing marginal utility.

Table 13.2. *Outcomes in utils*

State of the world	T	W
Person		
R	0.6	1
P	0.4	0.2

If each individual now assumes he has an equal probability of being R or P in either state of the world, then the von Neumann–Morgenstern–Marschak postulates of rationality dictate the following evaluations of the two possible states:

$$W_T = 0.5(0.6) + 0.5(0.4) = 0.5$$
$$W_W = 0.5(1) + 0.5(0.2) = 0.6$$

The state of the world without the progressive tax provides the highest expected utility, and would according to Harsanyi be selected by all impartial individuals. But, reply Pattanaik and Sen, P might easily object. He is clearly much worse off under W than T, and experiences a doubling of utility in shifting to T (while) R loses less than $\frac{1}{2}$. The utility indexes in Table 13.2 reveal P to be risk averse. Given a choice, he might refuse to engage in a fair gamble at having R or P's utility levels under T and W, just as a risk averter refuses actuarially fair gambles whose prizes are in monetary units. Although the Harsanyi welfare function incorporates each individual's risk aversion into the evaluations of the U_i, it does not allow for differences in risk aversion among the impartial observers who determine the social welfare function values. If they differ in their preferences toward risk, so too will their evaluations of social welfare under the possible alternative states of the world, and unanimous agreement on the social welfare function will not be possible [Pattanaik, 1968].

What risk preferences should an impartial observer employ when evaluating the different possible outcomes of the social choice process? Extending the logic of the Harsanyi approach it seems reasonable to suggest that each individual use not his own risk preferences, but assume he has an equal probability of having the risk preferences of every other individual. Suppose in our example one individual was risk neutral (N), the other risk averse (A). Their evaluations of the alternative states of the world might then look something like the figures presented in Table 13.3.

The elements of row N represent the simple expected values of states T and W occurring, assuming an individual has the same

Table 13.3. *Outcomes in utils (second round of averaging)*

State of the world	T	W
Person		
N	0.5	0.6
A	0.44	0.42

probability of being R or P and is risk neutral. Row A presents the lower evaluations that a risk-averter might place on these possible outcomes. The social welfare levels under these two states of the world, assuming each individual had an equal probability of being rich or poor *and of being risk averse or risk neutral*, would then be

$$W_T = 0.5(0.5) + 0.5(0.44) = 0.47$$
$$W_W = 0.5(0.6) + 0.5(0.42) = 0.51$$

The state of the world without the tax is again preferred, although by a narrower margin.

The same objection to this outcome can be raised, however, as was raised to the first. A risk averter will recognize that the the tax alternative favoring the rich has a greater likelihood of occurring under risk neutral preferences than under risk averse preferences. He might then object to being forced to accept a gamble that gave him an equal chance of having risk neutral or risk averse preferences, in the same way that he would reject a fair gamble of experiencing the utility levels of the rich and poor. This objection can be met in the same way as the previous objection, however. Reevaluate the two states of the world assuming each individual has an equal probability of being risk neutral or risk averse using the utility levels from the previous round of averaging as this round's arguments for the utility functions. If the utility functions are smooth and convex convergence on a single set of values for W_T and W_W can be expected.[3]

---

[3] Vickrey was the first to suggest repeated averaging of welfare functions to bring about consensus [1960, pp. 531–2]. Mueller [1973] and Mueller, Tollison, and Willett [1974a] have proposed using this technique explicitly with respect to answering the objections of Pattanaik and Sen

Here the reader may begin to feel his credulity becoming stretched. Not only is our ethical observer supposed to take on the subjective preferences of all other citizens, these preferences must be defined over both physical units like apples and money, and the interpersonally comparable cardinal utility units of each individual, and he must be prepared to engage in a potentially infinite series of mental experiments in arriving at *the* social welfare evaluation to which all impartial individuals agree. The price of unanimity is high.

Although this type of criticism cannot be readily dismissed, it must be kept in mind that what we seek here is not a formula for evaluating social outcomes which each individual can apply and come up with a unique number. What we seek is a way of conceptualizing the problem of social choice to which we all might agree, *and* which might help us arrive at agreement over actual social choices were we to apply the principles emerging from this form of mental experiment. In this context it pays to consider the Harsanyi approach alongside of Rawls' theory.

Both Harsanyi and Rawls obtain an ethical foundation for their analysis by relying on the intuitive notion that certain social choices *ought* to be made impartially.[4] Impartiality is introduced by assuming that these social choices are made by someone uncertain of his future position. And, as in Rawls, some form of interpersonal comparison is required by the individual who assumes this impartial frame of mind. These are the elements the two theories have in common. Harsanyi, however, would have the impartial observer try and envisage the subjective utility levels of each citizen under different social states and use these in making

to the Harsanyi welfare function. Vickrey [1960] sets up the problem of maximizing social welfare as choosing a set of rules for a community to which one is about to enter, and is uncertain as to one's position in it. The setting is obviously similar to that envisaged by Harsanyi and not surprisingly we find Vickrey arguing for a weighted summation of von Neumann–Morgenstern (or 'Bernoullian') utility functions. He resorts to repeated averaging in the event there is disagreement over the values of these weighted sums.

[4] For a highly critical discussion of the role intuitionism plays in Rawls' argument see Hare [1973].

his (ethical) social choice. If we accept the above criticisms against an equal weighting of each individual's utility, then the Harsanyi approach would fall back to relying on some (unequal) weighted sum of the individual utilities. For the repeated averaging of the different utility indexes does nothing more than reweight the social welfare function in favor of the worse off individuals. This can be seen most dramatically by assuming that one individual is maximin risk averse. Repeated averaging will then result in the selection of that state of the world that maximizes the welfare of the worst off individual [Mueller, Tollison, and Willett, 1974a]. A social welfare function that gives enough weight to the most risk averse individual preference function in the limit reflects this same extreme degree of risk aversion.

In evaluating the 'realism' of the Harsanyi approach, therefore, the issues are these: (1) Can one envisage individuals obtaining sufficient information about the positions and psychology of other individuals to allow them to engage in the interpersonal comparisons inherent in the approach? (2) Can individuals assume an impartial attitude toward all individuals in the community, and from this impartial stance agree on a set of weights (a common attitude toward risk) to be attached to the positions of each individual when making the social choice?

Viewed in this light one gains, perhaps, a better appreciation for Rawls' criticism of utilitarianism's greater complexity [1971, pp. 132, 320–5; 1974, p. 144]. Suppose, for example, society did make social choices by applying Harsanyi's social welfare function. Now suppose someone feels that his position is in reality worse off than it ought to be in a just society. To answer this objection one must say that his position was evaluated using his own preferences in the original position, and his gains were weighed against those of all others using a consensual set of weights, or mean degree of risk aversion. But since any amount of redistribution is consistent with some degree of risk aversion, how can the unhappy citizen verify that his subjective preferences have been truly envisaged, that his position has received its proper weight? Here the comparative simplicity of Rawls' lexicographic orderings defined on primary goods – for all their faults – comes shining through.

More formally, we can note, following Sen,[5] that a utilitarian welfare function of the type proposed by Harsanyi requires *unit comparability* of individual utilities, while a maximin decision rule as in Rawls requires only the comparability of utility levels. To operationalize the utilitarian social welfare function requires cardinal interpersonal utility comparisons, while ordinality will suffice in the case of maximin. Given the great reluctance of economists toward acceptance of the idea of cardinal interpersonal utility comparisons, one can well imagine the obstacles confronting a principle whose compliance requires a general consensus on a set of cardinal, interpersonal utility comparisons.

The objections which have been raised to the work of both Rawls and Harsanyi, and similar efforts along these lines suggest that the main value of these works, at least from the point of view of public choice, is not the principles these theorists derive from their analyses,[6] the real number one might assign to a social welfare function. Their main contributions lie instead in the insight they provide as to how collective decisions, at least of some types, *ought* to be made, and the implications these considerations have for actual democratic choice processes. Let us turn, therefore, to an approach to collective choice that is more positivistic in its orientation, and yet relies on the idea of impartiality.

B. The just political constitution

James Buchanan and Gordon Tullock [1962] develop a theory of Constitutional Government in which the constitution is written in a setting resembling that depicted by Harsanyi and Rawls. Individuals are uncertain over their future positions, and thus are led out of self-interest to select rules that weigh the positions of all other individuals.[7] If we think of individuals at the

---

[5] [1970*a*, pp. 145–6; 1974*a, b*; 1977*b*]. See, also, D'Aspremont and Gevers [1977].

[6] Buchanan makes this point in his review of Rawls' book [1972].

[7] [1962, pp. 77–80]. Leibenstein [1965] achieves the same effect by envisaging collective decisions being made by a group of aging individuals for their descendents.

constitutional stage as being utilitarians who implement the impartiality assumption by assuming they have an equal probability of being any other individual, then the rules incorporated into the constitution can be thought of as maximizing a Harsanyi-type of social welfare function [Mueller, 1973]. These constitutional rules, like Arrow's axioms, form the basis for the social welfare function.

As presented, the Buchanan–Tullock theory is at once positive and normative. They state that: 'The uncertainty that is required in order for the individual to be led by his own interest to support constitutional provisions that are generally advantageous to all individuals and to all groups seems likely to be present at any constitutional stage of discussion' (p. 78). And the tone of their entire manuscript is strongly positivist in contrast to, say, the works of Rawls and Harsanyi. But they also recognize the normative antecedents to their approach in the work of Kant and the contractarians (see, especially, appendix 1). Indeed, they state that the normative content to their theory lies precisely in the unanimity achieved at the constitutional stage (p. 14).

One of the important contributions of Buchanan and Tullock's book is to demonstrate the conceptual usefulness of the distinction between the constitutional and parliamentary stages of democratic decisionmaking. If unanimous agreement can be achieved behind the veil of uncertainty that shrouds the constitutional stage, then a set of rules can be written at this stage that allows individuals to pursue their own self interest at the parliamentary stage in full possession of knowledge of their own tastes and positions. This obviously requires that any redistribution which is to take place be undertaken at the constitutional stage where uncertainty over future positions holds (ch. 13). Here the similarity to Rawls is striking. Unlike Rawls, however, Buchanan and Tullock are able to allow individuals not just *more* information about themselves at the parliamentary stage, but full information. With redistribution and similar property rights issues out of the way, the only decisions left to decide at the parliamentary stage are allocational efficiency improvements of a prisoners' dilemma type. Unanimity out of pure self interest is at least theoretically possible, and Wicksell's voluntary exchange theory of government can reign at this level of decisionmaking.

Buchanan and Tullock do not argue for unanimity at the parliamentary stage, however, but instead develop their costs of decisionmaking framework for determining the optimal majority, as discussed above. They also develop other propositions about representative government (chs. 15 and 16), and still others can be developed using the Buchanan and Tullock mode of analysis.[8]

Despite its obvious importance to their theory, Buchanan and Tullock do not discuss the process by which the constitution gets written, or the procedure for selecting delegates to the constitutional convention to ensure that they all act in the disinterested manner required to achieve unanimity on the democratic rules and individual rights under which the society will operate. Although the long-run nature of these decisions would certainly move the individual's own calculus in the direction of an impartial observer, whether any group of delegates could abstract sufficiently from their own positions and ideologies to produce the kind of collective contract Buchanan and Tullock envisage must remain an open question.

C. Conclusions

The studies reviewed in this chapter do not present a more convincing argument that unanimity can be achieved on the basic constitutional or social welfare issues than Rawls' study of the social contract did. Indeed, it seems obvious from the debate that has surrounded the work of Rawls, Harsanyi, and Buchanan and Tullock, that general agreement on the specific principles that form the social contract or maximize the social welfare function is unlikely to be forthcoming. The veil of ignorance, the equal probability assumption, or similar mental constructs simply do not provide sufficient analytical structure for forging principles of

---

[8] The number of papers that have implicitly adopted the constitutional stage decision as a point of reference is large. See in particular Rae [1969]; Mueller [1971, 1973]; Mueller, Tollison, and Willett [1974*a, b*, 1976]; Abrams and Settle [1976]; Crain and Tollison [1976*b*].

justice or welfare that can garner consensual support. General agreement on a set of principles, which are abstract yet nevertheless sufficiently specific to be meaningful, has not been nor seems likely to be possible.

If these studies have failed to derive principles of justice to which all can agree, or to indicate how such a consensus can be reached, they have at least succeeded in indicating that consensual agreement upon the basic principles and rules within which a society operates is needed. Can a well-ordered society exist in which a consensus does not exist on the place of liberty, and the principles governing distribution in the society? Can a political constitution sustain support if citizens do not accept its rules and distributional implications as fair and just? While Rawls, and Buchanan and Tullock emphasize the need for consensual support for social and political institutions, Harsanyi rests the normative significance of the concept of social welfare on a consensual agreement among all individuals on the preferred social outcome.

Beyond simply emphasizing the importance of consensus, however, these studies have suggested how it might be reached. Despite all of the criticism of these works, the ideas of justice as fairness, impartiality, and equiprobability have survived largely unscathed. This is no mean achievement. For it suggests a shared view toward individualism, a shared view toward the setting in which social choice takes place, and further basic agreement on the underlying properties of the social decision problem. If agreement does exist at this intuitive level, then it should be possible to extend our shared intuitions and design a process for drafting a constitution which would achieve consensus. The studies reviewed here have not carried us very far in this process, but they have pointed us in the right direction. A logical place for collective choice work to proceed is in the design of such processes.

PART III

Normative and positive theories compared

14

Normative and positive theories of public choice contrasted

Rules for collective decision are needed, quite simply, because people live together. Their mere grouping into circumscribed geographic areas creates the potential and necessity for collective action. Some collective decisions can benefit all individuals involved; other decisions benefit only some. Even when everyone benefits, some do so more than others, raising an issue of how the 'gains from trade' are shared. Thus, collective choices can be grouped into two categories: those benefiting all members of the community, and those benefiting some and hurting others. These two categories correspond to the familiar distinction between moves from off the Pareto frontier to points on it, and moves along the frontier; to allocation and redistribution. Positive public choice, as positive economics, is most pertinent to analysis of decisions in the first group; normative welfare theory to decisions within the second.

It was one of Knut Wicksell's [1896] great insights to recognize the importance of the distinction between allocation and redistribution decisions, *and* to recognize the need to make these decisions by separate voting procedures. More fundamentally his contribution to the literature can be seen as the recognition of the necessity of combining a discussion of the characteristics of the outcomes of government action, the allocation or redistribution decisions, with the inputs from the citizens via the voting process

263

that bring these outcomes about. This latter contribution was virtually ignored by the profession for a half century until the public choice literature began to appear. It may be regarded as one of the cornerstone postulates of this literature.

Although Wicksell made use of the distinction between allocation and redistribution decisions, the focus of his analysis was on the former. The redistribution decisions were assumed to have been justly decided at some prior point in time. This left only the allocative efficiency improvements to resolve, decisions of potential benefit to all. Here Wicksell's work takes on a distinctly contractarian and individualistic tone. Each citizen took part in the collective decision process to advance his own ends, and via the *quid pro quo* of collective decisionmaking outcomes were reached to the mutual benefit of all. Voting achieved in the market for public goods the same outcome as exchange achieved in the markets for private goods. This contractarian, *quid pro quo* approach to government has underlain much of the positive theory of public choice and the public expenditure theory of public finance, most visably in the work of Buchanan and Musgrave.

The literature on real valued welfare functions indicates that if the Pareto postulate alone is introduced, 'normative' and positive theory lead to the same marginal conditions defining allocations along the Pareto frontier. To choose from among the set of Pareto-preferred points additional postulates must be introduced incorporating stronger value judgements than contained in the Pareto postulate. Most writers have shied away from making these additional value judgements, have stopped short of defining a social welfare function that will select from among the Pareto-preferred set. Those who have introduced additional value postulates, e.g. Harsanyi [1955] and Ng [1975], have invariably come up with additive social welfare functions whose arguments are the cardinal, interpersonally comparable utilities of the citizens. Thus, to go beyond the selection of some point from among the infinity of Pareto preferred points that might be chosen under the unanimity rule, a voting procedure is required that makes cardinal, interpersonal utility comparisons.

The same conclusion has emerged from the literature on Arrow-type axiomatic welfare functions. It was a major objective of Arrow's search to find a social welfare function that based its ordinal rankings of alternatives on the aggregation of individual ordinal rankings. That none was found indicates that interpersonal utility comparisons must be made either directly via the decision rule, or indirectly through restrictions placed on the preference domain, the types of issues that can be decided, and so on. One way or another value judgements involving interpersonal comparisons must be introduced.

As David Hume pointed out long ago, propositions concerning values cannot be derived from factual observations alone.[1] Some intuitive conceptualization of right and wrong, of acceptable and unacceptable is required. Thus, efforts to introduce values into collective choice in a nonarbitrary way become a search for a community's shared notions of justice and morality. Indeed, a community might easily be defined in terms of these shared values. Individualism, the Pareto postulate, the Arrow axioms, justice as fairness, and the golden rule are all essentially intuitive value statements, or notions of morality and justice. The social welfare function, or contract, or constitution embody and reflect these values.

Normative theory starts with the community and attempts to derive propositions based on its collectively held values. Treating the community as an 'organic' body, as *the* starting point, follows logically from the necessity of there being a commonly held set of values for there to be any community. While consensual agreement on the underlying value postulates may be necessary, there is no logical reason why unanimity must emerge from this consensus as *the* social choice rule. Indeed, when choices are to be made from points along the Pareto frontier, unanimity cannot be the collective choice rule. The redistributive property of all less-than-unanimity rules thus makes them the logical choice for selecting among Pareto efficient allocations. Majority rule emerges as a

---

[1] [1739]. See, also, Sen [1970*a*, pp. 56–64].

leading candidate for resolving distributional issues, and the disparagement of the unanimity rule in the normative literature is explained.[2]

We have seen, however, that it is precisely the redistributive property of decisions made under the majority rule that produces cycles. If the majority rule is used to decide redistribution questions, then some, presumably fair, process for breaking cycles must be agreed upon. More fundamentally, the normative justification for the majority rule rests on the assumption that individual issues, or the set of all issues over time, involve equal utility changes for each citizen. This assumption, in turn, implies a process for selecting and amending issues that is impartial insofar as it leads to issues satisfying this equal intensity assumption. Thus, the normative literature on majority rule handles the knotty question of incorporating justness into the decision process in the same way Wicksell did, by assuming that justice was introduced at some prior, and unspecified, stage of collective decisionmaking. How justness was introduced into the process, and what decision rule was used to express agreement on the fairness of the rules is not addressed in the literature on majority rule. But, from the work of Harsanyi, Rawls, and Buchanan and Tullock, we can surmise that the only analytically satisfactory way to select a set of fair decision rules is to choose them by unanimous agreement.

If normative theory studies processes for revealing commonly held values regarding interpersonal utility comparisons, positive public choice studies processes for revealing intrapersonal utility comparisons. For the bulk of the positive literature analyses the implications of various collective decision rules given individual preferences, and (often implicitly) a common value system. Thus, positive public choice focuses on decisionmaking at the parliamentary or legislative stage under the rules set at the constitutional stage. If values enter the public choice process, they enter at the

---

[2] Arrow [1963, pp. 119–20]; Barry [1965, pp. 323–4]; Baumol [1967, pp. 43–4]; Samuelson [1969]; Sen [1970a, pp. 24–6]. Given the egoistic man assumption, redistribution can be achieved under a unanimity rule only if individuals are or assume they are uncertain over their future positions [Mueller, 1977].

constitutional-social contract stage. Majority rule, logrolling, vote trading, point voting, the demand revealing processes, and so on are all examined in the positive public choice literature in terms of their efficiency at revealing individual preferences, their potential for reaching an equilibrium on the Pareto frontier. As with majority rule, to secure additional normative content to the outcome reached, or even in some cases to insure that it is Pareto optimal, additional assumptions are required about the nature of issues introduced and the process for proposing and amending them. Thus, the characteristics of the outcomes of the different voting rules are ultimately tied to the assumptions made about the constitutional stage of decisionmaking, even though this stage is not the main focus of the positive literature.

For this reason, much of positive public choice is implicitly, and sometimes explicitly as in the work of Buchanan and Tullock, in the contractarian tradition. If one starts with the individual, before the collective can be analyzed, it must, at least conceptually, be formed. The issues of what individuals make up the collective, and what questions it can resolve must be faced. If the state of anarchy is chosen as a starting point, as in much of the contractarian literature, then the issue becomes a decision on which individuals are to be joined by the social contract, and what rights assigned to the collective. Nowhere is the importance of this question more apparent than in the literature on fiscal federalism and voting-with-the-feet. If primary citizenship is assigned to the local community, then individuals in a community blessed with natural advantages or simply industrious neighbors have an important property right which can allow them to sustain their natural advantage over time. If primary citizenship is vested in the inclusive polity, citizens in unfavorably endowed local communities are able to tax those living in other local communities. How then is the writing of the social contract envisaged, as a pact among all members of the inclusive polity, which sets aside certain rights for the local polities? Or do the citizens first form a pact for the local polity, and then delegate authority over some issues to the larger one? The latter interpretation would appear to have more historical support for it, but the social contract is not supposed to be a historically based construct. The normative basis for the social contract should stem from the abstract principles from which it is derived, and these in turn must be relied upon to settle this question.

The contractarian underpinnings of the positive public choice literature may help to explain its emphasis on unanimous consent and Pareto optimality. If the polity is envisaged as a union of individuals, who, conceptually, have the option of not joining, then unanimous agreement on basic choices is required. But unanimity can be achieved, under individualist–egoistic assumptions, only for Pareto moves. Thus, in the positivist approach, Pareto efficiency and unanimity are ineluctably linked. In a voluntary association of individuals, unanimity is, potentially, always possible; all moves latently Pareto efficient.

The differences in starting points also explains the different approaches to the *status quo* apparent in the two literatures. The positivist works within a set of fixed rules and value consensus, and favors maintenance of the existing rules in the absence of clearly expressed preferences for change. The welfare theorist attempts to define the rules to be embedded in an ideal (perhaps new) constitution and sees no reason to give previous rules preference.

The way in which constraints on the issue set are introduced is also revealing. When assumptions about the value consensus and domain of choice are made explicit in the positivist literature, they come at the beginning of the discussion. Given these assumed constraints, the positivist often evinces a lack of concern in, or downplays the importance of, the impossibility theorems.[3] A. K. Sen's [1970*b*] impossibility theorem is disturbing to a positivist only in that it presumes that one individual's preference that another read a book the latter thinks distasteful would even enter into the social choice process.[4] The social welfare function texts, on the other hand, begin with an unlimited domain assumption, and work back to consider restrictions on the preferences included

[3] For example, Tullock [1967].
[4] Ng [1971]; Peacock and Rowley [1972]; Bernholz [1974].

in the welfare function's domain, after first deriving the impossibility results.[5] The suggestion that a basic agreement on some ends may be necessary for a normative collective choice process comes after the exploration of the infeasibility of not assuming such consensus.

This contrasting of perspectives helps clarify the apparently differing conclusions and emphases of the two approaches. It, also, may help to explain the interest in Rawls. For Rawls' theory is at once individualistic–contractarian and overtly normative. The unanimous agreement of all citizens for all time becomes *the* social preference ordering of the community, through the homogenization of tastes that occurs as individuals pass through the veil of ignorance into the original position, in the same way as Harsanyi derives a unique unanimous social welfare function, and Buchanan and Tullock a constitution.[6] In these works, the justice and impartiality other writers assume exists in the prior stages of collective decisionmaking becomes the basis for a consensual foundation to the social decision process.

In closing this comparison, some paradoxes and unresolved questions must be noted. Although the bulk of the positivist–contractarian literature discusses decisionmaking within an agreed social contract or constitution, the process by which this agreement is reached is almost never discussed. Buchanan and Tullock's book on the *Logical Foundations of Constitutional Democracy* devotes only a few pages to the constitutional stage, and here argues the plausibility of assuming unanimity due to uncertainty over future positions. Buchanan's [1975a] recent book, although devoted to the social contract, does not discuss the *process* by which actual constitutions are drawn.

Nor does the social welfare function literature discuss how agreement is expressed on basic values, even though, under the

[5] See Arrow [1963, pp. 74–91]; Vickrey [1960]; Sen [1970a, pp. 166–86].
[6] Some criticisms of Rawls are also revealing. Buchanan, the positivist-contractarian, objects to Rawls' extension of his theory of the social contract *process* to define actual *outcomes* of the process in terms of principles of justice [1972]. Welfare theorists Arrow and Sen do not object to this effort. They criticize only the form the principles take [Sen, 1970a, pp. 135–46; 1974; Arrow, 1973].

present interpretation at least, this literature is directly concerned with the functional embodiment of these values. Quite to the contrary. Barry and Samuelson are openly critical of unanimity, even when applied to the constitutional stage [1965, pp. 242–5; 1967]. Arrow accepts an interpretation of the social welfare function as a constitution, but seems not to feel it is literally agreed upon by citizens. Instead, he sees the implications of the social welfare function research as guiding ethically neutral public officials when making policy decisions.[7] But this interpretation reopens all of the old questions of value judgements, interpersonal utility comparisons, etc., that the new welfare economics sought to avoid. Given Arrow's own results, it is clear that the policymaker cannot easily find a decision rule consistent with an obviously agreed upon set of normative axioms. New axioms must be found. But what (who?) guides the policymaker in this search, the economist? Unless there is a general consensus over the policymaker's or economist's choice of value postulates, the spectre of multiple social welfare functions reappears. But can the policymaker, or economist, determine if a consensus exists, and what it is, if it is not somehow literally expressed?

It is fitting that we close with this query. For the basic challenge facing a community is achieving a consensus, or the dilemma of decisionmaking in its absence. Public choice has shed light on these issues, but much remains to be done. The positive literature is riddled with demonstrations of the instability, inefficiency or irrationality of various voting outcomes, the normative literature by impossibility proofs. But this should be neither surprising nor particularly discouraging. Indeed, it is precisely because it deals with some of the oldest and toughest questions a community faces, that public choice attracts so many fine scholars. And for this reason, one can remain optimistic about the field's future growth and development.

[7] [1963, p. 107]. Arrow expresses this view in reference to a quote from A. Bergson, who's position is closer to the contractarian philosophy, i.e. 'that the concern of welfare economics is to counsel citizens generally' [1954, p. 242].

BIBLIOGRAPHY

Abrams, B. A. and Settle, R. F. 'A Modest Proposal for Election Reform,' *Public Choice*, Winter 1976, **28**, pp. 37–53.

Alchian, A. A. and Demsetz, H. 'Production, Information Costs, and Economic Organization,' *Amer. Econ. Rev.*, Dec. 1972, **62**, pp. 777–96.

Alchian, A. A. and Kessel, R. 'Competition, Monopoly and the Pursuit of Money,' in *NBER*, *Aspects of Labor Economics*. Princeton: Princeton Univ. Press, 1962, pp. 157–75.

Aldrich, J. H. 'Candidate Support Functions in the 1968 Elections: An Empirical Application of the Spatial Model,' *Public Choice*, Summer 1975, **22**, pp. 1–22.

Aranson, P. H. and Ordeshook, P. C. 'Spatial Strategies for Sequential Elections,' in R. G. Niemi and H. F. Weisberg, eds., *Probability Models of Collective Decision-Making*, Columbus: Merrill, 1972.

Arrow, K. J. *Social Choice and Individual Values*. New York: John Wiley & Sons, Inc., 1951, rev. ed. 1963.

– 'Tullock and an Existence Theorem, *Public Choice*, Spring 1969, **6**, pp. 105–11.

– 'Some Ordinalist-Utilitarian Notes on Rawls' *Theory of Justice*,' *J. Philosophy*, May 1973, **70**, pp. 245–63.

Arrow, K. J. and Scitovsky, T., eds. *Readings in Welfare Economics*. Homewood, Ill.: Richard D. Irwin, Inc. 1969.

Ashenfelter, O. and Kelley, S. Jr, 'Determinants of Participation in Presidential Elections,' *J. Law and Econ.*, Dec. 1975, **18**, pp. 695–733.

D'Aspremont, C. and Gevers, L. 'Equity and the Informational Basis of Collective Choice,' *Rev. Econ. Stud.*, June 1977, **44**, pp. 199–209.

Axelrod, Robert, *Conflict of Interest*, Chicago: Markham, 1970.

Bagehot, W. *The English Constitution*, 2nd ed., London, 1905.

Barr, J. L. and Davis, O. A. 'An Elementary Political and Economic Theory of the Expenditures of Local Governments,' *Southern Econ. J.*, Oct. 1966, **33**, pp. 149–65.

Barry, B. *Political Argument*, London: Routledge and Kegan P., 1965.

– *Sociologists, Economists and Democracy*, London: Collier-Macmillan, 1970.

271

Barzel, Y. 'Private Schools and Public School Finance,' *J. Polit. Econ.*, January 1973, **81**, pp. 174–86.

Barzel, Y. and Silberberg, E. 'Is the Act of Voting Rational?' *Public Choice*, Fall 1973, **16**, pp. 51–8.

Barzel, Y. and Deacon, R. J., 'Voting Behavior, Efficiency, and Equity,' *Public Choice*, Spring 1975, **21**, pp. 1–14.

Baumol, W. J., *Business Behavior, Value and Growth*, New York: Macmillan, 1959.

– *Welfare Economics and the Theory of the State*, second edition, Cambridge: Harvard University Press, 1967.

Bell, D. *Coming of Post-Industrial Society*, New York: Basic Books, 1973.

Bennett, E. and Conn, D. 'The Group Incentive Properties of Mechanisms for the Provision of Public Goods,' *Public Choice*, Spring 1977, **29**, pp. 95–102.

Bentley, A. F. *The Process of Government*, Chicago: University of Chicago Press, 1907.

Bergson, A. 'A Reformulation of Certain Aspects of Welfare Economics,' *Quart. J. Econ.*, Feb. 1938, **52**, pp. 314–44.

– 'On the Concept of Social Welfare,' *Quart. J. Econ.*, May 1954, **68**, pp. 233–53.

Bergstrom, T. C. and Goodman, R. P. 'Private Demands for Public Goods,' *Amer. Econ. Rev.*, June 1973, **63**, pp. 280–96.

Bernholz, P. 'Economic Policies in a Democracy,' *Kyklos*, 1966, fasc. 1, **19**, pp. 48–80.

– 'Logrolling, Arrow Paradox and Cyclical Majorities,' *Public Choice*, Summer 1973, **15**, pp. 87–95.

– 'Logrolling, Arrow Paradox and Decision Rules – A Generalization,' *Kyklos*, 1974*a*, **27**, pp. 49–61.

– *Grundlagen der Politischen Ökonomie, Band II*, Tübingen: Mohr (Siebeck), 1974*b*.

– 'Is a Paretian Liberal Really Impossible?' *Public Choice*, Winter 1974*c*, **20**, pp. 99–107.

– 'Logrolling and the Paradox of Voting: Are they Logically Equivalent?' *Amer. Polit. Sci. Rev.*, Sept. 1975, **69**, pp. 961–2.

– 'On the Stability of Logrolling Outcomes in Stochastic Games,' Discussion paper No. 13, Universität Basel, January 1977*a*.

– 'Prisoner's Dilemma, Logrolling and Cyclical Group Preferences,' *Public Choice*, Spring 1977*b*, **29**, pp. 73–84.

Black D. 'On the Rationale of Group Decision Making,' *J. Polit. Econ.*, Feb. 1948*a*, **56**, pp. 23–34, reprinted in Arrow and Scitovsky [1969, pp. 133–46].

– 'The Decisions of a Committee Using a Special Majority,' *Econometrica*, July 1948*b*, **16**, pp. 245–61.

– *The Theory of Committees and Elections*. Cambridge: Cambridge University Press, 1958.

Blau, J. H. 'A Direct Proof of Arrow's Theorem,' *Econometrica*, Jan. 1972, **40**, pp. 61–7.

– 'Liberal Values and Independence,' *Rev. Econ. Stud.*, July 1975, **42**, pp. 395–402.

Blau, J. H. and Deb, R. 'Social Decision Functions and the Veto,' *Econometrica*,

May 1977, **45,** pp. 871–9.

Borcherding, T. E., ed. *Budgets and Bureaucrats*, Durham: Duke University Press, 1977*a*.

– 'One Hundred Years of Public Spending, 1870–1970,' 1977*b* in Borcherding [1977*a*, pp. 19–44].

Borcherding, T. E., Bush, W. C. and Spann, R. M. 'The Effects of Public Spending on the Divisibility of Public Outputs in Consumption, Bureaucratic Power, and the Size of the Tax-Sharing Group,' in Borcherding [1977*a*, pp. 211–28].

Borcherding, T. E. and Deacon, R. T. 'The Demand for the Services of Non-Federal Governments,' *Amer. Econ. Rev.*, December 1972, **62,** pp. 891–901.

de Borda, J. C. 'Mémorie sur les Elections au Scrutin,' *Historie de l'Académie Royale des Sciences*, 1781.

Bowen, H. R. 'The Interpretation of Voting in the Allocation of Economic Resources,' *Quart. J. Econ.*, Feb. 1943, **58,** pp. 27–48, reprinted in Arrow and Scitovsky [1969, pp. 115–32].

Braithwaite, R. B. *Theory of Games as a Tool for the Moral Philosopher*, Cambridge: The University Press, 1955.

Brams, S. J. and Fishburn, P. C. 'Approval Voting,' mimeo, 1977.

Brennan, G. and Buchanan, J. M. 'Towards a Tax Constitution for Leviathan,' *J. Public Econ.*, 1977, **8,** pp. 255–73.

Breton, A. *The Economic Theory of Representative Government*, Chicago: Aldine Publishing Co., 1974.

Breton, A. and Wintobe, R. 'The Equilibrium Size of a Budget Maximizing Bureau,' *J. Polit. Econ.*, Feb. 1975, **83,** pp. 195–207.

Breyer, F. 'Sen's Paradox with Decisiveness over Issues in Case of Liberal Preferences,' *Zeitschrift für Nationalökonomie*, 1977, **37.**

Brittan, S. 'The Economic Contradictions of Democracy,' *British J. Polit. Sci*, April 1975, **5,** pp. 129–59.

Brown, D. J. 'Acyclic Choice,' Cowles Foundation, New Haven, 1973.

– 'Aggregation of Preferences,' *Quart. J. Econ.*, Aug. 1975, **89,** pp. 456–69.

Browning, E. K. 'Collective Choice and General Fund Financing,' *J. Polit. Econ.*, April 1975, **83,** pp. 377–90.

Buchanan, J. M. 'The Pure Theory of Government Finance: A Suggested Approach,' *J. Polit. Econ.*, Dec. 1949, **57,** pp. 496–506.

– 'Federalism and Fiscal Equity', *Amer. Econ. Rev.*, September 1950, **40,** pp. 538–600.

– 'Federal Grants and Resource Allocation,' *J. Polit. Econ.*, June 1952, **60,** pp. 201–17.

– 'Individual Choice in Voting and the Market,' *J. Polit. Econ.*, Aug. 1954, **62,** pp. 334–43.

– 'The Economics of Earmarked Taxes,' *J. Polit. Econ.*, Oct. 1963, **71,** pp. 457–69.

– 'An Economic Theory of Clubs,' *Economica*, Feb. 1965*a*, **32,** pp. 1–14.

– 'Ethical Rules, Expected Values, and Large Numbers,' *Ethics*, Oct. 1965*b*, **76,** pp. 1–13.

– 'An Individualistic Theory of Political Process,' in D. Easton, ed. *Varieties of Political Theory*, Englewood Cliffs: Prentice-Hall, 1966, pp. 25–37.

– *Public Finance in a Democratic Process*, Chapel Hill: University of North

Carolina Press, 1967.
- *The Demand and Supply of Public Goods*, Chicago: Rand McNally, 1968.
- 'Notes for an Economic Theory of Socialism,' *Public Choice*, Spring 1970, **8**, pp. 29–43.
- 'Principles of Urban-Fiscal Strategy,' *Public Choice*, Fall 1971, **11**, pp. 1–16.
- 'Rawls on Justice as Fairness,' *Public Choice*, Fall 1972, **13**, pp. 123–8.
- *The Limits of Liberty: Between Anarchy and Leviathan*, Chicago: University of Chicago Press, 1975*a*.
- 'Public Finance and Public Choice,' *Nat. Tax. J.*, Deç. 1975*b*, **28**, pp. 383–94.
- 'A Hobbesian Interpretation of the Rawlsian Difference Principle,' *Kyklos*, 1976*a*, **29**, pp. 5–25.
- 'An Ambiguity in Sen's Alleged Proof of the Impossibility of a Pareto Libertarian,' mimeo, Blacksburg, 1976*b*.
Buchanan, J. M. and Goetz, C. J. 'Efficiency Limits of Fiscal Mobility: An Assessment of the Tiebout Model,' *J. Public Econ.*, April 1972, **1**, pp. 25–43.
Buchanan, J. M. and Tollison, R. D., eds. *Theory of Public Choice*, Ann Arbor: The University of Michigan Press, 1972.
Buchanan, J. M. and Tullock, G. *The Calculus of Consent*, Ann Arbor: The University of Michigan Press, 1962.
Buchanan, J. M. and Wagner, R. R. 'An Efficiency Basis for Federal Fiscal Equalization,' in Margolis, J., ed. *The Analysis of Public Output*, New York: National Bureau of Economic Research, 1970.
Bush, W. C. 'Individual Welfare in Anarchy,' in G. Tullock ed. *Explorations in the Theory of Anarchy*, Blacksburg: Center for the Study of Public Choice, 1972, pp. 5–18.
Bush, W. C. and Mayer, L. S. 'Some Implications of Anarchy for the Distribution of Property,' *J. Econ. Theory*, August 1974, **8**, pp. 401–12.
Cebula, R. J., 'Local Government Policies and Migration,' *Public Choice*, Fall 1974, **19**, 85–93.
- 'An Analysis of Migration Patterns and Local Government Policy Toward Public Education in the United States,' *Public Choice*, Winter 1977, **32**, pp. 113–21.
Clarke, E. H. 'Multipart Pricing of Public Goods,' *Public Choice*, Fall 1971, **11**, pp. 17–33.
- 'Multipart Pricing of Public Goods: An Example,' in S. Mushkin, ed. *Public Prices for Public Products*, Washington: The Urban Institute, 1972, pp. 125–30.
- 'Some Aspects of the Demand-Revealing Process,' *Public Choice*, Spring 1977, **29**, pp. 37–49.
Clotfelter, C. J. *Public Spending for Higher Education*, College Park: University of Maryland Press, 1976.
Coase, R. 'The Problem of Social Cost,' *J. Law and Econ.*, Oct. 1960, **3**, pp. 1–44.
Coleman, J. S. 'Foundations for a Theory of Collective Decisions,' *Amer. J. Sociology*, May 1966*a*, **71**, pp. 615–27.
- 'The Possibility of a Social Welfare Function,' *Amer. Econ. Rev.*, Dec. 1966*b*, **56**, pp. 1105–22.
- 'The Possibility of a Social Welfare Function: Reply,' *Amer. Econ. Rev.*, Dec. 1967, **57**, pp. 1311–17.
- 'Political Money,' *Amer. Polit. Sci. Rev.*, Dec. 1970, **64**, pp. 1074–87.

– 'Internal Processes Governing Party Positions in Elections,' *Public Choice*, Fall 1971, **11,** pp. 35–60.
– 'The Positions of Political Parties in Elections,' in Niemi, R. G. and Weisberg, H. F., eds. *Probability Models of Collective Decision-Making*, Columbus: Merrill, 1972.

Comanor, W. S. 'The Median Voter Rule and the Theory of Political Choice,' *J. Public. Econ.*, Jan.–Feb. 1976, **5,** pp. 169–77.

de Condorcet, M. *Essai sur l'Application de L'Analyse à la Probabilité des Decisions Rendues à la Pluraliste des Voix*, Paris, 1785.

Crain, M., and Tollison, R. 'Campaign Expenditures and Political Competition,' *J. Law and Econ.*, April 1976*a*, **19,** pp. 177–88.
– 'Public Choice as Positive Choice,' mimeo, 1976*b*.
– 'Attenuated Property Rights and the Market for Governors,' *J. Law and Econ.*, April 1977, **20,** pp. 205–11.
– 'The Influence of Representation on Public Policy,' *J. Legal Stud.*, forthcoming.

Dahl, R. A. *After the Revolution?* New Haven: Yale University Press, 1970.

Daniels, N. *Reading Rawls*, New York: Basic Books, 1974.

Davis, J. R. 'On the Incidence of Income Redistribution,' *Public Choice*, Spring 1970, **8,** pp. 63–74.

Davis, O. A. and Haines, G. H., Jr. 'A Political Approach to a Theory of Public Expenditures: The Case of Municipalities,' *Nat. Tax. J.*, Sept. 1966, **19,** pp. 259–75.

Davis, O. A., Hinich, M. J. and Ordeshook, P. C. 'An Expository Development of a Mathematical Model of the Electoral Process,' *Amer. Polit. Sci. Rev.*, June 1970, **64,** pp. 426–48.

Deacon, R. T. 'A Demand Model for the Local Public Sector,' *Rev. Econ. and Stat.*, May 1978, **60,** pp. 184–92.

DeMeyer, F. and Plott, C. 'The Probability of a Cyclical Majority,' *Econometrica*, March 1970, **38,** pp. 345–54.
– 'A Welfare Function Using Relative Intensity of Preference,' *Quart. J. Econ.*, Feb. 1971, **85,** pp. 179–86.

Diamond, P. 'Cardinal Welfare, Individualistic Ethics, and Interpersonal Comparisons of Utility: A Comment,' *J. Polit. Econ.*, Oct. 1967, **75,** pp. 765–6.

Dodgson, C. L. 'A Method of Taking Votes on More than Two Issues,' 1876, reprinted in Black [1958, pp. 224–34].

Downs, A. *An Economic Theory of Democracy*, New York: Harper and Row, 1957.
– 'Why the Government Budget is Too Small in a Democracy,' *World Politics*, July 1960, **12,** pp. 541–63.
– 'In Defense of Majority Voting,' *J. Polit. Econ.*, April 1961, **69,** pp. 192–9.
– *Inside Bureauracy*, Boston: Little, Brown, 1967.

Drèze, J. H. and de la Vallée Poussin, D. 'A Tatonnement Process for Public Goods,' *Rev. Econ. Stud.*, April 1971, **38,** pp. 133–50.

Escarraz, D. R. 'Wicksell and Lindahl: Theories of Public Expenditure and Tax Justice Reconsidered,' *National Tax. J.*, June 1967, **20,** pp. 137–48.

Faber, M. 'Einstimmigkeitsregel und Einkommensumverteilung,' *Kyklos*, 1973, **26,** pp. 36–57.

Fair, R. C. 'The Effect of Economic Events on Votes for President,' *Rev. Econ. Stat.*, May 1978, **60,** pp. 159–73.

Farquharson, R. *Theory of Voting*, New Haven: Yale University Press, 1969.

Fine, B. J. 'Individual Liberalism in a Paretian Society,' *J. Polit. Econ.*, Dec. 1975, **83,** pp. 1277–82.

Fisch, O. 'Optimal City Size, the Economic Theory of Clubs and Exclusionary Zoning,' *Public Choice*, Winter 1975, **24,** pp. 59–70.

Fishburn, P. C. *The Theory of Social Choice*, Princeton: Princeton University Press, 1973*a*.

– 'Summation Social Choice Functions,' *Econometrica*, Nov. 1973*b*, **41,** pp. 1183–96.

Fishburn, P. C. and Gehrlein, W. V., 'An Analysis of Simple Two-Stage Voting Systems,' *Behavioral Science*, Jan. 1976*a*, **21,** pp. 1–12.

– 'An Analysis of Voting Systems with Non-Ranking Voting,' mimeo, 1976*b*.

Flatters, F., Henderson B. and Mieszkowski, P. 'Public Goods, Efficiency, and Regional Fiscal Equalization,' *J. Public Econ.*, May 1974, **3,** pp. 99–112.

Fleming, M. 'A Cardinal Concept of Welfare', *Quart. J. Econ.*, August 1952, **66,** pp. 366–84.

Frey, B. S. 'Why do High Income People Participate More in Politics?' *Public Choice*, Fall 1971, **11,** pp. 101–5.

– 'The Political-Economic System: A Simulation Model,' *Kyklos*, fasc. 2, 1974, **27,** pp. 227–54.

– 'Politico-Economic Models and Cycles,' *J. Public Econ.*, April 1978, **9,** pp. 203–20.

Frey, B. S. and Garbers, H. 'Der Einflus Wirtschaftlicher Variabler auf die Popularität der Regierung,' *Jahrbücher für Nationalökonomie und Statistik*, 1972, **186,** pp. 281–95.

Frey, B. S. and Lau, L. J. 'Towards a Mathematical Model of Government Behavior,' *Zeïtschrift für Nationalökonomie*, 1968, **28,** pp. 355–80.

Frey, B. S. and Schneider, F. 'On the Modeling of Politico-Economic Interdependence,' *European J. Polit. Research*, Dec. 1975, **3,** pp. 339–60.

– 'An Empirical Study of Politico-Economic Interaction in the U.S.,' *Rev. Econ. Stat.*, May 1978*a*, **60,** pp. 174–83.

– 'A Politico-Economic Model of the United Kingdom,' *Econ. J.*, June 1978*b*, **88,** pp. 243–53.

– 'An Econometric Model with an Endogenous Government Sector,' *Public Choice*, forthcoming.

von Furstenberg, G. M. and Mueller, D. C. 'The Pareto Optimal Approach to Income Redistribution: A Fiscal Application,' *Amer. Econ. Rev.*, Sept. 1971, **61,** pp. 628–37.

Furubotn, E. and Pejovich, S. 'Property Rights and Economic Theory: A Survey of Recent Literature,' *J. Econ. Literature*, Dec. 1972, **10,** pp. 1137–62.

Garman, M. B. and Kamien, M. I. 'The Paradox of Voting: Probability Calculations,' *Behavioral Science*, July 1968, **13,** pp. 306–17.

Gehrlein, W. V. and Fishburn, P. C. 'Condorcet's Paradox and Anonymous Preference Profiles,' *Public Choice*, Summer 1976, **26,** pp. 1–18.

– 'The Probability of the Paradox of Voting: A Computable Solution,' *J. Econ.*

Theory, forthcoming.

Gibbard, A. 'Manipulation of Voting Schemes: A General Result,' *Econometrica*, July 1973, **41**, pp. 587–602.

– 'A Pareto-Consistent Libertarian Claim,' *J. Econ. Theory*, April 1974, **7**, pp. 388–410.

Goetz, C. J. 'Earmarked Taxes and Majority Rule Budgetary Processes,' *Amer. Econ. Rev.*, March 1968, **58**, pp. 128–36.

Goetz, C. J. and McKnew, C. R., Jr, 'Paradoxical Results in a Public Choice Model of Alternative Government Grant Forms,' in Buchanan and Tollison [1972, pp. 224–35].

Goodhart, C. A. E. and Bhansali, R. J. 'Political Economy,' *Polit. Stud.*, 1970, **18**, pp. 43–106.

Gough, J. W. *The Social Contract,* 2nd ed., Oxford: Clarendon Press, 1957.

Gramlich, E. M. 'The Effects of Grants on State-Local Expenditures: A Review of the Econometric Literature,' National Tax Assoc., *Proceedings of the Sixty-Second Annual Conference on Taxation, 1969* (1970), pp. 569–93.

Green, J. and Laffont, J.-J., 'Characterization of Satisfactory Mechanisms for the Revelation of Preferences for Public Goods,' *Econometrica*, March 1977*a*, **45**, pp. 427–38.

– 'Imperfect Personal Information and the Demand Revealing Process: A Sampling Approach,' *Public Choice*, Spring 1977*b*, **29**, pp. 79–94.

Greenberg, J., Mackay, R. and Tideman, N. 'Some Limitations of the Groves–Ledyard Optimal Mechanism,' *Public Choice*, Spring 1977, **29**, 129–37.

Greene, K. V. 'Some Institutional Considerations in Federal–State Fiscal Relations,' *Public Choice*, Fall 1970, **9**, pp. 1–18.

Groves, T. 'Incentives in Teams,' *Econometrica*, July 1973, **41**, pp. 617–31.

– 'On the Possibility of Efficient Collective Choice with Compensation,' Paper presented at the ASSA meetings, Atlantic City, 1976.

Groves, T. and Ledyard, J. 'Optimal Allocation of Public Goods: A Solution to the "Free Rider" Problem,' *Econometrica*, May 1977*a*, **45**, pp. 783–809.

– 'Some Limitations of Demand Revealing Processes,' *Public Choice*, Spring 1977*b*, **29**, pp. 107–24.

– 'Reply,' *ibid.*, 1977*c*, pp. 139–43.

Groves, T. and Loeb, M. 'Incentives and Public Inputs,' *J. Public Econ.*, Aug. 1975, **4**, pp. 211–26.

Guha, A. S. 'Neutrality, Monotonicity and the Right of Veto,' *Econometrica*, Sept. 1972, **40**, pp. 821–6.

Haefele, E. T. 'A Utility Theory of Representative Government,' *Amer. Econ., Rev.*, June 1971, **61**, pp. 350–67.

Hammond, P. J. 'Why Ethical Measures of Inequality Need Interpersonal Comparisons', *Theory and Decision*, Oct. 1976, **7**, pp. 263–74.

Hansson, B. 'The Independence Condition in the Theory of Choice,' *Theory and Decision*, Sept. 1973, **4**, pp. 25–49.

Hardin, R. 'Collective Action as an Agreeable n-Prisoners' Dilemma,' *Behav. Sci.*, Sept. 1971, **16**, pp. 472–81.

Hare, R. M. 'Rawls' Theory of Justice,' *Philosophical Quarterly*, April 1973, **23**, pp. 144–55, as reprinted in Daniels [1974, pp. 81–107].

Harsanyi, J. C. 'Cardinal Utility in Welfare Economics and in the Theory of Risk-Taking,' *J. Polit. Econ.*, Oct. 1953, **61**, pp. 434–5.

– 'Cardinal Welfare, Individualistic Ethics, and Interpersonal Comparisons of Utility,' *J. Polit. Econ.*, Aug. 1955, **63**, pp. 309–21, reprinted in Arrow and Scitovsky [1969, pp. 46–60].

– 'Can the Maximin Principle Serve as a Basis for Morality? A Critique of John Rawls' Theory,' *Amer. Polit. Sci. Rev.*, June 1975a, **69**, pp. 594–606.

– 'Nonlinear Social Welfare Functions,' *Theory and Decision*, Aug. 1975b, pp. 311–32.

– *Rational Behavior and Bargaining Equilibrium in Games and Social Situations.* Cambridge: Cambridge University Press, 1977.

Hart, H. L. A. 'Rawls on Liberty and its Priority,' *University of Chicago Law Rev.*, Spring 1973, **40**, pp. 534–55, reprinted in Daniels [1974, pp. 230–52].

Head, J. G. 'Public Goods and Public Policy,' *Public Finance*, 1962, **17**, pp. 197–221.

– 'Lindahl's Theory of the Budget,' *Finanzarchiv*, Oct. 1964, **23**, pp. 421–54.

Hildreth, C. 'Alternative Conditions for Social Orderings,' *Econometrica*, Jan. 1953, **21**, pp. 81–94.

Hinich, M. J. and Ordeshook, P. C. 'Plurality Maximization vs. Vote Maximization: A Spatial Analysis with Variable Participation,' *Amer. Polit. Sci. Rev.*, Sept. 1970, **64**, pp. 772–91.

Hirschman, A. O. *Exit, Voice, and Loyalty*, Cambridge: Harvard University Press, 1970.

Hobbes, T. *Leviathan*, London, 1651. Reprinted in *The English Philosophers*, New York: Modern Library, 1939, pp. 129–234.

Hochman, H. M. and Rogers, J. D. 'Pareto Optimal Redistribution,' *Amer. Econ. Rev.*, Sept. 1969, **59**, pp. 542–57.

– 'Pareto Optimal Redistribution: Reply,' *Amer. Econ. Rev.*, Dec. 1970, **60**, pp. 977–1002.

Hotelling, H. 'Stability in Competition,' *Econ. J.*, March 1929, **39**, pp. 41–57.

Hume, D. *Treatise of Human Nature* (1739), Oxford: Oxford University Press, 1941.

– *An Inquiry Concerning the Principles of Morals* (1751), Indianapolis, Bobbs-Merrill, 1957.

Hurwicz, L. 'On the Existence of Allocation Systems whose Manipulative Nash Equilibria are Pareto Optimal,' Paper presented at the Econometric Society Meetings, Toronto, 1975.

Inada, K.-I. 'The Simple Majority Decision Rule,' *Econometrica*, July 1969, **37**, pp. 490–506.

– 'Majority Rule and Rationality,' *J. Econ. Theory*, March 1970, **2**, pp. 27–40.

Intriligator, M. D. 'A Probabilistic Model of Social Choice,' *Rev. Econ. Stud.*, Oct. 1973, **40**, pp. 553–60.

Johansen, L. 'Some Notes on the Lindahl Theory of Determination of Public Expenditures,' *International Econ. Rev.*, Sept. 1963, **4**, pp. 346–58.

Joslyn, R. A. 'The Impact of Decision Rules in Multi-candidate Campaigns: The Case of the 1972 Democratic Presidential Nomination,' *Public Choice*, Spring 1976, **25**, pp. 1–17.

de Jouvenal, B. 'The Chairman's Problem,' *Amer. Polit. Sci. Rev.*, June 1961, **55**, pp. 368–72.

Kadane, J. B. 'On Division of the Question,' *Public Choice*, Fall 1972, **13**, pp. 47–54.

Kahn, A. E. *The Economics of Regulation: Vol. 1*, New York: Wiley, 1970.

Kasper, H. 'On Political Competition, Economic Policy, and Income Maintenance Programs,' *Public Choice*, Spring 1971, **10**, pp. 1–19.

Kats, A. and Nitzan, S. 'Global and Local Equilibrium in Majority Voting,' *Public Choice*, Summer 1976, **26**, pp. 105–6.

Kelly, J. S. 'Rights Exercising and a Pareto-Consistent Libertarian Claim,' *J. Econ. Theory*, Aug. 1976, **13**, pp. 138–53.

– *Arrow Impossibility Theorems*, New York: Academic Press, 1978.

Kemp, M. C. 'Arrow's General Possibility Theorem,' *Rev. Econ. Stud.*, 1954, **21**, pp. 240–3.

Kemp, M. C. and Asimakopulos, A. 'A Note on "Social Welfare Functions" and Cardinal Utility,' *Can. J. Econ. Polit. Sci.*, May 1952, **18**, pp. 195–200.

Kemp, M. C. and Ng, Y.-K. 'On the Existence of Social Welfare Functions: Social Orderings and Social Decision Functions,' *Economica*, Feb. 1976, **43**, pp. 59–66.

– 'More on Social Welfare Functions: The Incompatibility of Individualism and Ordinalism,' *Economica*, Feb. 1977, **44**, pp. 89–90.

Kendall, W. *John Locke and the Doctrine of Majority Rule*, Urbana: University of Illinois Press, 1941.

Kirchgässner, G. 'Ökonometrische Untersuchungen des Einflusses der Wirtschaftslage auf die Popularität der Parteien,' *Schweizerische Zeitschrift für Volkswirtschaft und Statistik*, 1974, **110**, pp. 409–45.

Kirman, A. P. and Sondermann, D. 'Arrow's Theorem, Many Agents, and Invisible Dictators,' *J. Econ. Theory*, Oct. 1972, **5**, pp. 267–77.

Klevorick, A. K. 'Discussion,' *Amer. Econ. Rev.*, May 1974, **64**, pp. 158–61.

Klevorick, A. K. and Kramer, G. H. 'Social Choice on Pollution Management: The Genossenschaften,' *J. Public Econ.*, April 1973, **2**, pp. 101–64.

Koehler, D. H. 'Vote Trading and the Voting Paradox: A Proof of Logical Equivalence', *Amer. Polit. Sci. Rev.*, Sept. 1975, **69**, pp. 954–60.

Kramer, G. H. 'Short Run Fluctuations in U.S. Voting Behavior, 1896–1964,' *Amer. Polit. Sci. Rev.*, March 1971, **65**, pp. 131–43.

– 'Sophisticated Voting Over Multidimensional Choice Spaces,' *J. Mathematical Sociology*, July 1972, **2**, pp. 165–80.

– 'On a Class of Equilibrium Conditions for Majority Rule,' *Econometrica*, March 1973, **41**, pp. 285–97.

Kramer, G. H. and Klevorick, A. J. 'Existence of a Local Cooperative Equilibrium in a Class of Voting Games,' *Rev. Econ. Stud.*, Oct. 1974, **41**, pp. 539–47.

Kuga, K. and Nagatani, H. 'Voter Antagonism and the Paradox of Voting,' *Econometrica*, Nov. 1974, **42**, pp. 1045–67.

Landes, W. M. and Posner, R. A. 'The Independent Judiciary in an Interest-Group Perspective,' *J. Law and Econ.*, Dec. 1975, **18**, pp. 875–901.

Leibenstein, H. 'Long-Run Welfare Criteria,' in Margolis, J. ed. *The Public Economy of Urban Communities*, Baltimore: Johns Hopkins Press, 1965, pp. 539–57.

- 'Allocative Efficiency vs X-Efficiency,' *Amer. Econ. Rev.*, June 1966, **56**, pp. 392–415.
- 'Organizational or Frictional Equilibria, X-Efficiency, and the Rate of Innovation,' *Quart. J. Econ.* Nov. 1969, **83**, pp. 600–23.

Lerner, A. P. *Economics of Control*, New York: Macmillan, 1944.

Levine, M. E. and Plott, C. R. 'Agenda Influence and Its Implications,' *Virginia Law Rev.*, 1977, **63**, pp. 561–604.

Lindahl, E. 'Just Taxation – A Positive Solution,' first published in German, Lund, 1919. English translation in Musgrave and Peacock [1958, pp. 168–76].

Lindeen, J. W. 'An Oligopoloy Model of Political Market Structures,' *Public Choice*, Fall 1970, **9**, pp. 31–7.

Lindsay, C. M. 'A Theory of Government Enterprise,' *J. Polit. Econ.*, Oct. 1976, **84**, pp. 1061–77.

Little, I. M. D. 'Social Choice and Individual Values,' *J. Polit. Econ.*, Oct. 1952, **60**, pp. 422–32.
- *A Critique of Welfare Economics*, Oxford: Clarendon Press, 1957, 2nd ed.

Locke, J. 'An Essay Concerning the True Original Extent and End of Civil Government,' reprinted in *The English Philosophers*, New York: Random House, 1939.

Loeb, M. 'Alternative Versions of the Demand-Revealing Process,' *Public Choice*, Spring 1977, **29**, pp. 15–26.

Lowi, T. J. *The End of Liberalism*, New York: W. W. Norton, 1969.

Luce, R. D. and Raiffa, H. *Games and Decisions*, New York: Wiley, 1957.

Ludwin, W. G. 'Voting Methods: A Simulation,' *Public Choice*, Spring 1976, **25**, pp. 19–30.

Lyons, D. 'Nature and Soundness of the Contract and Coherence Arguments,' in Daniels [1974, pp. 141–67] based on material from 'Rawls versus Utilitarianism,' *J. Philosphy*, Oct. 1972, **69**, pp. 535–45, and 'The Nature of the Contract Argument', *Cornell Law Rev.* (No. 6, 1974), **59**.

McConnell, G. *Private Power and American Democracy*, New York: Alfred A. Knopf, 1966.

McGuire, M. 'Private Good Clubs and Public Good Clubs: Economic Models of Group Formation,' *Swedish J. Econ.*, 1972, **74**, pp. 84–99.
- 'Group Segregation and Optimal Jurisdictions,' *J. Polit. Econ.*, Jan./Feb. 1974, **82**, pp. 112–32.

McGuire, M. and Aaron, H. 'Efficiency and Equity in the Optimal Supply of a Public Good,' *Rev. Econ. Statist.*, Feb. 1969, **51**, pp. 31–8.

McKelvey, R. D. 'Intransitivities in Multidimensional Voting Models and Some Implications for Agenda Control,' *J. Econ. Theory*, June 1976, **12**, pp. 472–82.

McMillan, M. L. 'Toward the More Optimal Provision of Local Public Goods: Internalization of Benefits or Intergovernmental Grants?' *Public Finance Quart.*, July 1975, **3**, pp. 229–60.

MacPherson, C. B. 'Market Concepts in Political Theory,' *Canadian J. Econ. and Polit. Sci.*, Nov. 1961, **27**, pp. 490–7.

MacRae, D. C. 'A Political Model of the Business Cycle,' *J. Polit. Econ.*, April 1977, **85**, pp. 239–63.

Malinvaud, E. 'Procédures pour la Détermination d'un Programme de Consommation Collective,' *European Econ. Rev.*, Winter 1970–71, **2**, pp. 187–217.

Marris, R. *The Economic Theory of Managerial Capitalism*, New York, Free Press, 1964.

May, K. O. 'A Set of Independent, Necessary and Sufficient Conditions for Simple Majority Decision,' *Econometrica*, Oct 1952, **20**, pp. 680–4.

Meltzer, A. H. and Vellrath, M. 'The Effects of Economic Policies on Votes for the Presidency: Some Evidence from Recent Elections,' *J. Law and Econ.*, Dec. 1975, **18**, pp. 781–98.

Migué, J.-L. and Bélanger, G. 'Towards a General Theory of Managerial Discretion,' *Public Choice*, Spring 1974, **17**, pp. 27–43.

Mill, J. S. *Considerations on Representative Government*, New York: Bobbs-Merrill, 1958.

Miller, G. J. 'Bureaucratic Compliance as a Game on the Unit Square,' *Public Choice*, Spring 1977, **19**, pp. 37–51.

– 'Institutional Inequality,' paper presented at the Public Choice Society Meeting, New Orleans, 1978.

Miller, J. C. III, 'A Program for Direct and Proxy Voting in the Legislative Process,' *Public Choice*, Fall 1969, **7**, pp. 107–13.

Miller, N. R. 'Logrolling, Vote Trading, and the Paradox of Voting: A Game Theoretical Overview,' *Public Choice*, Summer 1977, **30**, pp. 51–75.

Miller, W. L. and Mackie, M. 'The Electoral Cycle and the Asymmetry of Government and Opposition Popularity,' *Polit. Stud.*, 1973, **21**, pp. 263–79.

Milleron, J. C. 'Theory of Value with Public Goods: A Survey Article,' *J. Econ. Theory*, Dec. 1972, **5**, pp. 419–77.

Mueller, D. C. 'The Possibility of a Social Welfare Function: Comment,' *Amer. Econ. Rev.*, Dec. 1967, **57**, pp. 1304–11.

– 'Fiscal Federalism in a Constitutional Democracy,' *Public Policy*, Fall 1971, **19**, pp. 567–93.

– 'Constitutional Democracy and Social Welfare,' *Quart. J. Econ.*, Feb. 1973, **87**, pp. 60–80.

– 'Allocation, Redistribution and Collective Choice,' *Public Finance*, 1977, **32**, pp. 225–44.

– 'Voting by Veto,' *J. Public Econ.*, 1978, **10**, pp. 57–75.

Mueller, D. C., Philpotts, G. C. and Vanek, J. 'The Social Gains from Exchanging Votes: A Simulation Approach,' *Public Choice*, Fall 1972, **13**, pp. 55–79.

Mueller, D. C., Tollison, R. D. and Willett, T. D. 'The Utilitarian Contract: A Generalization of Rawls' Theory of Justice,' *Theory and Decision*, Feb./April 1974*a*, **4**, pp. 345–67.

– 'On Equalizing the Distribution of Political Income,' *J. Polit. Econ.*, March/April 1974*b*, **82**, pp. 414–22.

– 'Solving the Intensity Problem in a Representative Democracy,' in R. D. Leiter and G. Sirkin, eds. *Economics of Public Choice*. New York: Cyro Press, 1975, pp. 54–94, reprinted in Amacher, R., Tollison, R. and Willett, T. *Political Economy and Public Policy*, Ithaca: Cornell University Press, 1976, pp. 444–73.

Musgrave, R. A. 'The Voluntary Exchange Theory of Public Economy,' *Quart. J. Econ.*, Feb. 1939, **53**, pp. 213–38.

– *The Theory of Public Finance*, New York: McGraw-Hill, 1959.

- 'Approaches to a Fiscal Theory of Political Federalism,' NBER, *Public Finances: Needs, Resources and Utilization*, Princeton: Princeton University Press, 1961, pp. 97–122.

Musgrave, R. T. and Peacock, A. T. eds. *Classics in the Theory of Public Finance*, New York: St Martin's Press, 1967.

Nagel, T. 'Rawls on Justice,' *Philosophical Rev.*, April 1973, **82**, pp. 220–34, reprinted in Daniels [1974, pp. 1–15].

Nash, J. F. 'The Bargaining Problem,' *Econometrica*, April 1950, **18**, pp. 155–62.

Nath, S. K. 'Liberalism, Pareto Principle and the Core of a Society,' University of Warwick, 1976.

Ng, Y.-K. 'The Possibility of a Paretian Liberal: Impossibility Theorems and Cardinal Utility,' *J. Polit. Econ.*, Nov./Dec. 1971, **79**, pp. 1397–1402.

- 'Bentham or Bergson? Finite Sensibility, Utility Functions and Social Welfare Functions,' *Rev. Econ. Stud.*, Oct. 1975, **42**, pp. 545–69.

Niemi, R. G. 'Majority Decision-Making with Partial Unidimensionality,' *Amer. Polit. Sci. Rev.*, June 1969, **63**, pp. 488–97.

Niemi, R. G. and Weisberg, H. F. 'A Mathematical Solution for the Probability of the Paradox of Voting,' *Behavioral Science*, July 1968, **13**, pp. 317–23.

Niskanen, W. A. Jr, *Bureaucracy and Representative Government*, Chicago: Aldine-Atherton, 1971.

- 'Bureaucrats and Politicians,' *J. Law and Econ.*, Dec. 1975, **18**, pp. 617–43.

Nitzan, S. 'Social Preference Ordering in a Probabilistic Voting Model,' *Public Choice*, Winter 1975, **24**, pp. 93–100.

Nordhaus, W. D. 'The Political Business Cycle,' *Rev. Econ. Stud.*, April 1975, **42**, pp. 169–90.

Nozick, R. *Anarchy, State, and Utopia*, New York: Basic Books, 1974.

Oates, W. E. *Fiscal Federalism*, London: Harcourt Brace, 1972.

Olson, M., Jr, *The Logic of Collective Action*, Cambridge: Harvard University Press, 1965.

Oppenheimer, J. 'Some Political Implications of "Vote Trading and the Voting Paradox: A Proof of Logical Equivalence": A Comment,' *Amer. Polit. Sci. Rev.*, Sept. 1975, **69**, pp. 963–6.

Orbell, J. M. and Uno, T. 'A Theory of Neighborhood Problem Solving: Political Action vs. Residential Mobility,' *Amer. Polit. Sci. Rev.*, June 1972, **66**, pp. 471–89.

Ordeshook, P. C. 'The Spatial Theory of Elections: A Review and Critique,' presented at the European Consortium for Political Research Workshop on Participation, Voting, and Party Competition, Strasbourg, 1974.

Orzechowski, W. 'Economic Models of Bureaucracy: Survey, Extensions, and Evidence,' in Borcherding [1977a. pp. 229–59].

Ostrom, V. *The Political Theory of a Compound Republic*, Blacksburg: Public Choice Society, 1971.

Palda, K. S. 'Does Advertising Influence Votes? An Analysis of the 1966 and 1970 Quebec Elections,' *Can. J. Polit. Sci.*, 1973, **6**, pp. 638–55.

- 'The Effect of Expenditure on Political Success,' *J. Law and Econ.*, Dec. 1975, **18**, pp. 745–71.

Park, R. E. 'The Possibility of a Social Welfare Function: Comment,' *Amer. Econ.*

Rev., Dec. 1967, **57**, pp. 1300–4.

Parks, R. P. 'An Impossibility Theorem for Fixed Preferences: A Dictatorial Bergson–Samuelson Welfare Function,' *Rev. Econ. Stud.*, Oct. 1976, **43**, pp. 447–50.

Pattanaik, P. K. 'Risk, Impersonality, and the Social Welfare Function,' *J. Polit. Econ.*, Nov. 1968, **76**, pp. 1152–69.

– *Voting and Collective Choice.* Cambridge: Cambridge University Press, 1971.

– 'On the Stability of Sincere Voting Situations,' *J. Econ. Theory*, Dec. 1973, **6**, pp. 558–74.

– 'Stability of Sincere Voting Under Some Classes of Non-Binary Group Decision Procedures,' *J. Econ. Theory*, June 1974, **8**, pp. 206–24.

Pauly, M. V. 'Clubs, Commonality, and the Core: An Integration of Game Theory and the Theory of Public Goods,' *Economica*, Aug. 1967, **35**, pp. 314–24.

– 'Cores and Clubs,' *Public Choice*, Fall 1970, **9**, pp. 53–65.

Peacock, A. T. and Rowley, C. K. 'Pareto Optimality and the Political Economy of Liberalism,' *J. Polit. Econ.*, May/June 1972, **80**, pp. 476–90.

Penrose, E., *The Theory of the Growth of the Firm*, Oxford: Oxford University Press, 1959.

Pestieau, P. 'The Optimality Limits of the Tiebout Model,' in W. E. Oates, ed. *The Political Economy of Fiscal Federalism*, Lexington: Lexington Books, 1977, pp. 173–86.

Peterson, G. M. *The Demand for Public Schooling*, Washington: Urban Institute, 1973.

– 'Voter Demand for School Expenditures,' in J. E. Jackson, ed. *Public Needs and Private Behavior in Metropolitan Areas*, Cambridge: Harvard University Press, 1975, pp. 99–115.

Philpotts, G. 'Vote Trading, Welfare, and Uncertainty,' *Can. J. Econ.*, Aug. 1972, **3**, pp. 358–72.

Plott, C. R. 'A Notion of Equilibrium and its Possibility Under Majority Rule,' *Amer. Econ. Rev.*, Sept. 1967, **57**, pp. 787–806.

– 'Recent Results in the Theory of Voting,' in M. D. Intriligator, ed. *Frontiers of Quantitative Economics.* Amsterdam: North-Holland, 1971, pp. 109–27.

– 'Ethics, Social Choice Theory and the Theory of Economic Policy,' *J. Math. Soc.*, 1972, **2**, pp. 181–208.

– 'Path Independence, Rationality and Social Choice,' *Econometrica*, Nov. 1973, **41**, pp. 1075–91.

– 'Axiomatic Social Choice Theory: An Overview and Interpretation,' *Amer. J. Polit. Sci.*, Aug. 1976, **20**, pp. 511–96.

Pommerehne, W. W., 'Budgetäre Umverteilung in der Demokratie: Ein empirischer Test Alternative Hypothesen,' Discussion Paper 64, Konstanz, 1975.

– 'Institutional Approaches to Public Expenditures: Empirical Evidence From Swiss Municipalities,' *J. Public Econ.*, April 1978, **9**, pp. 163–201.

Pommerehne, W. W. and Frey, B. S., 'Two Approaches to Estimating Public Expenditures,' *Public Finance Quarterly*, Oct. 1976, **4**, pp. 395–407.

Puviani, A. *Teoria della illusione nelle entrate publiche*, Perugia, 1897.

– *Teoria della illusione Finanziaria*, Palermo, 1903.

Rae, D. W. *The Political Consequences of Electoral Laws*, New Haven: Yale

University Press, 1967.
– 'Decision-Rules and Individual Values in Constitutional Choice,' *Amer. Polit. Sci. Rev.*, March 1969, **63**, pp. 40–56.
– 'The Limits of Consensual Decision,' *Amer. Polit. Sci. Rev.*, Dec. 1975, **69**, pp. 1270–94.
Rapoport, A. and Chammah, A. *Prisoners' Dilemma*, Ann Arbor: Michigan University Press, 1965.
Rawls, J. *A Theory of Justice*. Cambridge: The Belknap Press of Harvard University Press, 1971.
– 'Some Reasons for the Maximin Criterion,' *Amer. Econ. Rev.*, May 1974, **64**, pp. 141–6.
Ray, P. 'Independence of Irrelevant Alternatives,' *Econometrica*, Sept. 1973, **41**, pp. 987–91.
Reimer, M. 'The Case for Bare Majority Rule,' *Ethics*, Oct. 1951, **62**, pp. 16–32.
Riker, W. H. 'Voting and the Summation of Preferences: An Interpretative Bibliographical Review of Selected Developments During the Last Decade,' *Amer. Polit. Sci. Rev.*, Dec. 1961, **55**, pp. 900–11.
– *The Theory of Political Coalitions*. New Haven and London: Yale University Press, 1962.
Riker, W. H. and Brahms, S. J. 'The Paradox of Vote Trading,' *Amer. Polit. Sci. Rev.*, Dec. 1973, **67**, pp. 1235–47.
Riker, W. H. and Ordeshook, P. C. 'A Theory of the Calculus of Voting,' *Amer. Polit. Sci. Rev.*, March 1968, **62**, pp. 25–42.
– *Introduction to Positive Political Theory*. Englewood Cliffs: Prentice Hall, 1973.
Rosenthal, H. and Sen, S. 'Electoral Participation in the French Fifth Republic,' *Amer. Polit. Sci. Rev.*, March 1973, **67**, pp. 29–54.
Rothenberg, J. *The Measurement of Social Welfare*, Englewood Cliffs: Prentice-Hall, 1961.
Rowley, C. K. and Peacock, A. T. *Welfare Economics*, London: Martin Robertson, 1975.
Runciman, W. G. and Sen, A. K. 'Games, Justice and the General Will,' *Mind*, Oct. 1965, pp. 554–62.
Russell, K. P., Fraser, J., and Frey, B. S. 'Political Participation and Income Level: An Exchange,' *Public Choice*, Fall 1972, **13**, pp. 113–22.
Samuelson, P. A. *Foundations of Economic Analysis*. Cambridge: Harvard University Press, 1947.
– 'The Pure Theory of Public Expenditure,' *Rev. Econ. Statist.*, Nov. 1954, **36**, pp. 386–9, reprinted in Arrow and Scitovsky [1969, pp. 179–82].
– 'Arrow's Mathematical Politics,' In Hook, S. ed. *Human Values and Economic Policy*, New York: New York University Press, 1967.
– 'Pure Theory of Public Expenditure and Taxation,' in Margolis, J. and Guitton, H. eds. *Public Economics*, New York: St Martin's Press, 1969, pp. 98–123.
– 'Reaffirming the Existence of "Reasonable" Bergson–Samuelson Social Welfare Functions,' *Economica*, Feb. 1977, **44**, pp. 81–8.
Saposnik, R. 'On the Transitivity of the Social Preference Relation under Simple Majority Rule,' *J. Econ. Theory*, Feb. 1975, **10**, pp. 1–7.
Satterthwaite, M. A. 'Strategy-Proofness and Arrow's Conditions: Existence and

Correspondence Theorems for Voting Procedures and Social Welfare Functions,' *J. Econ. Theory*, April 1975, **10**, pp. 187–217.

Scanlon, I. M. 'Rawls' Theory of Justice,' in Daniels [1974, pp. 141–67] as adapted from 'Rawls' Theory of Justice,' *University of Pennsylvania Law Rev.*, May 1973, **121**, pp. 1020–69.

Schattschneider, E. E. *Politics, Pressures and the Tariff*, Englewood Cliffs: Prentice Hall, 1935.

Schneider, F. 'Politisch-ökonomische Konjunkturzyklen: ein Simulationsmodel,' *Schweizerische Zeitschrift für Volkswirtschaft und Statistik*, 1974, **3**.

Schumpeter, J. A. *Capitalism, Socialism and Democracy*, third edition, New York: Harper and Row, 1950.

Schwartz, T. 'Vote Trading and Pareto Efficiency', *Public Choice*, Winter 1975, **24**, pp. 101–9.

Scott, A. D. 'A Note on Grants in Federal Countries,' *Economica*, Nov. 1950, **17**, pp. 416–22.

– 'Evaluation of Federal Grants,' *Economica*, Nov. 1952*a*, **19**, pp. 377–94.

– 'Federal Grants and Resource Allocation,' *J. Polit. Econ.*, Dec. 1952*b*, **60**, pp. 534–6.

Seidl, C. 'On Liberal Values,' *Zeitschrift für Nationalökonomie*, 1975, **35**, pp. 257–92.

Selten, R. 'Anwendungen der Spieltheorie auf die Politische Wissenschaft,' in Maier, ed. *Politik und Wissenschaft*, München: Beck, 1971.

Sen, A. K. 'A Possibility Theorem on Majority Decisions,' *Econometrica*, April 1966, **34**, pp. 491–9.

– 'Quasi-transitivity, Rational Choice and Collective Decisions,' *Rev. Econ. Stud.*, July 1969, **36**, pp. 381–94.

– *Collective Choice and Social Welfare*. San Francisco: Holden-Day, 1970*a*.

– 'The Impossibility of a Paretian Liberal,' *J. Polit. Econ.*, Jan./Feb. 1970*b*, **78**, pp. 152–7.

– 'Rawls versus Bentham: An Axiomatic Examination of the Pure Distribution Problem,' *Theory and Decision*, Feb./April 1974*a*, **4**, pp. 301–10.

– 'Informational Basis of Alternative Welfare Approaches, Aggregation and Income Distribution', *J. Public Econ.*, Nov. 1974*b*, **3**, pp. 387–403.

– 'Liberty, Unanimity and Rights,' *Economica*, Aug. 1976, **43**, pp. 217–45.

– 'Social Choice Theory: A Re-examination,' *Econometrica*, Jan. 1977*a*, **45**, pp. 53–89.

– 'On Weight and Measures: Informational Constraints in Social Welfare Analysis,' *Econometrica*, Oct. 1977*b*, **45**, pp. 1539–72.

Sen, A. K. and Pattanaik, P. K. 'Necessary and Sufficient Conditions for Rational Choice under Majority Decision,' *J. Econ. Theory*, Aug. 1969, **1**, pp. 178–202.

Sherman, R. 'Experimental Oligopoly,' *Kyklos*, 1971, **24**, pp. 30–48.

Shubik, M. 'On Homo Politicus and the Instant Referendum,' *Public Choice*, Fall 1970, **9**, pp. 79–84.

Siegel, S. and Fouraker, L. E. *Bargaining and Group Decision Making: Experiments in Bilateral Monopoly*, New York: McGraw-Hill, 1960.

Silberman, J. and Durden, G. 'The Rational Behavior Theory of Voter Participation,' *Public Choice*, Fall 1975, **23**, pp. 101–8.

Silver, M. 'Political Revolution and Repression: An Economic Approach,' *Public Choice*, Spring 1974, **17**, pp. 63–71.

Simpson, P. B. 'On Defining Areas of Voter Choice: Professor Tullock on Stable Voting,' *Quart. J. Econ.*, August 1969, **83**, pp. 478–90.

Slutsky, S. 'A Characterization of Societies with Consistent Majority Decision', *Rev. Econ. Stud.*, June 1977a, **44**, pp. 211–25.

– 'A Voting Model for the Allocation of Public Goods: Existence of an Equilibrium,' *J. Econ. Theory*, April 1977b, **14**, pp. 299–325.

– 'Equilibrium under a-majority Voting,' mimeo, Cornell University, 1977c.

Smith, J. H. 'Aggregation of Preferences and Variable Electorate,' *Econometrica*, Nov. 1973, **41**, pp. 1027–41.

Smith, V. L. 'Incentive Compatible Experimental Processes for the Provision of Public Goods,' paper presented at the NBER Conference on Decentralization, Evanston, Ill., 1976.

Smithies, A. 'Optimum Location in Spatial Competition,' *J. Polit. Econ.*, June 1941, **49**, pp. 423–39.

Spann, R. M. 'Collective Consumption of Private Goods,' *Public Choice*, Winter 1974, **20**, pp. 63–81.

– 'Rates of Productivity Change and the Growth of State and Local Government Expenditures,' in Borcherding [1977a, pp. 100–29].

Stigler, G. J. 'Director's Law of Public Income Redistribution,' *J. Law Econ.*, April 1970, **13**, pp. 1–10.

– 'General Economic Conditions and Natural Elections,' *Amer. Econ. Rev.*, May 1973, **63**, pp. 160–7.

Stokes, D. E. 'Spatial Models of Party Competition,' *Amer. Polit. Sci. Rev.*, June 1963, **57**, pp. 368–77.

Stubblebine, W. C. *The Social Imbalance Hypothesis*, PhD Dissertation, University of Virginia, 1963.

Sullivan, T. 'Voter's Paradox and Logrolling: An Initial Framework for Committee Behavior on Appropriations and Ways and Means,' *Public Choice*, Spring 1976, **25**, pp. 31–44.

Taylor, M. J. 'Graph Theoretical Approaches to the Theory of Social Choice,' *Public Choice*, Spring 1968, **4**, pp. 35–48.

– 'Proof of a Theorem on Majority Rule,' *Behavioral Sci.*, May 1969, **14**, pp. 228–31.

– 'Review Article: Mathematical Political Theory,' *British J. Polit. Sci.*, July 1971, **1**, pp. 339–82.

– *Anarchy and Cooperation*, New York: Wiley, 1976.

Taylor, M. J. and Herman, V. M. 'Party Systems and Government Stability,' *Amer. Polit. Sci. Rev.*, March 1971, **65**, pp. 28–37.

Taylor, M. J. and Laver, M. 'Government Coalitions in Western Europe,' *European J. Polit. Research*, Sept. 1973, **1**, pp. 205–48.

Thompson, E. A. 'A Pareto Optimal Group Decision Process,' in G. Tullock, ed. *Papers on Non-Market Decision Making*, University of Virginia: Charlottesville, 1966, pp. 133–40.

Tideman, J. N. 'Ethical Foundations of the Demand-Revealing Process,' *Public Choice*, Spring 1977, **29**, pp. 71–7.

Tideman, J. N. and Tullock, G. 'A New and Superior Process for Making Social Choices,' *J. Polit. Econ.*, Dec. 1976, **84**, pp. 1145–59.
– 'Some Limitations of Demand Revealing Processes: Comment,' *Public Choice*, Spring 1977, **29**, pp. 125–8.
Tiebout, C. M. 'A Pure Theory of Local Expenditures,' *J. Polit. Econ.*, Oct. 1956, **64**, pp. 416–24.
Tollison, R. D., Crain, M. and Paulter, P. 'Information and Voting: An Empirical Note,' *Public Choice*, Winter 1975, **24**, pp. 43–9.
Tollison, R. D. and Willett, T. D. 'Some Simple Economics of Voting,' *Public Choice*, Fall 1973, **16**, pp. 59–71.
Toye, J. F. J. 'Economic Theories of Politics and Public Finance,' *British J. Polit. Sci.*, Oct. 1976, **6**, pp. 433–47.
Tulkens, H. 'Dynamic Processes for Allocating Public Goods: An Institution–Oriented Survey,' *J. Public Econ.*, April 1978, **9**, pp. 163–201.
Tullock, G. 'Some Problems of Majority Voting,' *J. Polit. Econ.*, Dec. 1959, **67**, pp. 571–9, reprinted in Arrow and Scitovsky [1969, pp. 169–78].
– 'Reply to a Traditionalist,' *J. Polit. Econ.*, Dec. 1961, **69**, pp. 200–3.
– *The Politics of Bureaucracy*, Washington: Public Affairs Press, 1965.
– *Toward a Mathematics of Politics*, Ann Arbor: University of Michigan Press, 1967*a*.
– 'The General Irrelevance of the General Impossibility Theorem,' *Quart. J. Econ.*, May 1967*b*, **81**, pp. 256–70.
– 'A Simple Algebraic Logrolling Model,' *Amer. Econ. Rev.*, June 1970, **60**, pp. 419–26.
– 'The Paradox of Revolution,' *Public Choice*, Fall 1971*a*, **11**, pp. 89–100.
– 'The Charity of the Uncharitable,' *Western Econ. J.*, Dec. 1971*b*, **9**, pp. 379–92.
– *Logic of the Law*. New York: Basic Books, 1971*c*.
– *The Social Dilemma: Economics of War and Revolution*, Blacksburg: Center for Study of Public Choice, 1974.
– 'Comment' (on Rae, 1975), *Amer. Polit. Sci. Rev.* Dec. 1975, **69**, pp. 1295–7.
– 'Practical Problems and Practical Solutions,' *Public Choice*, Spring 1977*a*, **29**, pp. 27–35.
– 'The Demand-Revealing Process as a Welfare Indicator,' *Public Choice*, Spring 1977*b*, **29**, pp. 51–63.
– 'Demand-Revealing Process, Coalitions and Public Goods,' *Public Choice*, Spring 1977*c*, **29**, pp. 103–5.
– 'Revealing the Demand for Transfers,' in R. Auster and B. Sears, eds. *American Re-Evolution*, Tucson: University of Arizona, 1977*d*, pp. 107–23.
Tullock, G. and Campbell, C. D. 'Computer Simulation of a Small Voting System,' *Econ. J.*, March 1970, **80**, pp. 97–104.
Varian, H. R. 'Equity, Envy, and Efficiency,' *J. Econ. Theory*, 1974, **9**, pp. 63–91.
– 'Two Problems in the Theory of Fairness,' *J. Public Econ.*, April–May 1976, **5**, pp. 249–60.
Vickrey, W. 'Utility, Strategy, and Social Decision Rules,' *Quart. J. Econ.*, Nov. 1960, **74**, pp. 507–35.
– 'Counterspeculation, Auctions, and Competitive Sealed Tenders,' *J. Finance*, May 1961, **16**, pp. 8–37.

Wagner, R. E. 'Revenue Structure, Fiscal Illusion, and Budgetary Choice,' *Public Choice*, Spring 1976, **25**, pp. 45–61.

Warren, R. S. Jr, 'Bureaucratic Performance and Budgetary Reward,' *Public Choice*, Winter 1975, **24**, pp. 51–7.

Weatherby, J. L. Jr, 'A Note on Administrative Behavior and Public Policy,' *Public Choice*, Fall 1971, **11**, pp. 107–10.

Welch, W. P. 'The Economics of Campaign Funds,' *Public Choice*, Winter 1974, **20**, pp. 83–97.

Wicksell, K. 'A New Principle of Just Taxation, *Finanztheoretische Untersuchungen*, Jena, 1896, reprinted in Musgrave and Peacock [1958, pp. 72–118].

Williamson, O. E. *The Economics of Discretionary Behavior*, Englewood Cliffs: Prentice-Hall, 1964.

Williamson, O. E. and Sargent, T. J. 'Social Choice: A Probabilistic Approach,' *Econ. J.*, Dec. 1967, **77**, pp. 797–813.

Wilson, R. 'An Axiomatic Model of Logrolling,' *Amer. Econ. Rev.*, June 1969, **59**, pp. 331–41.

– 'A Game-Theoretic Analysis of Social Choice,' in Liebermann, B., ed. *Social Choice*, New York: Gordon and Breach, 1971*a*.

– 'Stable Coalition Proposals in Majority-Rule Voting,' *J. Econ. Theory*, Sept. 1971*b*, **3**, pp. 254–71.

Wittman, D. A. 'Parties as Utility Maximizers,' *Amer. Polit. Sci. Rev.*, June 1973, **67**, pp. 490–8.

Wright, G. 'The Political Economy of New Deal Spending: An Econometric Analysis,' *Rev. Econ. Statist.*, Feb. 1974, **56**, pp. 30–8.

Young, H. P. 'An Axiomatization of Borda's Rule,' *J. Econ. Theory*, Sept. 1974. **9**, pp. 43–52.

NAME INDEX

289

SUBJECT INDEX